Rome
STOOPS TO CONQUER

Rome
STOOPS TO CONQUER

by

DR. E. BOYD BARRETT

AUTHOR OF

"The Jesuit Enigma"
"While Peter Sleeps"
"The Magnificent Illusion," Etc.

JULIAN MESSNER, INC.
New York

TABLE OF CONTENTS

Foreword

"We must have in this country the right to speak
our honest thoughts or we shall perish."

Rome
STOOPS TO CONQUER

CHAPTER I

TWILIGHT REVOLT

FROM an insignificant group of 25,000 adherents, shepherded by thirty poor priests, in 1789, the Catholic Church of America has grown to be a congregation of 20,000,000, led by thirty thousand priests. From being propertyless, she has become a rich institution, whose wealth exceeds two billion dollars. From being a despised and scattered flock, she has become the most perfectly organized body in the world enjoying immense influence and power. Bearing in mind her material and spiritual autonomy, her individualism, her close-knit interests and definite aims, her sharp separateness from all other institutions, one must regard her as a unique entity in the nation, an entity whose swift and ceaseless growth indicates a great destiny.

The American people watched with concern and suspicion the development of the Catholic Church in this country. They strove to thwart her growth with contempt and occasional blows. They had little sympathy for her. Wrote Cardinal Gibbons in 1876: "Upon the Church's fair and heavenly brow her enemies put a hideous mask and in that guise exhibited her to the insults and mockery of the public." Fifty years later the same kind of injustice was complained of by Archbishop McNicholas[1]: "The Catholic Church has been

[1] Cincinnati, 1929.

1

held up to men as an object to be hated and feared. She has been described as anti-Christ; the epitome of evil. She has been scorned as an alien incapable of assimilating American ideals. She is said to await only the opportunity to effect the destruction of American institutions."

But neither animosity nor injury succeeded in stemming the tide of Catholicism. The battle was lost. Irony, contempt and blows failed of their purpose. The "mustard seed" has grown into a mighty tree. Today the American people are silent about the Catholic Church: silent and apprehensive.

The Catholic Church has dug herself securely into American life and her social status has improved from year to year. She is highly esteemed for her good citizenship. In a hundred walks of life Catholics rank as leaders. In the Great War Catholics were as foolishly patriotic as other citizens and as generous in the sacrifices they made. In commercial and civil life individual Catholics mix and mingle and their identity as Catholics is completely submerged until, perhaps, some practical interest of the Church crops up and then their religious affiliation is revealed.

The Catholic Church has gained in the esteem of religious-minded and conservative Americans because of two salient characteristics; namely, her consistency in moral doctrine and her constancy of purpose.

The Church has a moral code and has stuck to it. In no serious respect has she deviated from traditional morals. In an age of subversive and bewildering theories she has remained her sober, dogmatic self. With unwavering consistency she has opposed divorce, free love in all its forms, contraception in its modern mechanical forms, godless education and Marxism. On the whole she has been splendidly faithful to her duty of teaching "hard sayings" while other

. Churches have shamelessly compromised on many moral doctrines.

Her constancy of purpose in pursuing the ambitions which she holds to be legitimate is equally outstanding. From the first she has laid claim to a unique divine mission which entitles her to "teach all nations." She has held and still holds it her exclusive right and duty to teach Americans, "to make America Catholic" (Archbishop Ireland). In holding, as she holds, that she is "the pillar and the ground of truth" and that her teaching is inerrant and indefectible, she is perfectly logical in her conduct. Her ambition to dominate American thought and regulate American manners is self-confessed. "She has no secrets to keep back. . . . Everything in the Catholic Church is open and above board" (Cardinal Gibbons). She calls on all Americans to hear her voice and obey her counsels. Error has no rights in her eyes, nor is it ever lawful to hide the truth. No other church shares with her this sublime, if often misrepresented, intolerance.

The Catholic Church in America is strong; stronger than any other group; stronger perhaps than any possible confederation of groups. Her strength does not derive from her property alone, nor from the mere numbers of her children however many they be, but from the enduring cohesion which possesses her organization and from the mysterious, inflammable texture of the Catholic mind.

Her strength has grown apace under the remarkably able leadership of the present Pope, Pius XI. He has given the best of his singular ability to the supervision and direction of the Catholic campaign in America. For him our country is a battlefield on which is being waged the greatest struggle of the Church's history. The conquest of America is the supreme objective at which he aims. He despairs of the Old

World with its interminable outbreaks against the Church and the multiplicity of divisions between peoples that entail internecine strife among his children. Besides, the Old World is in receivership. Pius is well aware that the Catholic Church can never hope again to dominate the civilized world until America kneels, beaten and penitent, at her feet.

It is characteristic of the Pope's strategy in guiding American Catholics that he has launched them on Catholic Action, and that he has taught them to enlarge and remodel the Catholic Press.

Catholic Action is not avowedly politics, indeed, in theory is far removed therefrom. It is the share the laity takes in "the apostolate of the bishops"; work done by laymen and laywomen on behalf of the Church under obedience to their pastors. But in fact, a large proportion of Catholic Action partakes of politics, and is a political penetration, an infiltration into the political world of a new force and agency. In writing to the Knights of Columbus, Cardinal Pacelli, on behalf of His Holiness, delicately avowed this aim. He urged on the Knights to a widespread rally of Catholic manhood as necessary for "the practical solution of those problems of social and civil life which put such severe tests on the souls of Catholics."

In teaching American Catholics this new phase of Catholicism, this active phase, and in sanctifying *it* with his blessing, Pius XI rendered inevitable many significant changes in the life-course of this nation.

Of the new Catholic Press there will be much to say later on. It suffices for the moment to refer to its outspoken boldness and to its remarkable success in stirring up the spirit of the Catholic masses and awakening in them a sense of their immense power. Thanks largely to their Press, a seething energy fills American Catholics. From end to end of the land they are men of action, united, confident of the future, and militant. Of late they have given many remarkable displays of their mobility as a force to influence public manners. The Legion of Decency was such a display. At the word of the bishops ten thousand meetings were held; a hundred thousand inflammatory pieces were printed in the Catholic Press; ten million Catholics signed pledges. The move was so sudden and violent that a score of non-Catholic bodies were carried along with it and joined ranks with the Catholics. The energy and organizing genius of Catholic Action was demonstrated. No such stupendous social maneuver could be achieved by any other American group.

Writes the editor of the Catholic journal, *Commonweal*: "The Catholic Church today is positively active on a scale and with an intensity of disciplined energy which is of vital concern to all thoughtful men and women who wish to know something of the great forces which are contending today for the leadership and control of the thoughts and actions of mankind. . . . That the Catholic Church is, to say the least, certainly one of the major forces of the world . . . is generally admitted. Its own claim, of course, is that it is incomparably, uniquely, the supreme spiritual power in all the world." [1]

This "admittedly major force of the world" is focused today on the problem of the future of this country. The possibilities of the situation provoke deep and enduring interest. To minds that distrust Catholicism, what is called "the menace of Rome" looms greater than ever before. To minds that see in Catholicism the regenerative force of the world, the future is bright with hope.

[1] *The Catholic Church in Action*, p. 5.

The importance of mass meetings as well as mass movements in maintaining the morale of their subjects is well known to the Catholic hierarchy of America. No diocese is left long without a well-staged display of numbers and strength. The effect of these demonstrations on the Catholic mind is well illustrated by a story told of a poor woman who attended a vast meeting organized by Archbishop Curley at Baltimore in June, 1934, to celebrate "The Birth of Maryland." There were 70,000 priests, nuns, papal knights and laity present. The poor woman had come a long journey but what she witnessed compensated her for her pains. "When you see all this," she cried, "you can only say that the Catholic Church can do anything."

The purpose of the meeting was avowedly to remind the American people of the contribution which the Catholic Church had made in the person of Lord Baltimore, to the doctrine of religious freedom. The Jesuit editor of *America*, in commenting, described it as "another of those events which bear overwhelming testimony to the fact that the Catholic Church is bound up with all that is great in America's past, present, and future." His bold claim that America's *future greatness* already belongs demonstrably to the Catholic Church is indicative of the profound confidence that Catholics feel as regards the future career of the Church in this country.

What is the official view of the Catholic Church about America? What does she think of our moral condition? How does she envisage her duty towards us?

Frankly, the Church has a poor opinion of the social and moral status of the nation. She sees America hastening to destruction and decay. "America is in a sad state today with vast groups of our people clamoring for new gods, new standards of morality, and in their mad desire they are worshipping material wealth and deifying self." [1] The disease she diagnoses as Neo-Paganism. Americans are no longer godly; they are godless; godless in education, in social relations, in industrial relations, and largely godless in government. "The world . . . outside the Catholic Church . . . is almost entirely pagan, completely materialistic in its philosophy and outlook . . . with the breakdown of family life and the sanctity of marriage." [2] This disease permeates every walk of life and corrupts young and old alike. It is the forerunner of something still worse: Communism. Communism is militant bloody Paganism with its sword unsheathed to strike down the Church. "Bolshevism is already battering at our doors," cries Bishop F. C. Kelley.

Officially the Catholic Church sees America in the direst straits in the matter of morals and religion, and sees Catholicism as the only possible way of salvation for the nation. She sees in Catholic Action all that is left of true American Action. She sees herself as the last defender of true Americanism. She claims, for instance, that the banishment of religion from public schools is an invasion of the Constitution and that the endowment of purely secular education is an unrighteous as well as an un-American favoring of atheism.

Having consecrated the slogan "Catholic Action means American Action," the Church no longer regards any "interfering" on her part with American manners and customs as un-American. All that she does is, she claims, done in the best interests of America. Her program, a long and varied one, provides for the reform of theaters; the censorship of books and reviews; the prevention of birth control propa-

[1] Dean of Fordham University, Conferring of Degrees, 1934.
[2] President of Fordham University, *Ibid.*

ganda; the defeat of the eugenics movement; the introduction of religion into the public schools; the obtaining of State aid for sectarian schools; the reform of industrial relations in accordance with papal encyclicals; the re-establishment of diplomatic relations with the Vatican; the acquisition of a more than presidential *veto* on legislation and on the policy of the Foreign Office, etc. Even these items comprise but a part of the Church's program. In general that program constitutes the domination, for the good of America, of American thought, manners, and government by the Catholic Church.

The program, did it remain a mere matter of pious hope and a subject of prayer, would be harmless, but the American Catholic hierarchy is not content with passive Christianity. It is busy mobilizing all its forces to put across its program. It feels assured that it will outlive opposition and will succeed in the end. What are ten or twenty years in the life of the Catholic Church? What is a century for that matter? But confidence in the inevitability of victory does not damp its present ardor for immediate action. Thanks to the present disintegration of American life the hour for action has struck. There is today a Catholic camp where banners float and bugles blare. The great campaign has begun.

That the Catholic Church is deadly in earnest in campaigning to "save America from herself" cannot be doubted. It is fully in accord with her traditions and her psychology. In whatever country she may be, the moment she feels herself strong enough to dominate thought, conduct and government, she makes the attempt to do so. "The Church has always done so," writes Hilaire Belloc, "and always will, please God!" She regards it alike as her duty and her divine mission. She is subject to that "expansiveness" or, as it is called, apostolicity, which is the characteristic of the Catholic spirit.

The revolt, or revolution, or uprising—whatever it may be called—which she has engineered in our midst is the necessary result of her faith. It is a unique phenomenon in our history because no other church or organization is like the Catholic Church. It could not have happened sooner because heretofore the Catholic Church was not strong enough to make the attempt.

Its coming has been foretold in various terms. Dean Inge, the inveterate hater of the Church, wrote a decade ago: "The determined effort of the Roman Catholic Church to capture the great Republic of the West makes the most interesting chapter in modern religious history." Years later the Catholic poet Theodore Maynard wrote: "The plain fact is that America will soon become the decisive battle-ground of the faith." Maynard did not envisage the struggle as a revolution, though it is difficult to call it anything else. Yet, though a revolution, it is not formally seditious. The Church is under arms against those she considers the enemies of this nation, and so far she is fighting under the forms of lawful civic strife.

To American citizens who are not so profoundly apprehensive about the future of their country as is the Catholic Church, the present turmoil seems unjustifiable. They consider that the Catholic Church is aggressive. Catholics, they say, have not suffered any injustices or hardships. They have been favored if anything, and certainly enjoy the same privileges as other citizens. There is no discrimination against them or against their Church. Their case is not like that of the German Catholics under Bismarck when their rights and liberties seemed to be endangered by the Kulturkampf.

American Catholics, in assaulting the institutions, manners and morals of this country, are not conducting a war of defense but one of attack and aggression. It is from them that threats issue and not from the government or the major portion of the population.

Be that as it may, the revolt is in motion and the question to be asked is, how far is it likely to go? With what additional powers will the Catholic Church be satisfied? What is the ultimate objective at which she aims? Does she intend, should the power be hers, to change and modify the Constitution? Does she mean to discard the American principle of the separation of Church and State? In fine, does she aim at being *the established church* of the United States?

This last question, a disturbing one for non-Catholics, was authoritatively answered (as it then seemed) by Alfred E. Smith, the Catholic lay leader of America, during his presidential campaign in 1928. He stated more than once and unequivocally: "I believe in the American doctrine of the absolute separation of Church and State." This statement became known as Smith's *Credo*. It was accepted at once by American Catholics, lay and clerical, as their *Credo* also. They all said "Amen" to it. And since that time neither the hierarchy nor the laity have repudiated it. Indeed, we frequently find reiterations of Smith's *Credo* from important Catholic apologists. Thus recently Father Elliot Ross, the Paulist, wrote: "Catholics in the United States yield nothing to their fellow-citizens in their devotion to the American principle of religious liberty and separation of Church and State." [1]

Smith's *Credo* reassured American non-Catholics and silenced for the time being the taunt of "divided allegiance" that has for so long been uttered against Catholics. But Smith's

[1] *Commonweal*, March 15, 1935.

Credo did not solve the terrible dilemma of American Catholics. It was impotent to wipe out the Roman decrees and encyclicals which establish as Roman Catholic doctrine the desirability of the union of Church and State. In point of fact, Smith's *Credo* was heresy. Objectively at least, it was a bid to trick and deceive the American people into a false conception of Catholic doctrine on the relationship that ought to exist between Church and State.

A year after Mr. Smith's pronouncement, namely, in 1929, this writer ventured on a prophecy: "Pius XI . . . has no choice but to administer a sharp rebuke to his recalcitrant American Children and assert his authority. No doubt he will wait a little while until the election heat has cooled down. Perhaps too his rebuke will be indirect; there may be no mention of America at all in his encyclical but everyone will know for whom it is intended." [1]

On the last day of the following year, Pius XI issued his encyclical "Casti Connubii" in which he definitely repudiated the "absolute separation" heresy of Alfred E. Smith and enlarged upon the desirability of "union and association" between Church and State. He was in fact putting before the American Catholic Church the ultimate objective at which she should aim.

As this recent and really authoritative teaching of the Catholic Church on the burning question of the relationship of Church and State is vitally important, and as it is given the minimum of publicity by American Catholics, it may be well to quote it fairly fully.[2] It has obvious reference, as indeed has the whole encyclical, to American conditions, as viewed from the Vatican.

[1] *While Peter Sleeps*, p. 182.
[2] Cf. last pages of "Casti Connubii," December 31, 1930.

We earnestly exhort in the Lord all those who hold the reins
of power that they establish and maintain firmly harmony and
friendship with this Church of Christ so that through the united
activity and energy of both powers the tremendous evils, fruits
of those wanton liberties which assail both marriage and the
family and are a menace to both Church and State, may be
effectively frustrated.

Governments can assist the Church greatly in the execution of
its important office if in laying down their ordinances they take
account of what is prescribed by divine and ecclesiastical law, and
if penalties are fixed for offenders. . . . There will be no peril
or lessening of the rights and integrity of the State from its association with the Church. Such suspicion and fear is empty and
groundless as Leo XIII has already so clearly set forth.

Continuing, and making the teaching of Leo XIII his
own, Pius XI says:

"It is in the interest of everybody that there be a harmonious
relationship" between Church and State, and that "if the civil
power combines in a friendly manner with the spiritual power
of the Church it necessarily follows that both parties will greatly
benefit."

He adds:

"The dignity of the State will be enhanced and with religion
as its guide there will never be a rule that is not just; while for
the Church there will be a safeguard and defence which will
operate to the public good of the faithful."

Pius XI then holds up to the American people as "a clear
and recent example" the solemn Convention between the
Vatican and Italian Government whereby the latter "assigns

as civil effects of the sacrament of matrimony all that is attributed to it in Canon Law."

There follows the official Catholic teaching, from the lips of Pius XI, which blasts the Smith *Credo* and all the equivocal misrepresentations of Catholic doctrine that the American Catholic Church has foisted on the American people. Pius XI says: "This" [the Vatican-Mussolini pact] "might well be a striking example to all of how even in this our day, *in which sad to say the absolute separation of the civil power from the Church and indeed from every religion is so often taught,* the one supreme authority can be *united and associated* with the other without detriment to the rights and supreme power of either thus protecting Christian parents from pernicious evils and menacing ruin." (Italics are ours.)

To return to the questions asked earlier: Does the Church intend, should the power be hers, to change and modify the Constitution? Does she mean to discard the American principle of the separation of Church and State? In fine, does she aim at being *the established church* of the United States? One cannot doubt, in view of the present Pope's teaching, which indeed is simply the reiteration of age-old Catholic doctrine, that the answers should all be in the affirmative.

If the aim of Catholic Action is to fulfill the mission of the Church, to dominate and chasten the soul and the manners of America, why should Catholic Action stop short of setting up Catholicism in a position of supreme authority in this country? The uprising that has begun, the strong nation-wide Catholic movement "to save America," the revolt against the Neo-Pagan state of the nation, can have, logically, no other termination than that outlined above by His Holiness.

Translated into strictly Catholic thought and language, the foregoing ideas are well expressed by Michael Williams, one of the lay leaders of American Catholicism. Having stated [1] that the ecclesiastical statistics for 1934 "amply prove that the Church in the United States is advancing steadily and strongly, practically all along its far-flung front" and that "the epic of Christianity lies concealed beneath the surface of the statistics," he concludes: "Meanwhile all Catholics with even a modicum of imagination cannot fail to be thrilled with the vision of the vast Catholic force ... the force of the Church in action, permeating the national life, the leaven in its mass, uplifting its ideals, directing its way toward the only road which is consonant with humanity's true nature; the road of Christian civilization."

[1] *Commonweal*, editorial, May 17, 1935.

CHAPTER II

CATHOLIC ACTION

CATHOLIC Action is best described as the new phase of Catholicism. There was always something kindred to it in the Catholic Church, but it is only in recent times that it has become an instrument of social power which obtrudes itself daily on the notice of the public. In America it is a force that has to be reckoned with; a force that is applied here, there and everywhere. It does not always succeed, nor is it always wisely applied, but no thoughtful American can deny its startling significance.

In theory, Catholic Action is the work and service of lay Catholics in the cause of religion, under the guidance of the bishops. In practice it is the Catholic group fighting their way to control America. In this fight they are far from disregarding the noble cause of humanitarianism. Catholics can point to as many constructive works of charity as any other religious group. But the motif latent in Catholic Action is not pure humanitarianism. It is a sterner and more practical purpose.

In medieval times the Church gained supremacy in various countries through her influence over nobles and soldiers. Today she aims at the old supremacy by mass action of her organized subjects, and by systematic penetration of various groupings. Writing of the need of trained propagandists in the "apostolate of industry," the present Pope states: "Undoubtedly the first and immediate apostle of the working men must themselves be working men, while the apostles of the industrial and commercial world should themselves be employers and merchants. It is your chief duty, Venerable Brethren, and that of your clergy to seek diligently, to select prudently, and train fittingly these lay apostles amongst working men and employers."

Though Catholic laymen as such have no jurisdiction in the Church, they are today the chief agents in the work and development of the Church. They are ready and willing to help the great cause. Priests and bishops mingle with them, guiding and advising them, and taking the lead openly when important issues are at stake. But the heavy work, the spade work, is done by the laity, men and women, to whom "the Catholic Cause" appeals.

There was a time—it is now past—when only pious Catholics took part in the work of the Church. But today many Catholics who cannot qualify as pious are busy about Catholic Action. Catholicism, in America at least, has ceased to be a matter of religious observance. Catholicism now is something that partakes of clannishness, and that is constituted in large part by social and political and "club" affiliations. Among the hundreds of Catholic leaders who are outstanding for their loyalty to the cause are to be found quite a few who have little if any regard for Catholic doctrines or observances. Catholic Action would be a far less serious factor in this country were its only agents pious and devout Catholics. The starting point of the wave of Catholic Action in this country may be traced back to the inauguration of the National Catholic Welfare Conference in 1921. On that occasion Archbishop Hanna declared: "We have co-ordinated and united the Catholic power of this country. It now knows where and when to act and is encouraged by the consciousness of its unity.

We feel ourselves powerful because our reunion has become visible." From that day Catholic strength has grown apace, and Catholic organizations have multiplied.

In no country of the world is there such thoroughgoing organization as among American Catholics. Every class, every cross section of sex, occupation, age and local affiliation is appropriately grouped. From "hello-girls" to dentists, from poets to policemen, Catholics are billeted in their societies and taught to be "Catholic-conscious." There are clubs or guilds or confraternities of Catholic lawyers, nurses, writers, army officers, naval officers, customs officers, stenographers, factory girls, and so forth. Some societies are nation-wide, like the Holy Name, with 2,000,000 members; the Knights of Columbus, with 500,000; the Sacred Heart League; the National Council of Catholic Men; the National Council of Catholic Women; and the Catholic Daughters of America, to mention but a few.

New organizations spring into existence every month. Only last May (1935) a "Catholic War Veterans Association" was established under the patronage of Bishop Molloy of Brooklyn. Already it has several "posts" and it aims at becoming not only a nation-wide but an international organization. Women auxiliaries are attached to the "posts" under the snappy name of "Yeomanettes." "I am sure," announced the chaplain, Father Higgins, "that we will have the holy backing of Cardinal Hayes and that the entire hierarchy will like-, wise approve." Contemporaneously with the Catholic War Veterans, the Catholic College Graduates felt inspired to do more than they were doing for Catholic Action and to set up a new organization, so that their leadership in Catholic life might become more effective. Father Parsons S. J.,[1] explain-

[1] *America*, May 11, 1935.

ing the new move, writes: "After all the big trends are the result of big men and big influences, and we must not blame the graduate if he himself feels that the tremendous forces that are within him as a result of his Catholic culture have not been released for the benefit of his country and our civilization. . . . Organize! Pool the intellects and the wills of as many of the graduates as can be got together. Give them a common objective. Fire their imaginations with the vision of a great movement which takes its roots from deep within the traditions that formed our Western civilization. *Let them be daring. Let them be even revolutionary if the need be for that*," (italics ours).

The rank and file of Catholics realize very clearly the power that comes from union, and the importance of organization. As an example of Catholic insight into the value of standing together, I quote from the remarks made at a Bronx Holy Name meeting by one of the officers. "Catholic men," he said,[1] "should unite in order to be able to tell legislatures that *they must not* introduce bills which are inimical to the ideals of the family or the ideals of the Catholic Church. They should organize so as to be strong enough to insist that school teachers who teach 'pernicious doctrines' be removed."

The words "strength," "power," "organization" are an ever-present refrain in addresses delivered at Catholic society meetings. Speakers harp on these words and stir up in their hearers a sense of solidarity and a fighting spirit. According to Cardinal Hayes, it is "praiseworthy and important" for Catholics "to portray the majesty, the dignity, the power and the growth of Catholic life." To err on the side of modesty in such a matter is less a virtue than a sin.

[1] *New York Times*, January 27, 1935.

"We must have great numbers, but they must be intelligent numbers," said District Attorney William F. X. Geoghan at a Knights of Columbus rally in Brooklyn.[1] "It should be realized that with an increase in numbers we shall greatly increase our strength and power for good . . . We should bear in mind that in the future we may wish to seek State Aid for our Catholic educational system."

The scope of Catholic Action is so immense and varied that it is quite impossible to deal comprehensively with it in one chapter. It reaches out into every field, from literature to athletics, from interpreting Catholic liturgy to picketing consulates, from training Girl Scouts to heckling Communists. It opposes here; it supports there. It is constructive and destructive; it recompenses and it punishes; it fills mailbags and closes theaters. In later chapters we shall deal with some of its largest manifestations, in reference to Mexico, Birth Control, Neo-Paganism, and other matters. Here we shall deal mainly with its tendencies and characteristics.

As an example of the wide scope of a Catholic society devoted to Catholic Action, we may take the work done by the Catholic Daughters of America for the year 1933-34. During the year the members of the "courts" of this society subscribed $925,124 for educational and "benevolent" activities. Of this sum $20,000 went to Rome for "welfare work"; $21,000, for Catholic Church Extension; and $25,000 to the Knights of Columbus. During the ten years 1924-1934, almost $5,000,000 was subscribed by the Daughters for these and other like objects.

During the year in question, one hundred of the Daughters entered convents; others worked (in 45 states) in Convert Leagues; Social Study Clubs; Catholic Press, Welfare, and

[1] March 16, 1935.

Legislation Committees, and other such activities. Thousands
of members devote their time to organizing retreats; giving
catechetical instruction; and teaching in religious vacation
schools. It was considered by the Supreme Directorate that
the annual report demonstrated *"the unlimited resourceful-
ness and marvellous courage of the personnel of the C. D.
of A."*

Catholic Action is busy, all over the country, about libraries,
Catholic colleges, Newman Clubs, vocations, public morals,
politics of course, and every form of human activity. "A
Catholic bookshelf in the public library is the way Catholics
of Dubuque, Iowa, have solved the problem of the dissemination of Catholic literature," writes a correspondent to
America.[1] Elsewhere the same problem is solved by the sur-
reptitious removal of anti-Catholic books and the demand
on the part of Catholics for pro-Catholic books which forces
the hands of librarians. When colleges need funds to extend,
a meeting of laymen is arranged and a drive for funds is
organized. The more prominent Catholic laymen are "selected" by the local Church authorities to lead the drive.
Thus, recently, when Seyton Hall, South Orange, needed a
new gymnasium (to cost $250,000), one hundred and fifty
laymen were "selected" to collect the money. More nuns are
required and a group of Catholic ladies open a recruiting
office in the Bronx called "The Little Flower Mission Circle"
and ship four hundred girls to convents within nine years. At
Malvern, Long Island, the Board of Education decided, with
reason, that Newman Clubs in public high schools were against
the state law and forbade them. The pastor, Father Burke,
and a local politician, Major Murray, took up the challenge.
Father Burke made the extraordinary claim that Newman

[1] April 6, 1935.

Clubs are not "under the auspices of the Catholic Church" and the matter became a political issue in the local elections. Meanwhile Father A. J. Owen, a Jesuit, writes to *America*[1] urging Catholics to interfere in the affairs of public schools even though they do not (and of course should not) send their children to them. He finds fault with Catholics for neglecting to watch over the morals and religious interests of non-Catholic children. "This neglect on the part of Catholics in many communities has allowed subversive elements to control schools and has naturally led to abuses which are daily becoming more evident. Such abuses will continue until every Catholic realizes his right and duty to concern himself with the educational system his taxes indirectly and directly support. *The exercise of this right and the fulfillment of this obligation clearly come within the scope of positive Catholic Action.*"

This brings us to the burning topic of Catholic claims and Catholic Action in the field of Education.

Catholics lose no opportunity of denouncing State schools as godless and demoralizing. They insist that there should be religious education given to all. "Education without God," they say, "is Education without Education." They point out that "God is written into the Constitution" and that it is unconstitutional and un-American to exclude the teaching of God's word and the inculcation of divine worship in schools paid for by the citizens. It is to this point of view that Father Owen refers in his letter given above. Another prominent Catholic, Professor F. X. Polo, states the position thus: "An adequate method of bringing the necessary knowledge of God to American youth is the core of the question of including the teaching of religion in the curriculum of our splendid

[1] March 9, 1935.

public school system. It would be an astounding anomaly and a disastrous tragedy in the life cycle of America if we raised up at public expense a youth entirely ignorant of the God who is written very definitely into our fundamental law as the Creator and Author of the laws of Nature and the Source of our inalienable rights."

I dwell on this Catholic policy of "interfering" in the curriculum of public schools in order to contrast it with the definite stand against any interference whatsoever on the part of the State or the public with the curriculum of their own Catholic schools.

The Church has always opposed the setting up of a Federal Department of Education lest it might give Federal authorities the right to meddle with parochial schools or colleges. When Mussolini declared to the Pope that the State was supreme in education and that in this matter he was "intractable," the Pope (giving a lead to Catholic bishops the world over) replied: "We can never agree to anything that restricts or denies the right given by God to the Church and the family in the field of education. On this point we are not merely intractable, we are uncompromising."

In order to have complete control of the education of Catholic children, the Church in America had Catholic schools and colleges built, at Catholic expense, and of course with the sole object of accommodating Catholics. The State did not interfere, beyond pointing out that it could not constitutionally support such private sectarian schools with public moneys. To do that would be to endow a particular religious faith and to nullify both the letter and the spirit of the Constitution.

In time, as Catholics grew bolder, they began to make claims against the State, saying: "We educate 2,500,000

American children and save the State $265,000,000 yearly. In the meantime we pay taxes to support the Public Schools which our children do not attend. This is unfair. We are doubly taxed. The State should aid our schools." Writes Michael Williams[1]: "Catholics do call attention to the fact that *in justice they have the right* to compensation for the expense involved in setting up their own schools and in giving education in citizenship," (italics ours).

In other words, the Church demands that she have the exclusive right to decide when and where and how to erect schools (without any reference whatsoever to taxpayers) and that the taxpayer should be compelled to foot the bill. What in essence she demands is the imposition on non-Catholic citizens of the odious injustice of "taxation without representation."

Is the Church serious about this claim? The answer is to be found in the recent effort made in the Ohio Legislature to have the Davis School Aid Bill passed. This bill was designed to give "emergency aid" to the amount of about $2,000,000 to the Catholic parochial schools of Ohio. For two years the Catholics have prepared for the fight in the House of Representatives. In the elections they secured pledges from nearly fifty members to support the bill. In the Senate the Davis Bill passed, 17 votes for and 15 against.[2] However, it was blocked in the House of Representatives, 86 against and 42 for. Says the *Catholic News* [3]: "Bigotry and fear of political consequences combined to deny the Parochial Schools the temporary aid which they sought from the State." Catholics attributed the defeat of what they considered a per-

[1] *The Catholic Church in Action*, p. 284.
[2] May 15, 1935.
[3] June 1, 1935.

fectly just and constitutional bill to the venom and hatred of their enemies. They lauded a Protestant, Mr. H. H. Root, for printing and circulating at his own expense 75,000 postcards that were used in flooding the mailbags of members of the Houses, in favor of the measure.

A bill which was no less unconstitutional, though less serious in scope, the Kelly-Corbett Transportation Bill, designed to give Catholic schoolchildren the right to use public school busses in going to school, passed both Houses in Albany recently but was vetoed by Governor Lehman to the immense annoyance and disappointment of New York Catholics. Had it received the Governor's signature and become a state law, Catholic Action would have won its first skirmish against the "tolerance" provisions of the Constitution.

Needless to say the Catholic fight for state aid for parochial schools is only in its first phase. Every year, from now on, we shall see the fight renewed until victory is achieved.

Catholic Action is essentially optimistic, bold, and at times reckless. Nowhere is there a braver or more hopeful spirit than among American Catholics. They feel or proclaim they feel on the upgrade. "All is well" all the time with them. Among them critics and doubting Thomases are few and inarticulate. On his seventy-seventh birthday, which he celebrated recently, Mgr. Lavelle of St. Patrick's told reporters: "There has never been a period in our recollection when Catholics were more devoted to their duties and their Holy Faith." Catholics are marching into battle today with cheery songs on their lips. They pay little heed to the few croakers who mourn the "terrible leakages" in their ranks. Their *esprit de corps* is excellent.

Their boldness in planning is exceptional. Gigantic undertakings are faced without faltering. "We Catholics," writes

John Wiltbye, "undertake the most impossible things, and in the current patois, we generally get away with them." [1] Schemes that other organizations would shrink from undertaking are commonplace among Catholics. As an example we may take the March (1935) "Drive for Action" of the Knights of Columbus. This "mobilization" was planned to embrace the United States and Canada, and the two countries were divided up into twenty-six areas. Each area was placed in charge of a distinguished layman, a general, judge, senator, corporation president, ex-mayor or ex-governor. The purpose of the drive was manifold, embracing the chief items of nation-wide Catholic Action, and an increase of membership for the order itself. The mobilization headquarters was located in the Empire State Building, of which the Chairman of the Board, Mr. A. E. Smith, is a leading Knight. The Supreme Knight, Martin H. Carmody, put before the organization the purpose of raising the membership from 500,000 to 1,000,000, and added: *"The campaign is not simply for the purpose of getting new members for the Order but to supply a greater and stronger co-operation between the laity and the heads of the diocese and parish."*

His Holiness, through Cardinal Pacelli, wrote a long letter expressing "high approbation" of the Knights and keen interest in their work: "It is my earnest hope and fervent prayer that this laudable endeavor to enroll the Catholic manhood of North America in the ranks of the Knights of Columbus may be a brilliant success. . . . The need is great: the present challenges to Catholic Action."

In the first week of the "drive" about 10,000 new members were enrolled, which was claimed as a record: "the largest number of new members to join an organization in so short

[1] *America*, February 25, 1935.

a period in the history of fraternal movements" (Supreme Knight Carmody). Apropos of the drive, Mr. Michael F. Walsh, State Deputy of New York, speaking in the Columbus Club, Brooklyn (April 1), is reported in the Press thus: "When I appeal to you for increased membership, I hasten to explain that we are not anxious to bring within our ranks a mob thirsty for destruction. If we can attract other men into our organization we will have accomplished Catholic Action."

What is noteworthy about such Catholic enterprises is the speed with which "the call" is spread among Catholics in every corner of the country, and the enthusiasm with which Catholic journals, Catholic broadcasting stations and Catholic pulpits lend support in disseminating suitable propaganda.

We turn now to some characteristics of Catholic Action and consider it first under its punitive or retaliatory aspect. When Catholic sensibilities are "outraged" vengeance in some appropriate form is taken. When remarks made in Mexico by Ambassador Daniels were considered by Catholics here to be laudatory of the Calles regime, he was promptly denounced and a clamor for his recall was raised. Alderman Deutsch was brought to book by Catholics on a like charge. He did not see eye to eye with them about Mexico and he was chastened for it. Dr. Charles L. Fama, of New York City, was appointed to a public office by Mayor LaGuardia and it was recalled by Catholics that in times past he had "attacked" the Catholics. The Mayor was called upon to oust him from office. Alderman Hart, as Catholic spokesman, declared: "There is no room in this country for intolerance; there is no room on the payroll of this city for a bigot." Meanwhile the Board of Estimates withholds Dr. Fama's salary!

The Protestant Defense League tried to interest Senator Borah in investigating "religious persecution in New York" as a preliminary to the investigation of "religious persecution in Mexico" but the Senator declined to act. He is reported as telling the League that the investigation would be a "delicate" matter! The Press of New York displayed little inclination either to take up the cause of Dr. Fama or to back the demand of the Protestant League. What Heywood Broun wrote a few years back is still apparently true: "Every New York editor lives in terror of the Catholic group."

Those who have had the misfortune to deliver lectures or to publish articles critical of some phase of Catholicism have experienced in abundance the punitive character of Catholic Action—shoals of abusive letters, the majority of which are anonymous—offensive remarks over the telephone—cancellation of business deals—and threats of various kinds. No other religious group in America displays so sensitive a concern about "the honor" of its creed as does the Catholic. "Catholics," wrote Mr. H. L. Mencken, "take criticism very badly." He might have said that they do not take it at all; they refuse to take it and hurl it back at the critic's head.

The well-known sensitivity of Catholics to anything that even remotely seems to reflect on their religion brings about ludicrous situations at times. One of these situations is described in a paragraph of the *New Yorker*[1] entitled "Vegetables." The story has to do with a sister magazine, *Vogue*, belonging to the Condé Nast organization. It happened that *Vogue* purchased from Anton Bruehl a picture of a crib made out of vegetables. It was an interesting and quite inoffensive piece of art but a member of the Condé Nast staff expressed horror at the implied irreverence and warned that there

[1] February 16, 1935.

would be Catholic reactions if the picture were published. She, as a pious Catholic, considered it a sacrilege to build a crib out of vegetables instead of ordinary bits of straw and wood. Some of the Condé Nast people sided with her; more thought her view absurd. Back of the concern over the issue was the latent fear of Catholic Action. As a compromise it was decided to consult Catholic ecclesiastical dignitaries on the matter. These accomplished theologians examined the picture carefully and gave it their *imprimatur*. Also they admitted frankly that only in the United States could such a question and such a situation have arisen.

Sensitivity to the Church's honor, which flourishes in ignorant Catholics as well as in educated Catholics, makes it a perilous matter to give a lecture, however fair and impartial, on a Catholic subject unless one be a priest or a well-known Catholic. An incident will serve to illustrate the point. The present writer, in a public lecture, stated that professed fathers of the Society of Jesus took solemn vows in accordance with their Constitutions. He was at once interrupted by a militant Catholic who declared that it was a lie to say that the Jesuit Order had Constitutions. He added, which was not in question at the time, that he had known Jesuits all his life and that they were all saintly men. It was utterly useless to point out that the *fact* that there were Jesuit Constitutions was not derogatory to the Order and that the *fact* could be verified by visiting any important library and inspecting a copy of the said Constitutions of the Society of Jesus. The interrupter, according to the accepted practice of Catholic Actionists involved in a public argument, held his ground in holy contempt of facts.

In her book *My Fight for Birth Control*,[1] Margaret

[1] Page 321.

Sanger gives a comparatively recent example of the sinister in Catholic Action. It happened in connection with the raid on her Clinical Research Bureau on March 23, 1929. The police who searched her offices carried away confidential medical case records. When her lawyer protested to the magistrate that such records were "privileged," he ordered them to be restored. When they were returnd 150 case records were still missing and Mrs. Sanger never succeeded in recovering them. Whose records were they?

Soon Mrs. Sanger found out that the missing case records were those of Catholic women who had visited the clinic. Some of them came to tell her that "they had received mysterious and anonymous telephone calls telling them that if they continued to go to the clinic their cases would be exposed in the newspapers." Mrs. Sanger maintains that the raid was engineered by "high Church authorities" for the very purpose that was accomplished, namely, of frightening off from it Catholic clients under threat of publicity. Mrs. Mary Sullivan, policewoman, was the Catholic hero of the fray.

Catholic Action is usually, but not always, unanimously endorsed by Catholics. Once in a while a dissenting minority is vocal among them. This is the case in the Catholic opposition to the Child Labor Amendment. Mgr. John A. Ryan, *The Catholic Worker* of New York, and a few individual Catholics like Frank P. Walsh support the measure but their influence is inconsiderable against that of Cardinal O'Connell, the dean of the hierarchy, Archbishop Glennon of St. Louis, and the other bishops.

The Catholic case against the amendment is that if it were adopted the authority of Catholic parents over their children would be imperiled. Father Corrigan, representing Cardinal

O'Connell, gave evidence against the amendment at a legislative hearing in Boston and said that "if the Amendment became effective Washington authorities could decide whether a child should receive training in the religious faith of his parents." [1] The Catholic Press in general denounced the Amendment as "a practically irrevocable provision granting unlimited power over the youth of the country to Congress." In New York it is recognized that the defeat of the Amendment was due "to the combined forces of manufacturers and many Catholic leaders, political and clerical."

This opposition to a measure which appeals to the enlightened sentiment of the American people is an example of the narrow selfishness of Catholic Action. No matter how great the benefit of the Amendment to the people at large, the possibility of its endangering the Church's influence under some utterly unlikely contingency, suffices to make Catholics oppose it.

In summing up the meaning and significance of Catholic Action in America it would be unfair and ungenerous not to acknowledge the fine citizenship and noble humanity of millions of Catholics who help support Catholic hospitals and charitable institutions; Catholic vacation schools, where 250,-000 supplement their education; Catholic rural life bureaus and organizations; Catholic Boy and Girl Scout movements; and a thousand and one other undertakings of Catholic Action that improve the well-being of American citizens.

On the other hand, it is impossible not to see that Catholic Action as a whole is directed to the end of changing America, root and branch, into another people and another culture.

It goes on here, there, everywhere; restless and entirely irresistible; a potent and subtle force shaping anew our na-

[1] *New York Times*, February 15, 1935.

tional destiny. Yet there is no one, as it seems, capable of appraising its significance and dramatizing its meaning for the understanding of the people.

Myopic political observers who smoke thoughtful cigarettes in editorial watchtowers wax excited over symptoms of passing political currents in the Middle West, but have neither the vision to see nor the art to interpret the most momentous thing that is happening today. Even the depression itself, great as are the effects that it has produced, and great as will be, in all likelihood, its further effects, is a matter of less consequence to the destiny of America than is the ever-deepening surge of Catholic Action.

CHAPTER III

WINNING THE WORKER

THE Catholic Church, since her emergence as the most powerful society in America, has until recently been singularly inactive in the field of Social Justice. Although a large percentage of her followers belong to the laboring classes, the Church has taken little interest in their problems. Her policy has been to side with the moneyed and privileged class and to frown upon the proletariat. Some of her most conspicuous leaders, such as Cardinal O'Connell, for instance, have been mouthpieces for the principles of the bankers. Very few have consistently advocated industrial and social reform.

It is true that the Church has been shrewd enough to pay lip service to elementary principles of Social Justice. Thus in 1919 the bishops, in a pastoral, declared: "The laborer's right to a decent livelihood is the first moral charge upon industry." Catholic preachers and Catholic journals have from time to time referred to the social program of Leo XIII and his encyclical on Labor. One journal, *America*,[1] boasts that for a quarter of a century it has advocated "collective bargaining, the right of labor to organize, decent working conditions and a living wage for all." But though there be a few pastorals and paragraphs to the credit of the Church's interest in Social Justice, there was never a drive of Catholic

[1] February 16, 1935.

32

Action to curb the capitalist or defend the exploited worker. Such drives are reserved for objectives that the Church considers more important.

American labor, Catholic and non-Catholic, has not been blind to the indifference, and indeed the hypocrisy, of the Catholic Church. Here was a Church, wealthy and powerful, that professed to be "the friend of the poor" and that preached charity and justice, and yet favored the oppressor and neglected the oppressed. Workers beheld cardinals, bishops, monsignori gorgeously attired, ceremoniously waited upon, sumptuously banqueted, palatially housed, transported in limousines, sedulously careful not to hurt the feelings of their millionaire patrons and friends, and yet pretending at the same time to have the interests of the poor at heart! Their real interest was to safeguard the *status quo* in which they throve, to defend the social order that made the rich richer and the poor poorer. No wonder the Church, with her harsh denunciations of Socialism, became an eyesore to the American workers.

Pius XI, referring to the fact that so many Catholics have "deserted the camp of the Church and passed over to the ranks of socialism," alleging, as their reason for doing so, that "the Church and those professing attachment to the Church favor the rich and neglect workingmen," admits that "some" Catholics were unjust to their employees. "Such men," he added, "are the cause that the Church, *without deserving it*, may have the appearance and be accused of taking sides with the wealthy and of being little moved by the needs and sufferings of the disinherited." How many American Catholic workers would agree with Pius XI that the charge against the Church which he recapitulates is undeserved?

The answer that the Church makes, in this country and

elsewhere, to the charge that she has neglected the cause of the poor is to point to her hundreds of hospitals and charitable institutions, and her organizations (such as the St. Vincent de Paul Society) for distributing relief. But this answer is not to the point. In fact, it is no answer at all!

No one in his senses would condemn the Church for her works of mercy. So far as they go they are entirely admirable. But they do not even touch the fringe of the social problem. What comfort is it to the tens of millions of exploited workers to know that there is a Catholic food and clothes dole awaiting tens of thousands who are in uttermost distress? It would, on the other hand, be a comfort to them to know that the Catholic Church was fighting with all her might, tooth and nail, against the conditions that produce hunger and nakedness; that priests and bishops, with their coats off, were united in a mighty drive, at the head of their followers, to insist that justice be done to the workingman. But the Church never espoused the cause of the poor in the only manner that was worth while, either in this or in any other country.

The Catholic Church in America has been as cold and indifferent to and as neglectful of the worker as of the Negro. She is ready to admit, and actually does admit, her shameful neglect of the latter but not of the former. Yet everyone knows that the colored man and the grimy, toil-stained man have been treated by her with like indifference.

If it be true, as the most loyal of American Catholic apologists, Dr. James J. Walsh, writes, that "Cardinals represent the spirit of the Church," we have in Cardinal O'Connell's attitude towards capital and labor an insight into that spirit. The Cardinal, as we shall see later, is the epitome of old-fashioned snobbishness and conservatism; an unfailing friend of the aristocrat, the capitalist and the banker, and an unwavering opponent of the cause of labor. He has preached in his cathedral against the workers and lauded the rich. He had the effrontery, in 1930, to preach in the presence of Mr. Green and other officials of the A. F. of L. of the "interest of the Church in labor." The message he gave to the A. F. of L. was to surrender, or as he put it, to "co-operate with Capital."

Cardinal O'Connell, as dean and ranking leader of the hierarchy, for twenty years has guided the policy of the Catholic Church here. That policy has been to conciliate the rich and to milk the poor. The Church, which insists on "sharing the wealth" of all her children, looks askance at workers who teach socialistic doctrines of distribution of un-earned riches.

Writes a Catholic who professes his readiness to die for the Church or the Pope[1]: "We find no solid union of Catho-lics fighting against the present immoral capitalistic system. We find no solidarity of the faithful in an attempt to bring to this earth the City of God. No, we find only harmless 'clean-movie' drives! What kind of [Catholic] action is it that allows textile mill operatives to be treated like slaves? What kind of Catholicism is it that softly closes its eyes at the diurnal exploitation of the proletariat on the part of the capitalist overlords? You know what kind of Catholicism it is. It is that of which the Marxist can well say, 'religion is the dope of the people.' "

The writer, a student of Columbia University, quotes ef-fectively in his letter from great Catholic theologians who taught that poverty was a source of temptation and an evil state from which one should try to escape. He contrasts this teaching with that of Cardinal O'Connell and with the prac-

[1] New York *World-Telegram*, Correspondents' Column, June 5, 1935.

tice of the Church in America, and winds up: "Do not chide
Father Coughlin. Raise up twenty Coughlins. Instead of one
fighting priest let us have twenty fighting bishops. That is
what Catholicism means today!" It would be easy to quote
from scores of Catholic correspondents remarks similar to
those of the Columbia student. It is evident that there is
widespread shame among thoughtful Catholics over the conduct of the Church in regard to labor.[1]

But now a change or what looks like a change has come
about suddenly. What is its meaning? Whence comes the
reversal of the time-honored policy of avoiding any action
that capital would find disagreeable? Whence this seething
newborn zeal for Social Justice? Bishops, Jesuits, Calvert Associates and Knights of Columbus are tumbling over one
another in a mad rush to grasp the hand of the worker and
slap him on the back! Today nothing is too good for labor;
nothing too bad to be said about capitalists!

The plain fact is that the American bishops have taken
fright. They found that they had lost influence with their
own Catholic workers and were hated and despised by non-
Catholic workers. It became evident that they could never
hope to pursue successfully their great schemes unless the
workers were conciliated and persuaded to envisage the
Church with a more friendly eye. The situation had become
very desperate and only desperate remedies were worth
trying. The Church commenced her great campaign on the
industrial front forthwith, and proclaimed a "new deal" for

[1] Writes a Jesuit, R. J. Henle, in the *Commonweal* for June 14, 1935:
"There is no use imagining where we would be *had we taken seriously the
encyclicals of the great Leo in his own day instead of in the fortieth
year after.*"

Labor. She is determined to make a bid at being "the worker's Church."

The papal encyclical "Quadragesimo Anno" made a timely appearance. It was completed in May, 1931, and placed in the hands of the American bishops as an instrument of propaganda. It is an astute document, capable of being interpreted in a liberal sense; capable also of being employed as a check to radicalism. It enfolds splendid shibboleths and a few fiery phrases to arouse labor to a sense of the "progressiveness" of Rome. On the other hand, it is drawn up with an eye to conserving all the important interests of capital. It is both liberal and conservative; profound and platitudinous; practical and too general for application. It is called, for the purposes of Catholic propaganda, "a charter of freedom for the worker," but in reality it is a sheet anchor for the old social order of capitalism and competition.

The encyclical offered a glorious opportunity for priests with the gift of eloquence, or the itch to write, to win fame and publicity. Bishops and superiors let them go ahead, and "red" sermons were delivered under the high vaults of Catholic cathedrals. With obvious guilelessness the learned Jesuit Father L. K. Patterson wrote in *America*[1]: *"Now is the time for Catholic priests and scholars to speak out fearlessly in defense of Social Justice.* A mere banal enunciation of general principles is not sufficient; we must be ruthless in applying 'Quadragesimo Anno' to concrete conditions. Little or nothing in the New Deal seems radical in the light of that Encyclical. Indeed, one wonders if it goes far enough. . . . Educated Catholics, where do you stand? We can break the grip of privilege; and the sway of selfish groups; unhorse

[1] June 16, 1934.

the munition makers; if we but really desire to do so. Thus we will forestall the 'hatchet-man'!"

The "new deal" that the Catholic Church is offering to the American worker is propagandized by *The Catholic Worker* of New York. This clever and piously-bright paper plays up the "advanced" doctrines and dicta of the clergy. It gives Father Haas, for example,[1] two columns for his attack on the manner in which Section 7-A has been administered, and another column for his plea for a $2,500 a year "family wage" for workers. "All American workers must be assured of a yearly income that will maintain them at a decent standard of living and this amount should be set at not less than $2,500." [2]

The most revealing contribution (in the March issue) is one from a Jesuit, Father Winter, who is busy of late organizing unemployed in Denver. He started a "Catholic Worker's Protective Alliance" which he says "does the same work for the jobless as the Communists do, sending committees to the relief stations, insisting on fair play, visiting families who appeal to us." Father Winter has so closely copied the kindness and charity of the Communists that he proudly *boasts:* "They said Father Winter is a Communist but does not know it!" He goes on to report that many men have come back to the Church because "at last the Church is doing something for the unemployed." Then follows the revealing sentence which tells of some of his men who were formerly Communists: *"They give their coal, their food, their days and nights to the work, just as they did when they were with the Communists."*

Whether the American workers will be won over by the

[1] March, 1935.
[2] *Ibid.*

pious camaraderie of Dorothy Day of *The Catholic Worker*, the roseate promises of Father Haas, the pseudo-Communist charities of Father Winter, and the "red paragraphs" of the Pope's encyclical remains to be seen. But it is likely that the Church will have to devise some more original and some more substantial bait for them before they troop in millions to the shelter of her fold.

A contributor to the *American Mercury*[1] calls the Catholic campaign to win the workers a "counter-attack." "In the past few years, with Father Coughlin in the van, numerous Catholic leaders have been not at all backward in denouncing the present social order. They employ the Pope's words, in his famous labor encyclical, "the tyrannical despotism" of capitalism. Some of the statements of these priests and lay spokesmen sound more like Union Square diatribes than utterances of the most conservative religionists. To say the least, they have done their part well in the counter-attack of the Church."

We turn now to the encyclical itself, "Quadragesimo Anno," the basis of Catholic labor doctrine; the instrument that Pius XI put into the hands of the American Church for the conquest of the workers.

In effect it is both a treatise on industrialism and social ethics, and a political document. In its latter aspect, which we shall deal with in a subsequent chapter, it is Catholic Fascism; in its former aspect it is age-old Thomism, changeless, conservative and unimaginative.

We notice that Pius XI, early in his letter, lays claim to divine authority to teach the true eternal doctrine of industrial ethics. "We lay down the principle, long since clearly established by Leo XIII, that it is Our right and Our duty to deal authoritatively with social and economic problems."

[1] March, 1935.

We propose to omit from this brief analysis the many touching and edifying aphorisms on charity and morals, and the many laudatory references to Leo XIII and Pius X. "Economic life must be inspired by Christian principles" summarizes the mystical elements of the encyclical.

Pius XI does not lighten the burden of religious duty that his predecessors placed on the backs of Catholic workers. For instance, he insists that the labor unions they join should be Catholic, or at very least "Christian." Never may Catholic workers join "un-Christian" (Socialist) unions. If there be none but "neutral" unions, the workers must seek the permission of their bishops before joining. Pius writes: "These [neutral unions] should always respect justice and equity and leave their Catholic members full freedom to follow the dictates of their conscience and obey the precepts of the Church. *It belongs to the Bishops to permit Catholic workingmen to join these Unions,* where they judge that circumstances render it necessary, and there appears no danger for religion, observing however the rules and precautions recommended by Our Predecessor of saintly memory, Pius X."

Practically speaking, this paragraph (with the final ominous insistence on obedience to the reactionary Pius X's rules and precautions) excludes Catholic workers from all American labor unions. There is not one that meets all the requirements of Pius X and Pius XI.

Curiously enough, although Pius XI desiderates "Associations of Employers," he lays down no rules or precautions whereby the Catholic industrial magnate should go on his knees to his bishop before joining his "Association." There is one law for the poor Catholic worker and another for the Catholic millionaire!

In the papal estimation, "Associations of Employers" are

presumed to have "respect for justice and equity" while "Labor Unions" are presumed to have no such virtue.

"Quadragesimo Anno" contains, as we have stated, some fine outbursts of liberal sentiment. Pius XI waves the red flag in half a dozen paragraphs. With holy wrath he denounces certain financial monsters. He points a warning finger at some abuses of government. How he undoes all the good effect of this bravery we shall see later.

Here then is Pius XI, the friend of the worker. "The immense number of propertyless wage-earners on the one hand, and the superabundant riches of the fortunate few on the other is an unanswerable argument that earthly goods so abundantly produced in this age of industrialism are far from rightly distributed and equitably shared among various classes of men." [1]

Again: "It is patent that in our days not only is wealth accumulated but immense power and despotic economic domination is concentrated in the hands of a few. . . . This power becomes particularly irresistible when exercised by those who, because they hold and control money, are able to govern credit. . . . This accumulation of power, the characteristic note of the modern economic order, is a natural result of limitless free competition which permits the survival of those only who are the strongest, which often means those who fight most relentlessly, who pay least heed to the dictates of conscience . . . the whole economic life has become hard, cruel, and relentless in a ghastly measure . . . the intermingling and scandalous confusion of duties and offices of civil authority and of economics has produced crying evils and has gone so far as to degrade the majesty of the State." [2]

[1] *Paulist Press Translation*, p. 21.
[2] Pages 32, 33.

Again: "Certain forms of property must be reserved to the State since they carry with them an opportunity of domination too great to be left to private individuals without injury to the country at large." [1]

Again: "Every effort must be made that at least in future a just share only of the fruits of production be permitted to accumulate in the hands of the wealthy and that an ample sufficiency be supplied to the workingmen." [2]

Added to these resounding trumpet calls, we have many wise if unoriginal platitudes, for instance: "It would be well if various nations in common counsel and endeavor strove to promote a healthy economic cooperation by prudent pacts and institutions, since in economic matters they are largely dependent one upon the other, and need one another's help."

From the foregoing one might expect that His Holiness would proceed to declare that the capitalistic system was in general unjust; that the wage-contract in common use was neither just nor valid inasmuch as one party to the contract has to sign under moral duress; that "the superabundant riches of the fortunate few" should be forfeited and shared; that free competition should be ruthlessly restricted. But, to the reader's astonishment and disappointment, Pius XI goes on to justify the actual *status quo*. On every point indicated he retreats hastily from the advanced posts he seemed to have occupied, and takes shelter in downright reaction.

Here then is Pius XI, the upholder of the capitalist and the enemy of labor. "The [capitalistic] system is not to be condemned. And surely it is not vicious of its very nature." [3] Continuing, in an involved, casuistic sentence, he explains

[1] *Paulist Press Translation*, Pages 35, 36.
[2] *Paulist Press Translation*, Page 22.
[3] *Paulist Press Translation*, Page 32.

that "it violates right order" when it takes every advantage to itself and completely disregards social justice, the common good and the human dignity of the worker. Pius XI does not assert that this actually happens, nor does he admit that anything short of these enormities would be "a violation of right order."

As regards "free competition" he declares that "within certain limits it is just and productive of good results." He does not say what the "limits" are; only it should not be "the ruling principle" of economic life.[1]

Next as regards the vital matter of the wage-contract: "Those who hold that the wage-contract is essentially unjust and that in its place must be introduced the contract of partnership are certainly in error."[2]

Again: "Entirely false is the principle widely propagated today that the worth of labor and therefore the equitable return to be made for it, should equal the worth of its net result. Thus the right to the full product of his toil is claimed for the wage-earner. How erroneous this is appears from what we have written above concerning capital and labor."[3]

This condemnation is no doubt logical in the light of Thomistic principles of "ownership," but it is harsh in the light of modern conditions and modern conceptions.

Let us proceed further. When Pius XI declares that "the wage paid to a workingman must be sufficient for the support of himself and his family," he seems to be fair, if not generous, to the worker. But he follows up this declaration with the qualification: "It is right indeed that the rest of the family contribute according to their power toward the common main-

[1] *Paulist Press Translation*, Page 29.
[2] *Paulist Press Translation*, Page 22.
[3] *Paulist Press Translation*, Page 23.

tenance." He seems to imply that the employer is *not bound* to pay a full family wage to the father in the case where some of the children, or perhaps the wife, is earning.

Pius XI takes an unequivocal stand against "excessive" wages, if indeed such are ever paid. He says: "All are aware that a scale of wages too low *no less than too high* causes unemployment. . . . To lower *or raise wages unduly* with a view to private profit and with no consideration for the common good, is contrary to social justice." [1]

Pius XI is adamant as regards the rights of property-owners. "It belongs to commutative justice to respect the possessions of others." He teaches also that *"the misuse or non-use of ownership does not destroy the right itself"* . . . "it is unlawful for the State to exhaust the means of individuals by crushing taxes and tributes" . . . "man's natural right of possessing and transmitting property by inheritance cannot be taken away by the State from man."

Pius admits that the State may ("provided the natural and divine law be observed") specify more accurately what is licit and what is illicit for property-owners *"in the use of their possessions,"* but he hastens to add that "it is plain that the State may not discharge this duty in an arbitrary way." The encyclical has been written into the *Congressional Record* at the instance of Huey Long, whose "Share the Wealth" program it very pointedly blasts!

All this teaching implies that the "fortunate few" may continue to hold their "superabundant riches" with the Pope's blessing subject only to the obligations of charity and of "certain other virtues." In strict justice they are not bound either to use their wealth well or to make any use of it at all. With regard to superfluous income, if, instead of devoting it to the

[1] *Paulist Press Translation*, Page 25.

general good, the owner invests it "in searching favorable opportunities for employment, provided the labor employed produces results that are really useful," he meets all the demands of virtue. The State may of course tax property but not unduly, nor may the State interfere in an "arbitrary way" in directing how superfluous income or property be employed.

Such is a brief analysis of what has so falsely been called a "charter of freedom" for the worker and "the death-knell of the capitalist." It is precisely the kind of worker's charter that one might expect to emanate from the mind of a priestly capitalist and an infallible autocrat.

"Quadragesimo Anno" has, of course, been lauded to the skies by others than Catholics. There are few members of President Roosevelt's Cabinet who have not sung its praises. In a recent interview[1] Senator Gerald P. Nye called it "the most magnificent contribution to social and economic reconstruction which it had been my privilege to study." General Hugh S. Johnson referred to it as a document "unsurpassed by the mind of man."

None the less, it seems to the present writer that "Quadragesimo Anno" teaches "Social Order" rather than "Social Justice." No intelligent worker, who studied its contents, would be content to abide by its doctrines or would see in them any broadening of his hopes.

Nevertheless, on account of its "purple patches," coming as it does from a Pope of Rome, it makes an excellent basis for Catholic propaganda. One can figure a Catholic spellbinder addressing a mob of unemployed: "Hear what the Pope says —and you know how careful Popes are not to overstate a case! 'The whole economic life has become hard, cruel, and relentless in a ghastly degree'! What do you think of that?

[1] *America*, April 20, 1935.

Hear him again! 'Immense power and despotic economic domination is concentrated in the hands of a few'—he says 'despotic domination' and he means it! He says, 'In future a just share only of the fruits of production will be permitted to accumulate in the hands of the wealthy and an ample sufficiency must be supplied to the workingmen!' What about that? What's wrong with the Pope or the Catholic Church?"

CHAPTER IV

PUBLIC SAFETY

To ASSUME authority in the name of Public Safety has characterized from earliest times most forms of revolt, and it was in the name of Public Safety that the Catholic hierarchy of America launched their attack on American morals in the summer of 1934.

Addressing his archdiocese, Cardinal Hayes said: "Public Safety demands that we establish quarantine against epidemics, enforce measures against unsanitary conditions, and guard our water supply lest contagion, infection and contamination harm the physical well-being of our people. To be consistent we should be equally concerned about the general moral tone of the nation. A serious lowering of the moral standards of any community menaces the common good and weakens if it does not destroy the sanctions that guarantee peace and prosperity. . . . Evil motion pictures undermine the moral foundation of the State."

Other Catholic archbishops and bishops issued similar proclamations. In Boston, Father Sullivan, the Jesuit, as the Cardinal's spokesman, said: "The present campaign against indecent motion pictures is a campaign for the preservation of our national morality, the very foundation of our governmental structure, and for the preservation of our national ideals."

All through the land there was an assumption of authority
in the Fascist manner by the Church, and a "Call to Arms"
was issued. The Pope's blessing was obtained for the crusade,
and millions of Christian soldiers enrolled and pledged themselves to fight. "Militant action should be resorted to if
necessary" the bishops had declared. *The crusaders were
ready!*

The Legion of Decency *began* as an assault on supposedly
evil motion pictures. Pictures offered an immediate and con-
venient target for Catholic Action on a nation-wide scale.
There were movie theaters everywhere, in every town and in
every village. Every Catholic parish established its Legion
at the word of the bishops and got busy. The Liberties Union
Committee protested in vain that "religious censorship is subversive of the religious liberty clauses in our basic law." In
the First Humanist Church of New York City, Rev. Dr.
Charles L. Potter exclaimed: "It is bad in a democracy to
have one group set up a moral censorship over the rest. Who
gave the Roman Catholic Church . . . the right to dictate the
morals of this nation?" The Church paid no heed to such
rebukes. Where her interests are concerned she declines to
attach importance to theories of human rights and liberties.
Besides, had she not declared in her episcopal manifestoes
that *Public Safety* demanded and justified her intervention.

The Catholic bishops, in launching the League, called
salacious pictures "the country's greatest menace." What they
meant was that salacious pictures were an expression of what
they considered the country's greatest menace — Neo-
Paganism.

It is difficult to define Neo-Paganism. It is a questioning
of the worth of Christian ethics, and a practical disregard of
the conclusions drawn therefrom. It constitutes a grave threat

to Catholicism which stands or falls by the old standard of morals. Catholics like to say that there is an issue between Western Civilization and Neo-Paganism and that in fighting for the former they are defending law, order, art, social welfare, and of course the American Constitution. They invoke the sentiment of patriotism in their struggle with the ugly monster that threatens. They warn that Neo-Paganism means atheism, Communism, and devilry in every form. "Could Satan himself devise a more successfully insidious attack on our national morality and ideals than that which the gentlemen of the motion picture industry devised to reward us for the wealth we heaped upon them and the trust we reposed in them?" [1] The Catholic hierarchy are naturally fearful lest the contamination spread among their flocks. Were such to happen, the Church's influence and their influence would be undermined. Confessions revealed the havoc caused in souls by modern dances, modern literature, the theater, the bathing beach, the night club, Nudism, birth control, secular education, and other manifestations of American "naturalism." In a lament issued at Rome on the eve of Lent (1935), His Holiness declared: "The pagan tendencies in present-day life afflict all open and attentive eyes. For many people life is specifically and paganly given over only to pleasure, to the quest after pleasure, and to amusement that is specifically and paganly immodest, with an immodesty that often exceeds that of ancient pagan life, inasmuch as it is addicted to what is termed with a horrible word and horrible blasphemy, the practice and cult of Nudism."

In the early stages of the Legion's activities the boycott weapon was invoked. Cardinal Dougherty ordered "his"

[1] Rev. Russell M. Sullivan, Boston, July 22, 1934, *New York Times* report.

people to stay away from motion pictures good and bad. "Nothing," he said, "is left for us except the boycott. The Catholic people of this diocese are, therefore, urged to register their united protest against immoral and indecent films by remaining away entirely from all motion picture theaters." Archbishop Glennon allowed "his" people to frequent theaters which excluded *all* indecent pictures. "If the picture house," he said, "shows both types of pictures, we'll tell our people to stay away from both." To show the sweet reasonableness of his decision, he said that no employer would keep a man in employment on the grounds that he was sober two days a week, although drunk the other four.

Then labor kicked and warned the Church that to boycott theaters would mean more unemployment. In Philadelphia their leaders declared: "It is obvious that the blanket boycott if enforced as planned can only lead to hardship and unemployment not only among musicians but among operators, stagehands, ushers, ticket-sellers, doormen, managers, and all others employed in the theaters." The Church did not wish to antagonize labor anew, nor to alienate her Catholic children who found employment in the theaters, so she modified her stand and restricted the Legion's energies to boycotting specific films. Meanwhile, strange as it may appear, the bishops displayed little interest in what should have been their vital concern—the discrimination between "decency" and "indecency" in films. The great thing, in their eyes, was to have the mighty Legion going strong for the glory of God and of the Church, and to have a good number of movies banned. It did not matter much which!

The work of applying Catholic moral theology to the classification of movies into good, bad and indifferent was usually left to pious women who had no scientific training as moralists, but who were deeply interested in pruriency. They drew up the famous "lists." Of these the most important, in fact the "official" list, came from Chicago. It was drawn up by a young lady, unaided! This girl held in her hands, so to say, the moral consciences of millions of American Catholics. Her judgment on what might be naughty for young men and old, maidens and matrons, soldiers and sailors, nuns and priests and even bishops was final, and authoritative!

The ten million Catholics who pledged themselves solemnly, standing in the churches with uplifted hands, "to form a right conscience about pictures that are dangerous to my moral life" took the Chicago maid's word as to what constituted the eternal difference between good and evil, right and wrong in screen drama. For American Catholics she became a holy Delphian oracle.

In connection with the Legion of Decency there soon appeared another anomaly. In various dioceses "Councils" were set up to spread and perpetuate its work. For these Councils a personnel had to be chosen. The individual bishops were faced with a problem. Whom should they choose as members of their Councils? Devout, irreproachable, scholarly laymen who would, supposedly, be sensitive to the canons of decency? Or public men, politicians who knew more about polling votes and wangling jobs, than about the finer points of Catholic theology?

His Eminence Cardinal Hayes in setting up the Council of the Legion for the archdiocese of New York, gave a lead in this thorny matter by plumping for politicians and public men. He made Mr. Alfred E. Smith, his chairman, and added as councilors, ex-Mayor John P. O'Brien, Judge Alfred J. Talley, Martin Quigley, Arthur O'Leary, George Mac-Donald, and his own representative, Father E. R. Moore. His

Eminence thus officially vindicated the moral outlook of
Tammany Hall by entrusting to it a strong vote in the supervision of matters of conscience and chastity in his diocese.

We now broach the subject of the developments and the
objectives of the Legion.

In New York, although Father Moore, as the Cardinal's
mouthpiece, informed the Press that "The Legion has not any
intentions of setting itself up as a guardian of society and
public morals *at this time*," it soon began to show its hand.

In St. Patrick's Cathedral Father Graham announced that
the movement would be directed against the legitimate stage.
"You are urged," he told the congregation, "to ignore producers and authors who lend themselves only to plays that
are salacious." Working with two colleagues, Fathers Woods
and Furlong, Father Graham drew up a "White List" of
Broadway plays. Of thirty Broadway plays current at the
time, only four were passed as "white"! Next came the move
against Nudism. Speaking on behalf of the Archdiocesan
Council, Mr. Alfred E. Smith reminded the Press that the
Appellate Division had ruled that existing laws did not justify
conviction in cases of Nudism-cult, and added: "If, as the
learned Appellate Division ruled, the present penal law is
not adequate to prevent public mingling and exhibitions of
naked men and women, if such action is not an offence against
public decency, this Legion will ask the Legislature to speedily
remedy this defect in the law and make it so. It seems to us
inconsistent to make a stand for decency on the screen and
ignore this latest challenge to the enforcement of decency in
reality. *We cannot overlook indecency in the substance while
condemning it in the shadow.*"

The contention of Nudists that the nude human body is

[1] December 9, 1934.

distinct from the lewd human body is regarded by the Legion as a deceitful sophism. The contention that there is no more essential connection between morality and clothing than between morality and cheese is regarded by the Legion as a blasphemy. Though more and more of the scaffolding about the human body is being removed, with propriety, as the years go by, the Legion in accordance with the Church's view, holds that if *all* were removed the structure would suffer a (moral) collapse.

No doubt, the Legion was acting under a hint from Rome in making this assault on Nudism, for within a month of the date of the introduction of the Anti-Nudism Bill at Albany, His Holiness launched his scathing denunciation. Henceforth nudists may expect to experience the same kind of hostility from the Catholic Church that birth controllers have experienced in this country. The Catholic Church has said "No!" to this cult and her "No!" is final.

The New York Catholic "cleanup" has extended to the magazine stands, the burlesque theaters, and the red-light districts through the agency of the Public Welfare and Police departments. It is also engaged in dealing with "immoral literature." At a meeting of the Catholic Writers Guild (March 4, 1935), Monsignor Lavelle spoke as follows: "There should be a nation-wide movement to suppress pernicious and indecent books. If this were done, as far as literature is concerned, the effect would be the same as in the battle against indecent moving pictures." Mgr. Lavelle's views on what Catholic conduct should be with respect to literature were given in his letter read in all the churches of the diocese on February 3, 1935. These views were meant for the public in general as well as for Catholics: "Exclusion from homes of all books and pamphlets hostile to religion and good works

or that ventilate obscene news and licentious scandals. . . .
All our people, men, women, and children, should pledge
themselves not to buy or read anything that offends against
decency or that is obnoxious to *the enlightened Catholic
conscience.*"

One wonders what percentage of current books, published
in New York, would satisfy the Lavelle canon. By "enlightened Catholic conscience" Mgr. Lavelle means a Catholic conscience that is illuminated by grace and faith, in other
words, a devout and delicate conscience. The present writer
knows of no non-Catholic book that would not *offend* in
some manner or other such a conscience.

In Chicago, the anti-book campaign gives promise of being
vigorous when launched. Catholic student-sodalists, at a meeting that numbered five hundred, resolved: "In recent years
there has been a noticeable increase in the number of salacious
books and magazines in wide circulation resulting in the
moral tone of much of our modern literature becoming more
and more offensive to the sodalists. Therefore be it resolved
that the operation of the Legion be extended to decreasing the
number and circulation of the salacious books and magazines
to improve the moral tone of that part of literature which
has become offensive to our ideals." [1]

The threat voiced by the student-sodalists of Chicago,
namely, that of "decreasing the number and circulation" of
books that Catholics disapprove of, is no idle threat. The
general public would be amazed if they realized what power
the Catholic Church exercises over the book trade. In the first
place, publishers for the most part are in absolute terror of
publishing a book that is calculated to hurt Catholic sensibilities. They take shelter under the pretense that their policy is

[1] *New York Times,* July 9, 1934.

to publish only "tolerant" books, thereby accepting the Catholice viewpoint that *all books which are critical of Catholic practices or policies are intolerant*. Few publishers endorse in practice the foreword at the head of this book: "We must have in this country the right to speak our honest thoughts or we shall perish." [1]

Thus Catholics block books at the source by keeping most publishers under their thumbs, at least in so far as concerns books about Catholicism. But should some books, critical of Catholicism, filter through, their resources are sufficient to deal with the situation. Catholics have considerable influence with distributing agencies. Through them they hold up or hamper a book that they are determined to kill. Should the book get by the distributing agencies and reach the bookstores and reviewers, the Church pursues it still. Catholic ladies visit the bookstores and threaten the proprietors. "You have a book there that is offensive to Catholics! You know what Catholics will be compelled to do if you persist in selling it? You understand?" As regards reviewers, it is a sad but absolutely true fact that none of the *great* reviewers feel comfortable in handling a book that is "offensive to Catholics." It happens at times that they think it more prudent not to make any reference whatsoever to such a book in their columns.

In New York there is a diocesan Literature Committee that issues a *Book Survey*, a quarterly in which are listed "good books," namely, such as are inoffensive to Catholics, and at the same time have some claim to being "worth while." Dr. Blanche Mary Kelly edits the *Book Survey*.

Sometimes Dr. Kelly, or one of her censors, is too liberal and protests are made from shocked Catholics. Such protests

[1] *New York Times*, Editorial, March 6, 1935

led her last year (1934) to remove from her "White List" a book that had formerly appeared on it, a novel entitled *Livingstones* by a young Englishman, Derrick Leon. The excommunication of this book, which won for it a considerable amount of publicity, was referred to in the *Book Survey*. The reference concluded thus: *"We are sorry if anyone bought the book on our recommendation."*

Reporters elicited from Dr. Blanche Mary Kelly that on second thought and recensorship she had decided that the book offended against the second canon of the Literature Committee's qualifications for the "White List," namely, that a book must not "offend the Christian sense of truth and decency." By *Christian* is, of course, meant *Catholic*. The canon is the same as that of Mgr. Lavelle. "Enlightened Catholic conscience" and "Christian sense" are synonyms for a Catholic.

If the Catholic dream come true, and Catholic Literature Committees all over the country have the final say in what the American public may read, that public will be in a far worse case than peoples that lived under the Inquisition. For after all, the Literature Committees of the Inquisition were composed of scholarly Dominican and Franciscan theologians, men of learning and of such science as was then available. Whereas the modern lay Catholic Literature Committees are composed of men and women who are equipped neither with theology nor with much scientific or literary discernment.

Catholic indifference to the taste and judgment of non-Catholics was dramatically instanced by the exclusion from Boston of Sean O'Casey's play *Within the Gates*. Mayor F. W. Mansfield, a devout Catholic, declared that the play as published "was nothing but a dirty book full of commonplace smut." The Jesuit, Father Sullivan, as spokesman for the Legion, and for Cardinal O'Connell, said that *Within the Gates* was "a sympathetic portrayal of the immoralities described, and even more so the clear setting forth of the futility of religion as an effective force in meeting the problems of life." Catholicism of Boston gave O'Casey his answer by showing how religion (if it was religion?) could be "an effective force" in meeting the problems of its existence.

Catholics answer the charge that such censorship as Mayor Mansfield exercised is "arbitrary" by declaring that a much more arbitrary censorship is exercised by critics and stage managers who offer the public naughty plays to the exclusion of edifying ones. Actually the Catholic attitude might be voiced thus: "I am competent to judge in moral matters and no one else is. There is need of a judge; Public Safety demands one. Therefore, I will be the judge!" The mentality is, of course, obviously Fascist. What else did Mussolini or Hitler say in presence of another field of circumstances? "I am competent to rule the State and no one else is! There is need of a ruler; Public Safety demands one. Therefore I will be the ruler!" The assumption of authority to override the will of the majority, even though merely and sincerely for the good of public morals, is a dangerous precedent in a country like ours. It is un-American and in effect seditious.

It is curious that from the start no attempt was made by the hierarchy to define "decency" or to lay down the principles on which a definition should be based. Such a procedure would have invited discussion. An intelligent understanding of "decency" might have awakened doubts and hesitancies in the minds of Catholic laymen and laywomen. The bishops preferred to eschew theology, philosophy and psychology, and leave their followers under the impression that "hot stuff" in general is subversive of morals and indecent! They aimed, they said, "to bring productions up to right moral standards." But what are right moral standards in the portrayal of crime or of night club life? Is night club life so essentially evil that it may never be portrayed? Are gangster pictures immoral unless the gangster is made out to be a detestable skunk? If so, Macbeth was not written "up to right moral standards," for the murdering pair in it are far from hateful! It has been claimed[1] that the Catholic Church suffered "a humiliating defeat" in its anti-movie campaign and that the whole spectacle was Gilbertian and "illustrated vividly the bankruptcy of Church leadership and intelligence." The fact that box-office receipts showed no falling off is brought forward as a fact to substantiate this point of view.

On the other hand, Catholic leaders have claimed that the victory is complete and the objective gained. "Give credit where credit is due," says Father R. E. Moore.[2] "The producers have cooperated. Without this cooperation no clean-up would have been possible and let us not cavil about motives. Today the leaven of the nation's screen entertainment is immeasurably higher than it was before the Legion of Decency began its campaign." Rabbis and Protestant ministers, who took their part in the movement, also declare that the moral tone of the movies is higher. The producers say that the movement cost them $10,000,000 in expenses incurred by recasting some films and scrapping others.

In any case, the result of the campaign is not to be judged

[1] *American Mercury*, March, 1935, "The Troubles of American Catholicism."

[2] *New York Times*, February 5, 1935.

solely by improvement in moral tone. The campaign was a trial of strength for the Church and an exercise in mobilization. The Church succeeded in demonstrating both her power and her capacity in organizing. Today she is immensely stronger for the display she gave in these respects. Furthermore, she showed her skill in hoodwinking the public and seizing authority to put over her own moral views on the whole nation. Not a Jew or Protestant or freethinker in America but has had to submit to the Church's dictation as to what is right and what is wrong for him or her to witness or the screen.

In the name of Public Safety the Church has laid the foundations of a far-reaching censorship of manners and morals. What she has done in the field of the motion picture industry she will presently attempt and achieve in other fields, especially that of literature.

She means to be the official censor of America.

In time the turn of science and philosophy will come and the Church will take steps to eradicate "error" from the schools and universities. As I have already said, "error has no rights in her eyes." Being "the Pillar and the ground of truth," it is her mission and her duty to make truth prevail and to vanquish its contradictory. The day when the schools and colleges are purified in this sense is still far off, no doubt, but the Church is patient and long-lived.

What man in Boston wields more power that Cardinal O'Connell? Who in Chicago is stronger than Cardinal Mundelein? Who in New York City than Cardinal Hayes? In Philadelphia, Cardinal Dougherty is a power, and in Baltimore Archbishop Curley—and so on, in most of our great cities, the Roman pennant flies! At the voice of a priest the

Senate of the United States was cowed into rejecting the World Court on which it was set. We have seen but the beginnings of the age of priestly control. Our books, our theaters, our amusements are under the Church's scrutiny, and what force can prevent her from doing as she will "in the name of Public Safety"?

CHAPTER V

THE LADY NEXT DOOR

THE attack on the Catholic Church in Mexico has deeply stirred American Catholics. It challenges them. Their Catholic neighbor, the beautiful Lady Next Door, is being done to death. What are they to do about it? Can they refrain from helping her? She looks to them for aid—the Pope beseeches them on her behalf—their honor is involved.

Actually, it is more than the honor of the Catholic Church here that is involved; her safety is to some extent at stake. Should anti-clericalism triumph in Mexico it would seek to follow up its victory. Mexico being regarded as an outpost of American Catholicism, its fate is a serious matter for Catholics. In defending the Church south of the Rio Grande they are defending themselves.

This fact largely explains the special pleading of the Catholics here that the United States Government should make the cause of the Mexican Church her cause. "The honor of our own country is deeply involved," writes the editor of *America*,[1] "when a semi-protectorate of ours engages itself in a Communistic and atheistic drive against all dwellers in the land." What matter the niceties of diplomatic etiquette —the custom of non-interference in the internal affairs of a foreign country—when so much harm threatens? Did not

[1] April 6, 1935.

61

American businessmen interfere in Mexico in 1927 to protect their oil interests? Should not Catholics now do as much
to protect their religious interests? "Let us not be content
with expressing sympathy. They are crucifying Our Saviour
again in Mexico. We are on the sidelines. Let us unite and
fight." [1]

The campaign of American Catholics in defense of the
Catholic Church in Mexico began with the meeting of the
hierarchy in Washington, D. C., on November 16, 1934, at
which seventy-eight bishops, archbishops and cardinals were
present. A joint, unanimous pastoral was issued in which the
religious persecution of Mexican Catholics was reviewed and
described, and in which the signatories appealed, as American
citizens, to all Americans to inquire into the state of Mexico
and to make public profession of their faith in the principles
of religious freedom. "As American citizens we present our
plea that justice may be done, that all our fellow-Americans
may make themselves advocates of that common justice for
man which is the security of every man and of every nation.
. . . Compromise at home or abroad on the part of any of our
fellow-citizens with regard to those principles is, to us, most
reprehensible."

The bishops struck a note of warning, bidding America
look to the future. "The full consequences of the persecution
of the Church and of Catholics in Mexico can scarcely be
foreseen at the present time. They cannot but eventually be
very grave. Those who must flee from their own country
into ours bring with them a problem to which we cannot be
indifferent."

The bishops referred pointedly to a speech in which Ambassador Daniels seemed to express approval of the educa-

[1] William O'Dwyer (Holy Name Society), March 10, 1935.

tional scheme of the Mexican Government and complained that such speeches contained ideas "absolutely at variance with our own American principles . . . and gave color to the boast of supporters of tyrannical policies that the influence of our American Government was favorable to such policies."

In the course of the pastoral the bishops disclaimed any wish to provoke armed intervention, or any intention of employing their influence "either as bishops or as citizens to reach those who possess political power anywhere on earth and least of all in our own country to the end that they should intervene with armed force into the internal affairs of Mexico for the protection of the Church."

The punch of the pastoral lay in the sentence: "Our own country cannot view with indifference the persecution of religion, the exiling of its citizens, by a neighboring country."

The bishops' pastoral was well received by the Press and widely disseminated. For all its apparent mildness and guilelessness, it proved a war beacon. Instantly there followed an outburst of Catholic Action which exceeded in violence and intensity that which had greeted the bishops' denunciation of the movie industry five months before.

This great anti-Mexican campaign is dangerous and embarrassing for the country. Our trade with Mexico is considerable. We export $30,000,000 worth of goods to Mexico and import $37,000,000 worth. Relations between the two countries have been strained many times, and are "touchy." Only such a policy as President Roosevelt's "good neighbor" policy can guarantee peace. Never had we less reason to wish for a quarrel with a neighbor. Yet, like a thunderbolt, Catholic Action has broken over the country, and the air is filled with fierce denunciations of the Mexican Government.

From every Catholic pulpit, during November, December,

January, and through the spring, issued harrowing descriptions of the persecution of Mexican Catholics and denunciations of the barbarity and wickedness of President Cardenas and his party. Every Catholic paper, without exception, carried like copy. Over the radio the mighty voice of Father Coughlin proclaimed the iniquity of the laws enacted against the Mexican Church, and fanned the flames of righteous hate. The Paulists backed the crusade over Station WLWL. Then began a Catholic boycott of Mexican goods and a campaign to prevent Americans from visiting Mexico. The Mexican Consulate was picketed by Fordham students and the consul heckled whenever possible. Next came "mass meetings" and an agitation for "interdenominational condemnation" of the Mexican regime.

On November 27th, a statement was issued on behalf of 500 clergymen of "three faiths": Protestant, Jewish, Catholic. The statement to which all could agree and which all signed was, from the Catholic point of view, disappointingly mild. "We register alarm," it read, "at every restriction upon the right of Churches to function. . . . recognizing that freedom from religious and racial intolerance is not fully achieved in the United States, and in other countries of the world than Mexico, we acknowledge our responsibility to labor for its achievement everywhere."

The Episcopal Church failed to express corporate disapproval of the Mexican Government because she believes that the Catholic Church in Mexico has merited to some degree at least the chastisement she has received. Writes C. H. Mitchell,[1] in answering Catholic criticism of Episcopalian backsliding over Mexico:

[1] *Commonweal*, April 12, 1935.

Charges have been publicly made by members of the Episcopal Church against the Roman Catholic Church in Mexico . . . which so far have gone unanswered. . . . These charges are of a most serious nature. "The Mexican Roman Catholic Church," according to the "Witness," an episcopal journal, has engaged "in a counter-revolution, with archbishops, bishops, and priests leading private armies. On at least one occasion they set fire to a train and stood by while people were roasted to death and they have slaughtered in cold blood hundreds of opponents including not a few officers of our own congregations."

This letter was contributed to the Catholic *Commonweal* as a reply to the editor's charges against the Episcopalians and "as an aid to understanding the attitude of the Episcopal Church."

American Catholics have been even more disappointed at the indifference of Rabbi Wise and other prominent Jews to the plight of Mexican Catholics. They recall how ardently they protested the Jewish persecution in Germany and they expect a similar ardor among Jews in protesting Catholic persecution in Mexico. They do not pause to consider whether the merits of the cases are equal or not.

In January the Knights of Columbus swung into action. Five Supreme Knights, Carmody, Swift, Callaghan, McGinley and Donahoe, descended on Washington and presented a virtual ultimatum to Secretary Hull. They demanded, in the name of 500,000 Knights, that he should recall Ambassador Daniels, for the speech he made in praise of the Mexican educational system, and that he should warn the Mexican Government that diplomatic relations would cease between the United States and Mexico unless an immediate stop was put to the persecution of the Catholic Church.

Mr. Hull's reply was contained in a letter to Representative Higgins, of Massachusetts, who was associated with the Catholic ultimatum. "Notwithstanding the well-settled policies and views respecting religious worship and practices that obtain in this country, I know you understand that other nations are recognized as being entitled to regulate for themselves their internal religious conditions in such manner as they may deem proper and that, accordingly, it is not within the province of this government to intervene in the situation in Mexico to which you refer. The procedure you suggest would be tantamount to an effort to determine the course to be taken by another nation and would almost certainly provoke such resentment as to defeat the purpose which you wish to achieve."

An unsuccessful effort was then made to interest the President in the matter, but he diplomatically escaped from expressing any sympathy with the Catholic viewpoint. Recourse was forthwith had to Congress and the Senate and to the surprise of the country Senator Borah consented to sponsor a demand for an investigation into the religious situation in Mexico before the Foreign Relations Committee. This was indeed a triumph for Catholic Action.

Borah had now to bear the brunt of Press criticism. An editorial in the *New York Times*[1] said: "It would be hard to imagine a resolution more inexpedient at the present time or bigger with possibilities of mischief." The editor appealed to the Senate to have nothing to do "with burning questions of other countries" and to preserve the "good neighbor" policy of the President. The *World-Telegram* published a similar editorial. New York Catholics were exasperated over

[1] February 2, 1935.

these editorials and Father Joseph A. Daly expressed their exasperation over WLWL. He complained that these papers were vociferous about religious persecution in Germany and "mum on the question of Mexico." Father Daly then dealt with the *Times'* argument of "inexpediency." "Expediency is," he said, "supposedly associated with tact, with diplomacy, but very often expediency can become a mask behind which lack of courage and furtive dishonest maneuvering find their refuge." Father Daly hinted ominously that the thing which was saving the Calles-Cardenas regime was the United States embargo on the importation of arms into Mexico, and concluded, with warmth and mixed metaphor, "It is indeed a crying shame that justice and liberty, the decencies of human life, must be sacrificed upon the yellow altar of expedience and persecution permitted to run its bloody way to preserve a weak-kneed peace of mind!"

Floods of clerical eloquence were now pouring over the land. In Detroit, Bishop Gallagher made his contribution: "Our State Department ties the hands of the persecuted that they may be ruthlessly butchered. Just as the Turks seized Christian children and transformed them into ferocious Janissaries, the crack troops of the Sultans, so also our Ambassador Mr. Daniels, encourages the gang of godless, Christ-hating cutthroats to snatch Christian children from the arms of their parents and teach them to desecrate the altars of God and spit on the faith of their poor fathers." [1]

In mid-February there arrived in Washington from Mexico, where for four months he had been studying the situation, Mr. F. W. Williams, Navigator of the Fourth

[1] National Catholic Welfare Conference, "News Service," January 21, 1935.

Degree of the Knights of Columbus. Mr. Williams, an experienced journalist and "ferreting investigator," brought with him a sensational story. The Mexican Catholics were arming and preparing for an uprising. Arms were coming across the border steadily. The people only awaited the day and the signal to rise in their millions and overthrow the hated tyranny of Cardenas. Meanwhile 90 per cent of them were in favor of the Borah investigation!

Mr. Williams had hair-raising stuff to tell about the teaching of immorality and atheism to tender children in the Mexican State schools, and about agents from Moscow with $18,000,000 to spend on Communistic propaganda. "They've taken God out of the sky down there," he said. "Here is how God stands in the town of Chihuahua. I was there. I was at the opening of school. I heard the children say in salutation:

" 'Teacher, there is no God!'

" 'My child,' the teacher responded, 'there never was any God!' "

Catholics did not question the value of Mr. Williams' "first hand evidence" nor inquire how, within four months, he had discovered that 90 per cent of 15,000,000 ignorant people were in favor of a Senatorial investigation in Washington into their affairs. His story was readily believed, and added fuel to the fires started by eloquent prelates and priests. Then followed the "mass meeting" of forty (or fifty?) thousand called together, inside and outside the Convention Hall, at Philadelphia, by His Eminence Cardinal Dougherty.[1]

With the object of showing what kind of thing a Catholic "mass meeting" of protest is, we take the following account from *America:* [2]

[1] February 24, 1935.
[2] March 9, 1935.

The gallery inside was a vast horse-shoe of human beings; the main floor sparkled with color; it held a giant, combined Catholic girls' orchestra; nuns, regiments of blue-caped white-hatted nurses; white-plumed Knights of Columbus; Catholic men and women stretching far to the rear; an immense ocean of human faces.

On the stage His Eminence, Cardinal Dougherty, on his throne was flanked by red-robed Monsignori, scarlet-coated Papal Knights, little pages in black velvet. Thronged around the altar, which was surmounted by a towering painting of Our Lady of Guadalupe, were white-surpliced seminarians, priests, red-cassocked Monsignori. Not only did the scene strike the senses. It struck the soul. The enormous assembly was a colossal act of faith. . . . Should other dioceses fall in line, the giant outpouring of Catholic faith in Philadelphia may prove to have been the first tones of a new Liberty Bell ringing out freedom for Mexico.

The Cardinal attired in scarlet cape and biretta, surmounted by a canopy of crimson and gold and surrounded by his pages and knights, told his audience that "300 priests were known to have been killed by the government since the violent persecution began in 1926." He estimated that since 1929 some 5,000 Catholic laymen had been done to death. He described how the Mexican Government was stripping boys and girls of morality and religion; how the jails were filled with Catholics; nuns banished; the churches robbed of all their possessions; the minds and hearts of the children perverted; the country Sovietized. He said: "For the last number of years twenty or thirty Communistic Russian agents of the Third International, financed by Russia, have been received into Mexico by its government and in conjunction with government officials whom they guide and encourage along the path of Communism, are promoting the Soviet plan of uprooting religion, morality, respect for legitimate authority, and are showing how to plunder the rich in order to line one's pockets. Already the fat of sacrilege is dripping from bloody hands."

The Cardinal, as reported by the Press, dwelt at some length on Thomas Canabal, "the man-eater of Tobasco" who hated Christianity so much that he called his donkeys "Christ" and "Blessed Virgin"; his three sons, Lenin, Satan and Lucifer; and "introduced sex education in the schools and had it taught in a manner too obscene and too revolting to tell."

In addition, the Cardinal quoted the "Russian agents" as boasting that "within five years they would clean up the mess of religion in Mexico and then pass into the United States to continue their work."

Archbishop Curley, of Baltimore, has achieved the difficult task of surpassing all the other prelates in the vehemence of his attitude with respect to the Mexican question. "The question involved," he said,[1] "is larger than that of religious persecution if such a thing were possible. It is one of fundamental human rights; more particularly it is one of the protection of American rights."

In urging diplomatic intervention by the United States he invoked the "Public Safety" plea, that had been invoked in the war against the movies and Neo-Paganism. "We would not," he said, "remain indifferent to a serious epidemic or contagious disease south of the Rio Grande; we cannot remain apathetic in face of the constantly increasing forces in the Republic of Mexico that would Sovietize that nation and constitute a menace to American rights."

Some time later, in addressing sodalists in Washington, he

[1] February 17, 1935.

delivered a bitter attack on our President, accusing him of exercising his personal influence against the Borah investigation and threatening him with the withdrawal of the Catholic vote in the next presidential election.

Apparently it never occurs to Archbishop Curley that the "American rights" he is so eager to have defended in Mexico are much more in jeopardy at home, as a consequence of the sectarian paroxysms that he works so hard to stir up. It is probably an inconvenience for American Catholic visitors to Tobasco, if there be any such, to go without Mass on Sunday, but it would be still more inconvenient for Presidents of this country to be obliged to sell their foreign policy in exchange for Catholic votes.

In small matters, as well as great, Catholic Action is busy in the fight to save the Mexican Church. Because the Rotary International decided to meet in Mexico this year, Catholics resigned in numbers; and the Bishop of Dubuque has forbidden his priests to have any connection with the Rotary in future. The Bishop of Los Angeles has formulated a complaint against two Mexican consuls, Alejandro V. Martinez, and Hermolao E. Torres, for "interfering" in American affairs by using pressure on American Catholics against joining in the prayers for Mexico.

The Mexican "good-will" broadcast over the NBC network was greeted by thousands of letters of protest from Catholics. A lecturer in Elmira who, as a Catholic, discussed Mexico, lost his connection with his lecture bureau, because the local priests took his remarks as "insults." In every possible manner and in every direction, American Catholics are striving to foment trouble between this country and Mexico. As the Jesuit editor of *America* puts it [1]: "*Everywhere Catho-*

[1] April 6, 1935.

lics are militantly making the country aware that in this Mexican protest they mean business."

Amid all the "war-propaganda" and scheming and agitating of American Catholics, one finds one who in the matter of Mexico has kept his head to some extent—Mgr. John L. Belford, of Brooklyn. He would have the Mexican Church look out for itself and fight its own battles. "We ought," he said, "to implore the Bishops and priests of Mexico living here, there, and elsewhere in hiding to go back and face a firing squad if necessary. . . . It is only by a baptism of blood that the Church of Mexico can be rescued." Apparently Mgr. Belford places little credence in the tales recounted by Cardinal Dougherty, and others, of 300 priests and 5,000 Catholic laymen slaughtered by Mexican "Christ-haters."

From the foregoing account of Catholic Action in the United States, on behalf of the Mexican Church, it is patent that the American hierarchy and American Catholics in general have made the cause of the Mexican Church their own. They absolve it from blame. They identify themselves with its conduct and policy. What then is the record of the Mexican Church? And what are the complaints of the Calles-Cardenas government against it?

The Mexican Foreign Minister Portes Gil, in an interview with Mr. S. L. A. Marshall of *The New York Times*,[1] admitted that his government was anti-clerical and Socialist, but denied that it was anti-religious. "No other religion among many," he said, "which are practiced in Mexico has presented any complaint to this government, alleging its ministry has been handicapped." He explained that under the Constitution religion should be taught by the parents at home and not in the schools, the purposes of which were to propa-

[1] March 20, 1935.

gate the scientific view of life and to develop in the children
the consciousness of the social equality of all Mexicans. He
denied that the Socialism taught was anti-religious, and
asserted that it was "pro-Mexican" and "pro-social justice."

The charge, based on history, that Portes Gil made against
the Catholic Church was to the effect that "considering itself
a hegemony superior to the civil power, it has continued to
interfere in the interior policy of Mexico."

He referred to the correspondence left by Maximilian and
his empress who had been introduced into Mexico by the
Church. This correspondence revealed "their difficulties in
dealing with a clergy that was determined to dominate and
subdue a government that was favorably disposed towards
the Catholic religion!" Portes Gil claimed that the Mexican
Church continued to use its wealth and power to increase its
influence in temporal affairs, and that it had not mended its
ways.

Next there were specific charges of sedition and conspiracy
against individual Mexican clergy, in particular against Archbishop Flores, Apostolic Delegate, and Bishop Manrique y
Zarate. These bishops were said to be active in fomenting
disaffection, promoting armed conspiracy and seeking the intervention of the United States.

Archbishop Flores admitted discussing matters with the
American hierarchy and stated: *"It is a right and duty based
on Catholic solidarity that peoples should help each other in
case of necessity. If this is interpreted as anti-patriotic I believe nobody can cast the first stone."*

The Mexican Government charged that a certain Mexican
Catholic, Señorita Sofia, was busy conspiring in the United
States on behalf of the Mexican bishops. Letters to her had
been seized, and it was known that she traveled from bishop

to bishop. Archbishop Flores explained: "With my recommendation she presented herself to Bishops in the United States and Canada and consulted the N.C.W.C. on the best means to organize lectures." He added words of praise of her piety and enthusiasm for culture. Naturally he made no admission regarding her reputed interest in getting arms across the border.

One of the charges against Bishop Manrique was based on his connection with "The Third Message to the Civilized World" which contained the passage: "Will you be such egoists and cowards as to be unwilling to expose your lives and earthly goods to peril to save these innocents from the grip of men so perverse and degenerate? *Don't ask me how to contend against these infamous men. If threatened with violence we must defend ourselves and our children with the feeble elements at our command.*" This passage was interpreted as being an incitement to rebellion.

The complaints of Mexican governors and others against the Church are, in general, those of obstructing and opposing the State. Governor Calles of Sonora, on banning all priests from his State, issued the following statement: "Since my taking over the government of the State of Sonora clerical elements have been the cause of tenacious propaganda against the official schools. Latterly those obstructionists have gone to the extent of publishing absurd and criminal notices to the effect that the Federal Government intends to give the children sexual education suggesting a disgraceful idea such as displaying them nude in public classes."

The social case against the Church is that she has kept the people of Mexico in ignorance and that as a result of her educational system in the days of her power 85 per cent of

Mexicans were illiterate. This percentage has been greatly reduced since the government has been secularized.

Disregarding minor matters, it is undeniable that the Mexican Church has striven in the past to control the government, to make education subservient to piety, to amass wealth and property, and to invoke armed assistance to perpetuate her ambitious status. In general it appears that she has consistently subordinated the common good to her temporal interests. Meanwhile the native Mexicans have retained a large part of the pagan superstitions of their race.

It is for the sake of this Church and this clerical tradition that American Catholics are striving to embroil our country in a foreign venture. It is in testimony of American Catholic Action that Archbishop Diaz, the Indian prelate of Mexico City, writes: "God bless that numerous United States public who have sympathized with me *in our common endeavor.*" [1] Hope is born in His Grace's heart that he will hear the refrain: "The Yanks Are Coming!" to the quick tread of ten thousand feet of United States Marines, and that with their coming he will see the renascence of the old-time clerical domination over Mexico.

The Catholics of the United States would have been better advised and have acted more patriotically had they negotiated a truce between Calles and Flores through bankers. Flores himself admits that when trouble threatened the Church in 1918 it was a letter to the Mexican Government from Mr. J. P. Morgan (which he claims to have seen and read) that safeguarded the Church from attack. Flores also holds that the more recent truce between Calles and the Church, which Ambassador Morrow (Morgan's former lawyer) negotiated,

[1] March 8, 1935.

was due to the same source. What Mr. J. P. Morgan "fixed" in 1918 and 1927 he could again fix. Has he been asked to do so? Or is it that he has been asked and has refused, in order to stimulate the Catholic rampage and embarrass Mr. Roosevelt?

CHAPTER VI

A FIGHTING PRESS

UNTIL recent years the Catholic group in America was handicapped by the lack of an efficient Press. Such papers and journals as it possessed were, for the most part, pious bulletins of little interest even to Catholics. Their circulation was limited and their influence was almost nil. They were no help to the Catholic cause. Many of them were so indifferently edited, so bereft of erudition and literary merit, that educated Catholics were ashamed of them.

Today the general aspect of the Catholic Press is different. It is a virile Press and efficiently managed. It has advanced and improved in many respects. Technically it is a hundredfold better than the old Press. In point of literary merit and scholarship it still leaves much to be desired but it registers great gains. In point of enthusiasm and pep for the Catholic cause it is perfect. It seethes with fiery energy. It is eager, active, militant. It boasts of the "flaming zeal" of St. Paul, and records that "if St. Paul were alive today he would be a journalist."

The change is due to the inspiration and direction of His Holiness, Pius XI, who possesses an enlightened understanding of the power of the Press and who realized clearly that an efficient Press was needed to co-ordinate and stimulate the Catholics of this country. Catholic Action, on which his heart is set, requires the backing of a Press. Bishop Griffin, of Springfield, Illinois, expressed the Pope's views when he said[1]: "Catholic Action without a strong Catholic Press may be compared to a strong man endeavoring to function on crutches. We need a strong, fearless, Catholic Press. We must have such a Press if Catholic Action is to succeed as His Holiness expects it to succeed." The same thought, expressed differently, made the subject of the address of the president of the Catholic Press Association, Joseph J. Quinn [2]: "Catholic Action must have a voice if it is to live, it must speak if it is to carry on. The support of the Catholic Press is the first and most essential activity in the program of Catholic Action. . . . Catholic Papers will be the carriers of the burning energy of Catholic Action for the new generation."

Thanks to Pius' continued interest and encouragement, the bishops, priests, and laity of the United States have done everything humanly possible to organize the Press. It is fully realized now that a Catholic Press is essential to develop solidarity among Catholics; to perfect their organic unity; to keep them informed and enthusiastic about Catholic Action and to preserve discipline among them. Significantly it is likened to the Catholic school by the Jesuit editor of *America:* [3] "No less truly than the Catholic School, although possibly in a lesser degree, a strong Catholic Press is necessary for the preaching of the gospel of Justice and Charity."

The comparison that the Jesuit makes between Catholic education and Catholic journalism gives us an insight into the Catholic conception of the function of the latter. The purpose of the Church in launching so many hundred Catholic papers

[1] February, 1935.
[2] 1934.
[3] February 9, 1935.

and practically forcing them upon their Catholic followers, is not to foster the love of art and literature nor to give Catholics academic delight in reading discussions of highly speculative theories of science and philosophy. The bishop's purpose, and that of the Pope who stands behind them in the Press drive, is grimly practical. There is work to do—Catholic Action—and the work needs the stimulus of printed thought and emotion. They mean the Catholic Press to function as an organ of persuasion, encouragement and inspiration. They want it to be a militant Press, a Press that in turn praises, criticizes, threatens and attacks. It schoolmasters with rod in hand. It points out mistakes and imposes tasks. It is relentless and severe. Always it is alert to the interests of the great Cause. "Were we dependent," writes the editor of *America*, "upon the secular Press for the truth about legislation which can be used against the Church and against Catholic interests, our cause would be lost." [1]

It would be unfair to pretend that the content of the better-class Catholic journals, such as the *Catholic World*, the *Commonweal* and *America*, makes no appeal to the intellect and to the aesthetic sense. At times these journals contain interesting and beautiful pieces, well written and thoughtful, but these flickers of light are infrequent. The tenseness and moroseness of propaganda pervades all Catholic journals, high and low alike. In general, the Catholic Press is a war Press and betrays the throbbing militancy and excitement that fills the Catholic camp.

It is important, at this point, to bring to light how Pius XI stepped in to identify himself in the most practical and intimate manner with American Catholic publications. He makes no pretense of diplomatic aloofness in the part he plays. To

[1] February 9, 1935.

be sure, he is technically a foreign Prince, one who has no claim to be heard "as an American Citizen," one who if sensitive to all the proprieties would hesitate to urge on American citizens the adoption of his views on political questions. But what do we find? We find it as an accepted maxim among American Catholics that the Press is "the mouthpiece" of the Pope. Thus Bishop Floersh, of Louisville, declared [1]: "The Catholic Press may be regarded as the mouthpiece of the Head of the Church . . . it is Our Holy Father himself who gave this title to it."

When visited by Mr. Reid of the Catholic Press Association, Pius XI frankly stated: "The Catholic Press is my voice. I do not say that it makes my voice heard, but it is my voice itself." [2] In these words the Pope takes responsibility for all the moral, social and political campaigning; for all the militancy; for all the punitive activity; for all the threats and caustic attacks that characterize the Catholic Press of America.

But does the Holy Father know much about this Press? In his pastoral (1935) Bishop Gibbons, of Albany, related how in his audience with the Pope in the previous December (1934) "nothing seemed to interest him more than our diocesan weekly," and how he had inquired into details of management and editorship. "He was visibly gratified," continued Bishop Gibbons, "when I assured him, in answer to his question, that the subscribers with few exceptions honestly paid their subscriptions."

Mgr. Smith, of Denver, in an interview with the public Press, gave an account of an audience he had had with the Pope, in which he described the activities and methods of the *Register* chain of Catholic papers, with its circulation of

[1] February, 1935.
[2] *America*, February 16, 1935.

350,000. The Pope expressed himself as highly pleased and declared that "the problem of circulating Catholic papers in America is solved." He was particularly interested in the manner in which Catholic journalists were trained and prepared for their work.

The task which the bishops had to face in reorganizing and developing their Press was no slight one. There was an immense field of twelve million Catholic readers to supply. They had to be educated into purchasing and reading Catholic literature. Old habits of reading purely secular papers had to be broken down and a new habit formed. The people were of various nationalities and interests. Regard had to be had for color as well as age and occupation. Journals calculated to interest the Negro would naturally interest no other class. The expense involved was immense. But the bishops faced the task and succeeded.

One of the most important decisions they made, to secure the success of the Catholic Press drive, was to allocate one month, February, every year as "Press month." During this month an intensive campaign for the Catholic Press is conducted. Every bishop addresses a pastoral letter to his priests and people urging upon them their duty to read and support the diocesan paper and to work for its expansion. From every pulpit in the land the admonition is heard: "Buy your diocesan paper! Read your own Catholic news!"

In their pastoral letters of the current year (1935) many of the bishops used their ecclesiastical authority to impose new methods of increasing circulation. "Cooperate with the business manager of the paper in his plans to increase circulation. Let there be organized in each parish a corps of solicitors who will make a house to house canvass for subscriptions . . . *convince merchants that it is good business to advertise in the paper*," wrote Bishop Gibbons, of Albany. Bishop O'Reilly, of Scranton, "threatened" his priests with "enquiry on the occasion of his official visitation" as to how they had co-operated in boosting his diocesan paper. Bishop Floersh ordered the pastors to form committees in each parish, and Bishop Rohlman gave a similar order, adding: "The reverend pastors must send the names of the representatives [the Committee] to the Chancery Office without delay." Bishop Laval, of New Orleans, asserted that the reading of the Catholic (diocesan) paper "is not merely optional but a matter of duty." Bishop Armstrong, of Sacramento, going still a step further, conjured his flock "to support the diocesan paper through patronage of the advertisers" and called this support "*a necessary and most useful form of Catholic Action.*"

In New York archdiocese, Mgr. Lavelle, on behalf of the Cardinal, strongly urged "subscription to and perusal of the Catholic periodicals, weekly and monthly" and added: "We have many of these and they are all good. I mention without exclusion our own New York publications—The Catholic News, The Catholic World, The Messenger of the Sacred Heart, The Rosary Magazine, America, The Commonweal. Periodicals like these will keep the people informed of the contemporary history of the Church, her trials, her triumphs, her needs. Above all they will make for a noble loyalty that never fails."

The value of this free advertising is naturally considerable. Mgr. Lavelle's letter was read at every Mass throughout the archdiocese on Sunday, February 3 (1935). It therefore reached the ears of about 2,000,000.

Special stunts are tried in some dioceses to work up circulation. In Cleveland, Bishop Schrembs enrolled 30,000 school and college children in a crusade for his *Catholic Uni-*

verse Bulletin. He held a preliminary meeting of 4,000 in
the public auditorium, and had an enlarged copy of the paper
fifteen feet in length on display above the stage. The crusade
of 1934 netted 20,000 additional subscribers. The 1935 crusade aimed at making every Catholic in the diocese subscribe.

The decision of the bishops to allocate February to the
cause of their Press, was not the only important move they
made. Through the N.C.W.C. they established a Catholic
News Agency, called the N.C.N.S. (National Catholic News
Service). This agency supplies interesting items of information to Catholic papers of America as well as to Catholic
papers of fourteen foreign countries. It is an efficient and
reliable service and has done much to make the Catholic
Press more up-to-date.

Besides the N.C.N.S. there is a Catholic Press Association,
which dates back a quarter of a century, but which was of
small importance until recent years. It holds an annual convention at which Press problems are frankly discussed. The
convention for 1935 was held in Atlanta, Georgia. A time-
worn question was raised, namely, that of establishing Catholic dailies. The Rt. Rev. Mgr. Peter M. H. Wynhoven,
editor of *Catholic Action of the South*, New Orleans, advocated the setting up of Catholic dailies, saying: "Catholic
daily newspapers are of an imperative importance, in fact a
condition *sine qua non* for Catholic Action to become real and
effective." The chairman, Father Parsons, wound up the discussion by declaring the project of a nation wide Catholic
daily "desirable, but relatively and psychologically impossible." In comment the *Catholic News*[1] in an editorial states:
"It is our opinion that a good substitute for a national Catholic
daily is the efficient chain of diocesan weeklies that covers the

[1] June 8, 1935.

whole country. The better they are supported and read by clergy and people the more conversant will American Catholics be with the Catholic viewpoint everywhere." One of the delegates to the convention, Mgr. Albert E. Smith of the Baltimore *Catholic News,* remarked on the tone of Catholic papers and advocated editorials "with a modified wallop."

It is remarkable that during the depression only one Catholic journal failed while a dozen new ones were started. One of the latter, *Catholic Missions,* boasted of reaching a circulation of 2,500,000 in its first issue.

Circulation is, of course, but one of the problems that a Press has to solve. For such a Press as the Catholic Press there is another even more serious one: that of establishing itself in the respect of the general public so that it may reach and influence the secular non-Catholic mind. In this respect the Catholic Press is a lamentable failure. Most of the Catholic papers are utterly unknown to non-Catholics, and for that matter are with difficulty obtained. Only *America* and the *Commonweal* are known by name, and even these journals are seldom read by non-Catholics. Frankly they are uninteresting to any but Catholic minds; that morose tenseness about Catholic affairs, to which I have already referred, is calculated to alienate all but Catholics. As the editor of the *Commonweal* frankly confesses: "Catholic Press activity is still largely an affair of Catholics talking among themselves and not reaching the great public adequately and effectively." [1]

Catholic editors are too impatient, too hot-tempered, too absorbed in petty and passing incidents that relate to the affairs of the Church, to rise to the plane on which they might by lucid and artistic writing interest the general public in Catholicism. There are many things in the cosmos of

[1] June 8, 1935.

Catholic activity that if philosophically discussed would win
attentive readers. But when, as in *America* and the *Commonweal*, really good articles are wedged in among hot-tempered and often bitter propaganda, and excited comments on
petty incidents, the effect is to irritate and disturb minds
seeking the pleasure of reading informative and thoughtful
writing. The Catholic Press cannot hope to establish itself
as part of the national literature until it ceases to be politico-
religious propaganda. It is no exaggeration to call it propaganda. Catholics themselves admit the fact. "Catholic literature," writes Father Talbot, S.J., co-editor of *America* (July
6), "of any type whatsoever, is propagandistic. We do not
conceal its nature nor do we wish to pass it over the counter
in any masquerading guise."

Turning now to examine its *genre* more closely, we take
in turn four prominent and typical papers: the *Catholic
News*, the *Catholic Worker*, the *Commonweal*, and *America*.
About each we will say a few words, with a view to bringing
out the characteristics of the Catholic Press.

The *Catholic News*, which was established in 1886, is thus
blessed by Cardinal Hayes: "I am pleased to recommend to
the faithful of the diocese the Catholic News, a friendly, interesting, and newsy weekly well known to Catholic New
York. The Catholic News because of its long years of useful
service in a truly Catholic spirit, enjoys a welcome at many
a Catholic fireside." [1]

If a champion golfer, or boxer, or speller (boy or girl)
happens to be a Catholic, that is "copy" for its columns. If
a distinguished European Catholic has ever been to America,
or mentions the word "America," that is "copy" also. A nun's
jubilee, or the fact that two, three, four, five or six members

[1] January 17, 1925.

of the same family enter religion; that is first-rate "copy" for this fireside, Holy Family, journal. Sermons, pious stories, edifying conundrums, a religious "believe it or not," tales from the missions, meetings of Catholic alumni, and so forth belong to the *Catholic News*. It makes money on boarding house announcements, and advertisements inserted by Catholic dentists, opticians and clothiers. In its editorial columns it is sound and fierce in its denunciations of "stage filth" and critics of Catholicism. Lastly it prints Father Gillis' syndicated *"Sursum Corda"* column.

Under these words from the Mass, Father Gillis reviewed Theodore Dreiser's *Tragic America*.[1] The review was, in the eyes of Dreiser, so foul and insulting that he had it reprinted and offered it as an advertisement to leading New York newspapers but they refused it. In part it said: "As Catholics, Mr. Dreiser, we lament the fact that you are a renegade from the faith. If anyone needs religion you do. . . . You rejected religion. And don't fool yourself about the reason. As a boy when you went to Mass didn't you sometimes hear from the gospels: 'Blessed are the pure of heart for they shall see God'? And with your active mind didn't you realize that contrariwise: 'Cursed are the impure of heart for they shall see only the devil'? That's your plight, Mr. Dreiser. You see all men as devils and all the earth as a hell because you carry around the devil and hell inside you. It is not unkind or un-Christian to tell you this."

The *Catholic News* printed this review, and has printed much else of a like kind "in its long years of useful service in a truly Catholic spirit" (Cardinal Hayes).

The *Catholic Worker*, to which we shall have frequent occasion to refer, is a recent publication, edited by Dorothy Day

[1] February 6, 1932.

and Dorothy Weston, in the cause of Catholic labor. It has rapidly increased its circulation to 70,000 at the time of writing. It admits candidly how its circulation is helped. "Father Benedict has interested 160 of his boys at St. Benedict's school in 'The Catholic Worker,' and each volunteered to take ten copies to sell on the streets of Newark. We are hoping that other schools will follow his example in bringing the paper to the man on the street. Cathedral High School takes 2,300 copies each month and many of the girls pass on their copies to their families or friends." In unison with all Catholic papers, the *Catholic Worker* repeats: "One of the most essential parts of Catholic Action is the sponsoring the Catholic Press."

The *Catholic Worker* is on the whole good-tempered and fair. Its piety is, however, exaggerated and the vision it gives of Catholicism is unreal. It plays up, to the uttermost, anything strongly red that is said by the clergy and professes that its chief aim is to spread a knowledge of Pius XI's teaching. The *Catholic Worker* shows signs of independence at times. It supported the Child Labor Amendment in spite of the opposition of the hierarchy and argued strongly in its columns that the Amendment was in full accord with Catholic doctrine. Of all the Catholic Press in America (since the sad demise of the *Fortnightly Review*), it is the most human; the paper that conceives best its appeal to the public mind. It sells for one cent, each month, in Union Square, hawked about by threadbare Catholic workers. The spirit of a Catholic Fabian Society is behind it.

The lay leader of Catholic journalists, Mr. Michael Williams, edits and has edited for ten years, the *Commonweal*. His avowed purpose is "to provide a worthy instrument of Catholic intellectual action."

Mr. Williams is an old, experienced journalist and excels in the make-up of his journal. He has written books on Catholic doctrine and enjoys expounding theology. "There is an obligation laid down on every Catholic to be a propagandist," writes Father Talbot, and Mr. Williams has chosen theology as his especial 'sphere. He has no training in the science and it is seldom that his expositions are accurate or fully orthodox, but his intention of doing the best he can for the Church is never in doubt. He claims that the *Commonweal* is not "Catholic propaganda," but it would be difficult to find a single issue that is not an apology for the Church and Catholicism. "The *Commonweal*," he told a staff writer of the *World-Telegram*,[1] "is not directly under ecclesiastical authority or censorship. Of course a Bishop might interpose if he thought we were confused about some principle or other or if we began to pretend we were spokesmen for the Church."

Mr. Williams, of course, should know that every Catholic, lay or clerical, who writes about Catholic doctrine and expounds it in public is "under ecclesiastical censorship" and is bound by Canon Law to submit his writings before publication to the bishop of his diocese. Even when a bishop does not fulfill his duty as a censor, the writer is still obliged to conform to the Church law—a law that no individual bishop can abrogate.

Mr. Williams' position as a lay editor, even though he be decorated with the St. Bonaventure medal for distinguished service in the cause of the Church, is a delicate one. He has not the authority to lead—that belongs to the bishops. Always he must follow. He must sit on the hedge on the occasion of questions turning up on which the bishops have not pro-

[1] April 20, 1935.

nounced. This weakness and hesitancy characterize his editorial policy.

The *Commonweal* espouses the cause of "Interdenominationalism," which is unsavory to the palate of Rome, and fair play for the Negro, which is a covert reflection on the senior pastors of the Church in this country. He means well but he is forever "putting his foot in it." In controversy he is ill-tempered and violent. On behalf of his religious fads he invites his readers to try sackcloth and ashes and to take their vacations in monastic cells. The "old-timers" laugh at his essays in mysticism and turn to the pages of Upton Sinclair to learn "the true story" of Mike Williams. The finances of the *Commonweal* have been helped along by the Calvert Associates, also by Messrs. B. Altman & Co. (Fifth Avenue, New York), who occupy a perennial half-page of advertising space and receive in the "Communications" column flattering letters for so doing.

America, the New York Jesuit publication of most importance, is smartly and tartly edited by Father Wilfrid Parsons. Father Parsons writes well and slickly. He is not candid in his apologetics, nor for that matter profound, but he scores points neatly and adopts a plucky stand on many questions. His journal is less sloppy than the *Commonweal*. Father Paul L. Blakely S.J., and The Pilgrim save it from mediocrity. Like all American Catholic journals it is frightfully—and needlessly—pugnacious and bitter. One could not imagine "Christians" of the character of Gandhi or Tagore writing the violent effusions that characterize its pages. The intemperance of tone is hard to reconcile with the long-headed patience that supposedly marks the true sons of Ignatius Loyola. But we should, perhaps, make allowance for the fact that 1535 and 1935 are far apart, as are the America Press and the original Manresa wherein the first Jesuit book was composed.

Lest it be thought that the criticisms of violence and intemperance are overstrong, let me quote a few examples of *America's* controversial methods. The first example I take from the issue of February 2, 1935. The article in question, an editorial, was entitled: "Will Rotary Go to Mexico?" This editorial was apropos of the acceptance by President Robert L. Hill of the Rotary International of an invitation to hold the annual convention of Rotary in Mexico City. The editorial indulges in browbeating, threatening, insinuating motives, and concludes with the dogmatic statement: "By going to Mexico Rotary will simply be aligning itself with the enemies of religion."

At the date of writing about five thousand Rotarians are enjoying their visit to Mexico City and watching with amusement processions of Catholic students calling for the downfall of the Mexican Government.

But to return to the article. We quote the following sentences: "Rotary will be well advised to change its mind. A storm of disapproval will descend upon it if it does not. . . . The officers of Rotary are not unaware of the deep suspicion with which their society has been viewed abroad by many Catholic authorities even to the extent of a Papal prohibition to priests to belong to it. . . . Those who have held that Rotary is a Masonic-dominated society will feel themselves fully justified when seeing it persist in going down to do honor to the atheistic Government of Mexico which is largely Masonic of the Grand Orient variety."

Under "Note and Comment" (April 27) we find an attack

upon Ambassador Daniels because he spoke over the radio in praise of Mexican scenery. The editor asks what would be done in the case of Ambassador Dodd were he to speak in praise of German scenery and urge Americans to visit Germany? Would he not be rebuked by the State Department "for making himself a salesman for German travel"? Then follows: "Before us lies a clipping from the Mexico City 'Excelsior' for April 8, and in it is a verbatim account of a radio speech by Ambassador Josephus Daniels, addressed, 'To my fellow-Rotarians in the United States' from the Foreign Office and in the presence of the Foreign Minister. All that Mr. Dodd did not do is done by Mr. Daniels and more. His undignified appeal reads like a page from a travel-agency bulletin. But about the misery of the people, the agrarian troubles, the industrial strikes, the religious persecution, the character of the generals and politicians, he is politely silent. One thing he does mention is interesting: the Rotarians will be received by the President of the Republic at the Foreign Club, which as revealed by Carleton Beals in the *Nation*, is 'a gambling den which is corrupting the people of Mexico City.' Is there no limit to the humiliations which Mr. Daniels will inflict on our own nation in Mexico?"

In the same issue of *America* and under the same heading "Note and Comment," there is a further paragraph on Mexico, this time about a good-will broadcast from Mexico to United States over NBC. The broadcast included "a poem recited behind music" which in the opinion of *America* was obscene. *America* quotes the terms of the license to broadcast which state that programs should be "of public interest, convenience or necessity," and claims that the Mexican good-will broadcast program should be canceled. *America* says:

"alien propaganda by a foreign government is certainly not in the public interest . . . the type of poem recited . . . is certainly not to public interest, convenience or necessity."

As a result of *America's* article, a group of Congressmen petitioned the Communications Commission to investigate, and quoted the poem that offended *America*. The "obscene" verse or verses at once became public property, and all the more attention was drawn to the "obscenity" on account of differences of translation from the Spanish, one by the National Broadcasting Co. and one by Father Parsons.

The NBC translation ran:

> But my greatest pleasure
> Was when she disrobed her flowing gown.
> Like a flexible branch
> She disclosed her beauty.
>
> An early rose
> Which had broken loose from its bud
> Boasting of all its beauty.

Father Parsons' translation brought out the "obscenity" more deliberately:

> But my greatest delight
> Was when she stood naked
> Of her flowing garment;
> And like a bending branch
> Of a willow, uncovered to me
> Her beauty, an unfolding rose
> Which breaks its bud and displays all its loveliness.

The song was an old Spanish one, of the time of Chaucer approximately. It was sung in Spanish which told indeed of an unclad maiden love-making on a shore beneath the stars, but it was no more "obscene" than a thousand other love songs ancient and modern—the ancient ones were perhaps often sung by St. Ignatius Loyola himself in his romantic youth. It was because the song was part of a "goodwill" effort, made by a government that American Catholics hate, that it was made the occasion of such a disedifying and stupidly bitter rumpus.

To conclude. The Catholic Press in its present phase is a fighting Press. Its effort is expended in stirring up Catholics to more and more Action so that the great victory may be achieved. It is reckless, truculent and violent in its methods. Part of it descends to vulgar abusiveness; part of it is almost maniacal in its fury. The more civilized and cultured part of it, that of New York, that we have dealt with is, to say the best of it, strong and harsh propaganda.

CHAPTER VII

INFILTRATION OF CATHOLIC THOUGHT

THE defeat of Alfred E. Smith in the presidential election of 1928 served as a rude awakening to Catholics. The outburst of anti-Catholic sentiment at the time demonstrated clearly that the American mind was out of tune with Catholicism. It was thought by Catholics that this was due chiefly to ignorance, and a resolution was adopted at a convention of the National Council of Catholic Men (Cincinnati, 1929) to initiate an "enlightenment campaign." Forthwith the radio, platform and press were employed to reveal to the American mind "what the Catholic Church really is." The effort to inject the Catholic viewpoint into American consciousness has continued to the present day.

Catholics have been clever and energetic in this propaganda, though how far they have succeeded in their purpose is a matter of question. Under the able supervision of the National Catholic Welfare Conference, Catholic ideas and Catholic news items have poured into the public mind through a thousand channels. In the pages of the public Press reports of Catholic ceremonies, functions, speeches, activities and so forth have mysteriously outnumbered and outspaced reports of all non-Catholic religious events combined. On the air Catholics have considerably more than their proportionate share of time. Within the week following Easter Sunday (1935), Catholics secured three international broadcasts: one for the Pope's Mass at St. Peter's; one for a "Five Cardinals" Peace Plea; and the third for the Notre Dame Alumni celebration. There was no other religious international broadcast save those of the Catholics.

Not only have Catholics succeeded in putting their case boldly and frequently before the public, but they have set up virtually impassable barriers against criticism. The hidden influence of the Church is used effectively in preventing the presentation of the opposing case. On the plea that criticism of the Church is bigotry and intolerance, she "insists," usually successfully, that American editors close their pages to it. If they do not obey when she insists she chastises them through her Press and radio service and in other ways.

The mainspring of Catholic propaganda is the teaching that only Catholic thought and Catholic morals can save America. It keeps hammering on the topic that "Catholicism is good for America"; that Catholicism is the best form of citizenship; that Catholicism is necessary to the country's welfare; that doctrines, such as birth control, which the Church condemns are "un-American and unpatriotic." These ideas were forcibly promulgated by one of the Supreme Knights of Columbus, Mr. William Larkin, in a nation-wide broadcast (March 17, 1935). He said: "Never since the dawn of recorded time has there been greater need of the dissemination of the principles underlying Catholic Action than at this very moment when false prophets and purveyors of anti-American propaganda under the guise of ameliorating the ills that sorely afflict humanity would set class against class, blot out the deity from the heavens, introduce the ethics of the barnyard into every relation of life, and trample underfoot the Constitution of our country and everything that is most precious and sacred to the heart of America."

In support of these ideas there is immense emphasis on the patriotism of Catholics past and present, on their unswerving loyalty to the Constitution and the principles of Americanism, and on their civic services to the country. We are reminded again and again that Catholics did their part, and more than their part, in the Great War; that in the War of Independence and in the Spanish-American War they likewise did their part. Catholic pageants are arranged to celebrate patriotic themes, such as the Birth of Maryland; the anniversary of the Treaty of Paris; the fighting at Fort Niagara; and of course the labors of Fra Junipere Serra. "We were here all the time," say the Catholics. "We were here in pre-colonial days in the persons of Jesuit missionaries. We were here in the persons of Lord Baltimore and his men in Colonial days, and stood out for religious liberty. In the War of Independence in the person of Captain John Barry we founded the American Navy, and in the person of Charles Carroll we signed the Declaration. Our theologian, Cardinal Bellarmine, supplied Jefferson with his best ideas on Democracy for the writing of the Constitution. We helped to build and create the country by our brains and thews. What other Church made larger contributions than we did? Are we not the most American of all religions?"

Catholic apologists, were they concerned about their propaganda being strictly logical, should of course demonstrate that the American Catholics who took their part in building the nation, did so precisely *because they were Catholics and on account of their religion,* but it would be quite impossible to do so. How could they prove, for instance, that the philandering Captain John Barry "founded the American Navy" because of his Catholicism? How could they show that it was on account of his Catholicism, and not on account of fear for the material well-being of himself and his followers, that Lord Baltimore favored religious freedom? However, propaganda need not be logical to be effective, and on the whole Catholics have succeeded in satisfying the American mind that they did their share of good patriotic work in the past.

There is a striking anomaly in Catholic propaganda in this country, to which attention must be called. In general it is the Church, and the activities of Catholics, that are publicized and boosted rather than the Catholic religion itself. Catholic life rather than the Catholic faith is explained and praised. The ethical ideas of the Church are expounded but not the dogmas of religion. Neither Catholic philosophy nor Catholic theology, save in a few particulars, are taught. What effort, for instance, is made to impart to the American mind the Catholic doctrine of *the supernatural?* The Catholic conception of "divine grace" receives no attention by Catholic apologists. Einstein's difficult theory of relativity is popularized, but not that of St. Thomas Aquinas on grace. Catholics who boost the Pope and his encyclicals, and other great Church celebrities, with the purpose of making America Catholic-minded, do not attempt to impart the fundamentals of Catholicism to the American consciousness.

Let us take for consideration a simpler and more concrete Catholic doctrine than that of grace, namely, the doctrine of papal infallibility. It is certainly all-important for Catholics to explain fully and clearly and convincingly the reasons for holding that the Pope is infallible. Catholics expect American non-Catholics to admit the superiority of their ethical doctrines, those, for example, that concern birth control, divorce, sterilization, on the grounds that these doctrines are "infal-

lible." But why should American non-Catholics accept them
as "infallible"? Why do not Catholics prove them to be such?
Why seek to force upon the American mind ethical teachings
labeled "infallible" without justifying the authenticity of
the label? Why not prove, once and for all and clearly, that
His Holiness is the sole authoritative interpreter of the natural law before attempting to persuade the American public
to accept his interpretations?

It is rather the end-results of Catholic thought that reach
the American mind than the Catholic principles, learning
and reasoning which precede the conclusions. On account of
this defect the Catholic case, as presented to America, is superficial and unsubstantial. Worse still: even the "end-results"
of Catholic thought are often inaccurately expounded by
American Catholic apologists. A spurious Catholicism is
popularized.

Let us take, as example, the Catholic thought on "sterilization." Educated Americans would like to have *the full story*
of why the Church is against "sterilizing the unfit." To the
average man it seems highly reasonable to render innocuous
(in respect of propagation) one who is diseased with a taint
that is at once serious and transmissible. If such a man con-
sents freely to being sterilized, why should he not be sterilized? And even if he do not consent, why should he not for
the common good be compulsorily and legally sterilized (sup-
posing such a law to be in force)?

In his encyclical "Casti Connubii" (1930), Pius XI gives
briefly—and none too clearly—the Catholic doctrine but he
does not tell the whole story of Catholic thought on the
matter, nor of course does any American Catholic. Pius XI—
in answer to the question, "Is it lawful for an individual to
have himself sterilized?"—affirms that "it is not lawful"

unless sterilization be necessary "for the good of the whole body." "Private individuals have no other power over the members of their bodies than that which pertains to their natural ends, and they are not free to destroy or mutilate their members or in any other way render themselves unfit for their natural functions." As reasons for this teaching Pius succinctly says: "Christian doctrine establishes and the light of human reason makes it most clear."

Catholic thought is unlikely to conquer the American mind unless it be more fully expounded and justified!

Again, Pius XI teaches that the State has no authority to interfere with the natural rights of subjects who are guiltless of crime. Advocates of eugenics "against every right and good, wish the civil authority to arrogate to itself a power over a faculty which it never had and can never legitimately possess." "Man has a natural right to enter matrimony" and so long as he is guiltless of crime the State cannot deprive him of this right even though "according to the norms and conjectures of [scientific] investigations he would through hereditary transmission bring forth defective children."

The one exception that the Pope makes (or seems to make) is in the case of those guilty of a grave crime. In this case the Magistrate can "mutilate the body" by way of punishment. To punish past misdeeds sterilization is permissible but to prevent future evils it is not lawful. Pius XI quotes St. Thomas: "No one who is guiltless may be punished by a human tribunal either by flogging to death, or mutilation, or by beating."

Catholic doctrine is thus entirely hostile to the eugenics program, but *Catholic thought remains unexplained*. Everyone knows that the lopping off of "members," ears, nose, hands and feet, etc., was a common practice in medieval times, and that the services of eunuchs were much in demand. The deprivation of an organ was a matter of small account. For a long period the Vatican choir owed much to "castration." When did the new severity in the application of principles begin? And why? Mr. Michael Williams, who often likes to go one better than the Pope, assures us that "even if the transmission of criminality, abnormality, and deficiency were a matter of iron and predictable law, she [the Church] would maintain that the social problem thus created could not be solved by the mutilation of the potential undesirable parents." [1] Needless to say, Mr. Williams has no authority to make such an absurd assumption, even in his pious endeavor to spread "Catholic thought."

A pregnant and characteristic Catholic idea that issues from the Pope's condemnation of eugenics is that *the family is more sacred than the State*," but this idea, which if properly expounded would influence many American minds, is neglected, like so many other important ones, by Catholic apologists.

Father Coughlin, more than any American Catholic who ever lived, has served to popularize Catholic thought, not only on Social Justice, but on the kindred subject of Communism. He has been the occasion also of the exposition of the Catholic idea of a cleric's place in public life. His Catholic critics have taken occasion to flood the public Press with the teachings of Canon Law and the customs of the Church. "It should be remembered," said Cardinal O'Connell,[2] "that no individual priest has the right to speak for the whole Church: that he has absolutely no right to commit the Church to any particular philosophy of economics. His mission is to preach

[1] *Commonweal*, March 15, 1935.
[2] Boston, December 9, 1934.

the word of God . . . The priest's place is in the sanctuary where he is to preach the word of God."

Father Edward V. Dargin, a canonist of New York Archdiocese, received a tremendous Press when he set about showing the American public that Father Coughlin was infringing the statutes of Canon Law. Non-Catholic America was treated to discourses on a Catholic subject that hitherto had been wholly unknown to them. They were told about decisions of Sacred Congregations and the enactments of the Baltimore Council. Around the devoted neck of Father Coughlin has been hung quite an immense sheaf of lessons in Catholicism by alert propagandists.

It will suffice to remind readers that Catholic thought on the social problems of birth control, divorce and public decency is well disseminated. That upon crime prevention is perhaps less well known.

To the Catholic mind there will always be crime, but its amount can and should be lessened by the proper education of youth in Christian ideals and conduct. To prevent or forestall crime is therefore the work of the educator. And what is the Catholic thought on education? "School and Church naturally go together. The school, as Father Drinkwater puts it so well, 'is far more than a place where definite teaching is given; it is a place or a group of people where a definite religion is being lived.' Mere religious instruction and facilities for giving it can never satisfy us (Catholics); we want our children to be brought up in what we call a Catholic atmosphere, breathing the air of religion, seeing signs of religion all about them, being taught by men and women who not only believe but practice their religion." [1]

Unfortunately in practice, Catholic education fails to keep

[1] From *Tablet*, London, quoted in *America*, February 25, 1935.

Catholics from crime. It fails even to get Catholics on the honor lists in art, literature and science. The Catholic schools and colleges of America, in spite of the tremendous sacrifices made to build and support them, have proved a terrible disappointment to Catholics. They have failed to produce more than a very few Catholic writers and Catholic scientists; they have failed egregiously to produce Catholic leaders; they have failed to bring credit on Catholic lore and Catholic philosophy. Writing in the *Commonweal* [1] a scholarly Catholic states: "There probably has never been in modern western history so culturally and socially ineffectual a minority, in ratio to the mass, as the twenty-odd millions of Catholics in the United States. A priest-editor once referred to this mass of American Catholics as the Church, not Militant, but Dormant. A great part of the responsibility for this condition, and some truth does lie in the charge, must be placed on our institutions of higher learning, their failure, in a broad generalization, to provide the nucleus of a homogeneous leadership, the leaven of a true culture."

Mr. McCarty goes on to show how the real work of promulgating Catholic culture amid "the un-Catholic leviathan" is held up by the lack of life and formation in Catholic education. He draws attention to the fact that Catholic thought owes more to Yale, Harvard, Princeton, Chicago and Colorado than to the Catholic colleges. Yale is producing work on the medieval religious drama; Harvard and Princeton on medieval literature and art; Chicago on Chaucer, and Colorado University on medieval philosophy. He concludes his article: " 'By their fruits ye shall know them': we [Catholics] have little reason in education for pride or complacency."

Still the infiltration of Catholic thought goes on in spite of

[1] June 28, 1935

the lack of scholarship, and of enterprise in research into the foundation of Catholic culture, among American Catholics.

In furtherance of the exposition of Catholic thought in history and sociology Hilaire Belloc and G. K. Chesterton are frequently invited to write for our Catholic journals, and are brought over here to lecture. Hilaire Belloc makes a bold and striking defense of the Catholic "Guilds of Workers" of the Middle Ages. He says: "The guilds fostered by the Church were rent by the divisions of Christendom following the so-called Reformation and workingmen were gradually dispossessed by predatory capitalists from any control over the means of production."

On the higher levels of literature and drama Catholic intelligenzia have striven to effect an entrance for Catholic thought. The Catholic Book of the Month Club affords all the encouragement it can to writers of books like *Death Comes for the Archbishop* who disseminate Catholic ideas and the Catholic viewpoint no matter what their religious faith may be. The Catholic Poetry Club, which has "the largest membership of any poetry society in the world," publishes a bimonthly *Spirit* devoted to verse. Among the members of its honorary committee are many non-Catholics. In the region of drama and pageant there is great activity among the faithful. There are, in the vicinity of New York, several "Passion Plays," one of the most ambitious of which is *Veronica's Veil* with a cast of 300 under the direction of a Passionist priest, Father Conrad Eiben. Father Eiben aims at making *Veronica's Veil* a national institution to rival the original Passion Play of Oberammergau.

Another Passion Play, *On the Road to Calvary*, is staged at Corona, Queens. Its managing committee comprise Borough President George U. Harvey, District Attorney Charles P. Sullivan, County Court Justices Peter M. Daly, William B. Hazelwood, and other men of political influence.

Pilate's Daughter (Brooklyn), with a cast of 125 women, has run for eighteen seasons. At the initial performance of the last season 1,800 attended. Pageants that are strictly religious are held within the churches. Such a pageant marking the opening of a drive for funds for the Catholic missions, was held in St. Patrick's Cathedral on January 20th, last. There was a colorful procession of children, boys and girls, 405 in all, dressed as nuns, brothers and priests. The procession proceeded around the cathedral and was reviewed by His Eminence Cardinal Hayes, who was seated on his crimson and gold throne, surrounded by pages dressed in medieval costumes, of green, scarlet, white and blue. Seventy-five religious orders of nuns and thirty-four of men were represented by the children. The old-time glory and pomp of Catholic ceremonial was displayed in miniature. The various costumes and habits were accurately reproduced, and the children walked with folded hands (and some of them with downcast eyes) in the manner of strictly cloistered celibates. The cathedral was crowded and many non-Catholics were present.

In an effort to help on the infiltration of Catholic thought into the American mind, the liturgy of the Church has of late been cultivated and studied. What is known as "the liturgical movement" has votaries among the elite of the Church. Many serious-minded Catholics hold that the seductive beauty of the Catholic liturgy would draw many to the bosom of the Church were it better known. They are impressed by the belief of English Catholics that "England will be converted through Catholic liturgy." New York Catholics have founded a "Liturgical Arts Society," the members of which lecture to Catholic groups on the history and significance of the Church's liturgy. Here and there an American bishop insists on a fuller and better liturgical setting for the sacraments, and calls for their administration in the solemn manner prescribed by the Church. But the majority of American bishops have no time for what they consider superfluous "foppery."

In a thoughtful letter to the *Commonweal*,[1] G. B. Neale refers to the matter: "Is the liturgical movement gaining ground? Yes, among a very, very limited number. These are generally the same few who make retreats and are at every Catholic affair. The others could not even explain what 'liturgical' means nor grasp any value from an exposition of its importance." Yet, in the opinion of the writer, the Liturgical Movement is better calculated to disseminate true Catholic thought than the majority of Catholic Action movements. In the liturgy of Mother Church there is found the sublime art and mysticism that is compatible only with love for and devotion to truth. A thoughtful American would be far more impressed by hearing, seeing and *feeling* High Mass, duly solemnized, than by the most magnificent parade of white-plumed Knights of Columbus that ever was staged. In High Mass he would sense the presence of lofty and noble thought: maybe he would admit it to be a divine conception. The parade he would regard as cheap and vulgar and material.

If Catholics fail to grasp the propaganda value of the Mass, it is because mysticism is dead among them. As G. B. Neale adds, in the letter already quoted: "To the great mass of Catholics mysticism is practically unknown—even repudiated.

[1] June 15, 1934.

They consider mysticism all right for priests and religious, but 'Let us be practical' is their attitude."

We come now to Catholic apologetics as a mode for disseminating Catholic thought and for making America "Catholic-minded." There are many guilds and leagues, such as the "Catholic Evidence Guild" and the "Trinity League," that are specially devoted to refuting erroneous statements about Catholicism and spreading "the truth" about it. Their methods are on the whole virile to the point of pugnacity. Many of the exponents of Catholicism are of limited ability, of unstable temper, and deficient in knowledge of Catholic doctrine. Strange to say, Catholic colleges and universities give their Catholic students a very ineffectual training in religion.

Be that as it may, the fighting element of Catholic propagandists command the air. On Station WLWL the Trinity League functions weekly. With the co-operation of a press-clipping bureau it attacks all statements derogatory to Catholicism which appear in the Press and in magazines. As descriptive of the activities of the League we quote the following from the *Catholic News* of New York.[1] "In the course of his addresses [during January, 1935] Dr. Sullivan [President of the League] called attention to publications found in Harper's Magazine, the American Mercury, the Watchman, the New York Times, the New York American and other issues of the Press. The articles, short stories and editorials to which he referred carried misrepresentations of Catholic doctrine and subject matter offensive and repugnant to all Catholics. Dr. Sullivan criticized, refuted, and corrected these Press excerpts by stating the authoritative position of the

[1] February 16, 1935.

Catholic Church in regard to each. On the other hand he lauded Dr. Nicholas Murray Butler, president of Columbia University, on the latter's zealous work in vigorously protesting against the encroachments of irreligious groups into schools and universities. As a result of these broadcasts the Trinity League has received letters from many of the offending publishers who apologized for the appearance of such obnoxious material and promised to be more censorious in the future." The founder of the League, Father Paul B. Ward C.S.P., aims at making it a national organization "to combat atheism."

The "letter-writing apostolate" of Catholics needs but a passing reference here. It consists in the sending of corrective, abusive and punitive epistles to the writers and publishers of such articles as Dr. Sullivan "refutes and corrects." It is hard to see how it furthers the great cause of making America Catholic-minded.

There are a thousand channels, other than those listed above, through which some element or phase of Catholicism is presented to the public of this country. Catholic propaganda is as varied in form as it is limitless in extent. It is interesting to note however the zeal of some Catholics in the matter. "As Catholics," writes Dorothy Day, "we must be class-conscious. . . . Conscious of a definite class to which we adhere . . . a firmly rooted sense of solidarity. There should be a thousand free workers' colleges throughout the country to bring Catholic thought to the man in the street. We must get rid of bourgeois and communist propaganda in our text-books; we must found Farming Communes where Catholic thought can flourish in a pure environment, untainted by the materialistic jungle without. . . . . Catholics must consider it their duty to raise their voices in Trades Unions especially where they have lost the lead. They must think it important to fill key positions in social organisms of all kinds. Catholics must grasp the plough."

The American mind is receptive, and some at least of "the Catholic outlook" is registered therein. Among educated Americans there is an awakened interest in the traditions of Catholicism. The philosophy of life of primitive Catholic peoples, such, for instance, as that which inhabits the Aran Isles, is studied with sympathy. No longer is the malicious and ribald version of Catholicism accepted as true.

Probably the infiltration of Catholic thought would have progressed further if Catholic apologists had more confidence in their audience and were more candid in their expositions. They have, beyond a doubt, a marvelous story to tell, the story of an ancient Church that has satisfied countless millions and sheltered within her arms the greatest scholars and artists of several hundred years of Western Civilization. The religion and the culture perfected by these minds were mystical, and noble and logical in their philosophy. The harshness, autocracy and wordliness of the Church belong to the picture and should not be concealed. The incredibility of the dogmas that evolved as the Church advanced in years does not detract from the glory of her progress through the ages. Though repugnant to reason, the faith as a faith still "hangs together." When studied and *lived* it carries its own conviction with it.

One marvels at the obtuseness of Catholic apologists expecting a large sale for an expurgated text on this great theme! Surely it cries for candor and frankness in the telling.

Until Americans are convinced that they are getting *all the facts*, good and bad, about the Church and Catholicism, the infiltration of Catholic thought will meet sullen resistance in their minds, and Catholic culture will remain unintelligible · to them.

CHAPTER VIII

INTERDENOMINATIONALISM

PERHAPS the most significant manifestation of the policy of the Catholic Church in this country at the present moment is her apparent trend towards Interdenominationalism. True, the Church does not go far in this direction but she goes sufficiently far to lead the public to believe that she has abandoned her old-time policy of splendid isolation. She is catering to the popular sentiment in favor of the churches "pulling together." Her voice is raised with the loudest in disparagement of "intolerance and prejudice" as un-American and un-Christian. She has gone beyond her earlier program of "exploring the areas of possible co-operation [with other Churches] in social and civic fields." With hesitating step and uneasy conscience she has entered "the commonwealth of brotherhood."

The interdenominationalism of American Catholics is all the more surprising when we recall the uncompromising aloofness from every form of heresy that has from time immemorial been the attitude of the Catholic Church. It is not so long since Leo XIII rapped Cardinal Gibbons on the knuckles because he dared to open a "Parliament of Religions" in Chicago. Even more recently (1928) the present Pope, Pius XI, wrote congratulating the president of the International Union of Catholic Women's Federations for denying membership to Catholic women's groups that were affiliated with non-Catholic groups. He said: "In order that your Union may retain the truly Catholic character and preserve its sole aim and full agreement with the instructions of the Holy See it is necessary that none of the affiliated associations become a member of neutral organizations or women's federations. . . . Therefore, it was entirely correct of you to reaffirm the principle that your Union is not permitted to admit to membership any organization affiliated with neutral associations." It would appear then that American Catholics must have some grave reason for cultivating Interdenominationalism, in defiance of the Roman tradition and teaching. In America today it is quite a common thing to find rabbis, priests and Protestant divines on the same platform advocating moral protests and furthering moral drives. They cooperate for the furtherance of decency and religion. They celebrate one another's jubilees. They discuss reforms of various kinds in conference. Mgr. Lavelle or some rabbi summons an "Inter-faith Conference" and when Peter, Martin and Jacob have lunched together and drunk cocktails they sit round a table devising plans to strafe the devil. Were such a thing to happen in Italy; were Catholic priests of the Eternal City to lunch and talk morals and cleanup campaigns with Methodist ministers and rabbis, the Holy Father would be horrified. Yet, in theory at least, Catholic doctrine is the same for Italy as for America. What Mgr. Lavelle does here should be sinful, if it be a sin in the shadow of St. Peter's.

And what of "Brotherhood Day"? This celebration is an outcome of the work of the Conference of Jews and Christians. Its national chairman is Dr. John H. Finley. "Brotherhood Day," he said, "should be practiced not only one day in the Calendar Year but every day." [1] He read messages in praise of the movement he represents from President Roosevelt, Mgr. Lavelle, and Rabbi Stephen Wise. Mr. Michael Williams, representing Catholic opinion, said [2]: "There was need for a commonwealth of brotherhood today when terrible prophets are arising now to lead the masses astray. . . . He emphasized that the purpose of Brotherhood Day was not only *to bring representatives of the various faiths together to talk but also to work together*" (italics ours).

Of course, every patriotic citizen will say: "Fine! An excellent thing! Protestants, Jews and Catholics should team up and pull the religious plow together!" But what seems good in the eyes of a patriotic American citizen may seem, and actually does seem, very wicked in the eyes of a sincere Roman Catholic theologian. The latter looks upon rabbis and Protestant divines as the most "terrible prophets" of all. He would remind Mr. Williams that his "commonwealth of brotherhood" idea was heretical and damnable however agreeable it might be to American taste.

Catholics, like Mr. Williams, Father Riggs, Father Elliot Ross and other pronounced interdenominationalists are, of course, greeted with tumultuous applause by non-Catholics when they take a step forward in the cause of Interdenominationalism. Dr. S. Parkes Cadman blesses and lauds them to the skies, and even the sourest Baptist minister claps his hands. Does not such applause give them a hint to pause and consider what they are doing? Without being invidious, it might be suggested that the lines of the poet Tom Moore apply:

[1] *New York Times*, February 24, 1935.
[2] *New York Times*, February 24, 1935.

Unprized are her sons 'til they learn to betray,
Undistinguished they live if they shame not their sires.

"Brotherhood" clergymen know instinctively that orthodox Romanism is against them and it is only when orthodox Romanism is repudiated that tears of joy well up in their eyes!

Many sermons were preached in the various pulpits of the city on "Brotherhood Day" (February 24, 1935). One of these deserves notice as illustrating the point at issue. Rabbi Isadore Aaron, of Brooklyn, said: "The greatest tragedy is the fact that when we compare two religions we tend to stress their differences instead of their similarities. We worship one God. We even conduct our services in a similar manner. We base our lives on: 'thou shalt love thy neighbor as thyself.'" To the plain man, innocent of Roman theology, this sounds good. But is it good to the Roman theologian?

The Roman theologian will quote in reply the text about "scandalizing the little ones" and prove that if only "similarities" are stressed the little ones will be deceived and led astray! They will as a result be devoured by "ravenous wolves." He will insist that it is *the points of difference* that matter not the points of similarity! As a good salesman sells his refrigerator against competing brands on "points of difference," namely, on points of superiority, on absences of defects, etc., so the theologian sells his religion on points of superiority and on absences of defects.

The Roman theologian will assert further that his "love for his neighbor" forces him to safeguard his neighbor from falsehood and heresy, and that it is his unremitting task to remind all the world of the errors of other religions and the differences between his "uniquely true" religion and all the rest.

Furthermore, the Roman theologian will insist that any line of conduct, such as friendly association and co-operation with heretics in sacred matters of morals, which may seem to condone heresy, is "inherently evil" and, like murder, *per se* bad and sinful and blasphemous.

"Brotherhood Day" has not been considered sufficient by ardent interdenominationalists, and "300 *recognized leaders* in religion and welfare work," namely, the "National Committee for Religion and Welfare Recovery," have issued a call for "Loyalty Sunday," October 6th, on which day (or on the preceding day for Jews and Sabbatarians) it is suggested that there be a 100 per cent attendance in churches and synagogues of churchgoers. The call includes quotations from letters and writings of "moral and religious leaders" among whom the Pope gets a place of honor, side by side with Roger Babson and Robert Millikan, and Nicholas Murray Butler. "The movement recognizes and *respects* differences of creed and church but urges a co-operative action for fundamental moral values *upon which all are agreed*" [1] (italics ours).

Will the Catholic clergy co-operate? Will Mgr. Lavelle agree to swop compliments with Rev. "Billy" Sunday, and pool moral values with Rev. Christian Reisner? Will he lend a hand in filling heretical churches with heretics on October 6th for the sake of "Brotherhood" and "Loyalty"? Does he not agree with Newton D. Baker of the National Conference of Jews and Christians that "every ignorance and every prejudice among us is a danger"? Why should a few old encyclicals be allowed to stand in the way of American "co-

[1] *New York Times*, March 3, 1935.

operative action for fundamental moral values"? "To limbo with encyclicals!" as Al Smith in effect said.

One of the offshoots of the National Conference of Jews and Christians is the annual tour of a "Tolerance Trio," a Catholic priest, a rabbi, and a Protestant clergyman, to benighted districts of the country, to give displays in the modern art of religious tolerance. "I was delighted," writes Father T. Lawrason Riggs,[1] "to accept the invitation of the National Conference of Jews and Christians to tour the South as the Catholic member of a 'good-will team, for Justice, Amity, and Understanding among Protestants, Catholics and Jews in America' starting on January 27th last. My pleasure came, however, largely from the prospect of three weeks association with my good friends [Rev.] Dr. Clinchy [Presbyterian] and Rabbi Lazaron."

The "Tolerance Trio" appeared on various public platforms, mostly in colleges, and asked each other prepared questions and answered each other, usually, with prepared jokes which (according to Father Riggs) provoked "satisfactory laughter."

Father Riggs was apparently bent upon dissipating the idea of "alleged political aims of Catholicism"; Rabbi Lazaron on proving that Jews are not "clannish." Question and answer were on burning topics:

Dr. Clinchy to Father Riggs: "Didn't the Pope tell you to vote for Al Smith?"

Father Riggs answers: "No, *the Pope is not interested in American politics*, as non-Catholics generally seem to think. As a matter of fact many Catholics did not vote for Al Smith."

Father Riggs is asked: "Do Catholics believe that all Protestants and Jews are going to hell?"

[1] *Commonweal*, April 12, 1935.

He replies: "No. We believe that no one loses his soul who does not knowingly sin against the Light. With repentance anyone will be saved if he follows the Light."

Such answers are "half-truths" and no more. Father Riggs and his like can never dissipate "ignorance and prejudice" by lack of candor. The Pope is intensely preoccupied about American politics and busy about them as we shall see later.

The "Light" to which he refers, according to Catholic doctrine, manifests to mankind in general the truth of Catholicism, and any man who, getting an inkling of the truth, fails to follow it up, sins against the "Light" and goes to hell. The dogma "extra ecclesiam nulla salus" (outside the Church there is no salvation) is Rome's answer to Father Riggs!

In Brooklyn (March 18th) before a "Parents and Teachers Association" meeting Father Riggs expressed disapproval of his brother priest, Father Coughlin, on the grounds that Father Coughlin did not make clear what were his own and what the Church's views. It never struck him to make clear what were his own and what the Church's views in regard to his "Tolerance" stunt. At the same meeting he went on record (according to the *New York Times* report) as agreeing with Jews and Protestants that "no denomination or group of sects should be permitted to control extra-curricular work any more than scholastic . . . they should all strive for complete co-operation [in school affairs] they felt." Like every other Catholic interdenominationalist, Father Riggs is "caught in the net" and conveniently forgets his Catholic doctrine, and what Popes have written on education. The Pope, of course, insists on absolute control of both the scholastic and extra-curricular education of all Catholics, and tolerates no interference either from other religious groups or even from the State.

Let me give a recent example [1] of how "Interdenominationalism" leads the Catholic clergy into the morass of heresy. On May 12th (1935), there was issued a "Joint Statement" signed by "250 leaders in Three Faiths" to protest against threatened curbs on Free Speech. The first signatory was Mgr. John A. Ryan (Professor of Moral Theology at the Catholic University, Washington, D. C.). About eighty other Catholic priests are reported to have signed the statement, which included many such sentences as those that follow:

"Our forefathers felt that the only safeguard to liberty for all was freedom of expression. This is the very essence of Americanism."

"Let us beware lest in the name of Americanism we allow the destruction of our most precious American traditions. Both the Fascists and the Communists deny the rights of free speech in countries which they control *but we should abhor their common practice in this regard and should scorn to adopt their methods of suppression in our free land.*"

"We therefore call upon the people of our respective faiths to arouse themselves at once to these dangers which threaten our American liberties and to exert their immediate influence as citizens for the preservation and maintenance of the rights and responsibilities of free speech, free assembly, and a free press, and the encouragement of free communication of mind with mind as essential to the discovery of truth and the maintenance of our American form of government."

These sentiments are, of course, wholly admirable and wholly American but *they are not the sentiments of Roman Catholicism.* From the Roman Catholic point of view they are heretical. The Roman Catholic doctrine is that "error has

[1] *New York Times*, May 13, 1935.

no rights"; that doctrines which the Church considers false or offensive, such, for instance, as Birth Control, Sterilization, Socialism, Communism, etc., *should be denied the privilege of the press and the privilege of free exposition.* What, for instance, does the present Pope say of Communistic propaganda? Elsewhere I have quoted his words: "We cannot contemplate without sorrow the heedlessness of those who seem to make light of these imminent dangers [of Communism] and *with stolid indifference allow the propagation far and wide of these doctrines.*" [1]

Evidently the Pope does not "scorn" the method of suppression but would adopt it and very stringently limit free speech! Again, let us note that Italian Fascistic practice of suppression of free speech, as regards matters inimical to the interests of religion, is to be attributed largely to papal influence with Mussolini.

It is no use for Monsignor Ryan and other Catholic priests to pretend that the American practice of free speech and free assembly is in accord with Roman Catholic doctrine. It is not! And when they play at "Interdenominationalism" they play fast and loose with their faith. Father Quitman F. Beckley calls "the developing rapprochement between the different religious groups in America" a "movement in the right direction." [2] That may be so. It may surely be a step oriented towards the ultimate good of America. But it is certainly not a movement which leads in the direction of orthodox Roman Catholicism.

A more coherent effort at interdenominationalism than that of Mgr. Lavelle and Father Riggs was attempted five years ago in Iowa University. It took the form of a School of

[1] "Quadragesimo Anno."
[2] *Commonweal*, June 14, 1935.

Religion. The idea was to provide students with the opportunity to study living religions under the teaching of their living clerical representatives, Jewish, Protestant and Catholic. Dignitaries of the three faiths agreed to co-operate to this end, and the State Board of Education of Iowa approved the project. The courses in this School of Religion counted for the taking of degrees. Father Takkenberg was appointed as Professor of Catholicism; Dr. Farbridge, of Judaism; and Rev. Dr. Hawley, of Protestantism. All went well for a time. From 1927 to 1930 the results were gratifying. Then Father Takkenberg, with the approval of his ecclesiastical superiors, withdrew. In *America*[1] he gave the reasons for the Catholic withdrawal. He complained that Catholics were duped and that Protestants gained most from the School of Religion. "I cannot help feeling," he wrote, "that in the eyes of the learned or thoughtful people outside the fold *Catholicism will generally appear to best advantage if it remains unaffiliated with any Protestant movement.*"

Rome long since realized what the Iowa priest only found out after three years' experience of interdenominationalism (and what Mgr. Lavelle and Fathers Riggs and Ross will eventually discover), that Rome profits more by exclusiveness than by working in harmony with other groups.

What probably happened at Iowa University, and what inevitably happens when interdenominationalism gets going, is that the non-Catholic parties begin to believe in the Catholic pose of "broadmindedness" and "tolerance" and venture on a little friendly criticism that has a spice of realism in it. Then the fat is in the fire!

It is one thing for a Catholic to comment on his Church in a loving fault-finding manner without "giving away" any-

[1] February and March, 1931.

thing of moment. It is another thing for a Catholic to listen in silence and patience while a heretic (even the most friendly of heretics) *exposes* some of the faults of the Church. At once the Catholic is up in arms and "brotherhood" is forgotten!

A neat example of a "Tolerance Trio" priest (Father Elliot Ross already referred to), and a friendly interdenominational Protestant, Claris Edwin Silcox, in grips was revealed in Father Ross's review of a *Report* [1] edited by Mr. Silcox. The review is a subtle admixture of meaningless "I am in hearty accord-s" and "I believe this book attributes too much importance to-s."

Mr. Silcox indulges in spicy references to the friction caused by the Catholic doctrine on contraception, mixed marriages, civil liberty and authoritarianism. Father Ross counters in each case. As regards the Catholic doctrine on contraception he says "that Catholics condemn contraception and some Protestants sanction it produces no more friction than that Catholics condemn divorce and Protestants do not." He attributes such friction as arises to *political animus*, completely ignoring the insulting terms used by the Church against contraceptionalists.

When Mr. Silcox quotes with approval a Protestant view that "there will never be peace between Protestants and Catholics so long as the Catholic Church maintains its present attitude on mixed marriages," Father Ross answers: "As a matter of fact very few non-Catholics are involved in the consequences of the canon law on marriage." Everyone knows that there are thousands of mixed marriages yearly, and that the terms imposed by Rome on the non-Catholic spouse are

[1] *Report* on the relations between Jews, Catholics and Protestants, issued by the now defunct Institute of Social and Religious Research. The review appeared in the *Commonweal*, March 15, 1935. The Institute was allied to the National Conference of Jews and Christians.

from his or her viewpoint insufferably humiliating! Mr. Silcox quotes a French Catholic writer of importance, namely Louis Veuillot, as saying: "We demand liberty from you in the name of your principles; we deny it to you in the name of yours," and inquires: "What can be done with a demand like that?" This passage, which is found in the epilogue, so incenses Father Ross that he writes: "The Epilogue is the least satisfactory section of the book—in fact so unsatisfactory that for many Catholics it will spoil the whole study." Mr. Silcox was hitting below the belt when he referred to Catholic notions of civil liberty!

Mr. Silcox might have hit harder and lower had he thought of quoting Lord Acton, instead of Louis Veuillot. Lord Acton, perhaps the ablest of Catholic historians, admitted that "for four centuries Rome taught that no Catholic could be saved who denied that heretics should be burned."

Father Ross is further incensed when Mr. Silcox "puts the question in the mouth of the Protestant majority: 'Can democracy really endure if one group is educating its children for freedom while an influential minority in its midst continues to educate its children for authority?'" Father Ross claims there is a logical fallacy in the question and continues, with what seems to us an amazing lack of sincerity and candor: "There is no necessary contradiction between political freedom and religious authority. Catholics accept their religion from Rome, their politics—*leaving aside for the moment a very few politico-moral questions* such as compulsory sterilization of the feeble-minded—they choose for themselves" (italics ours).

Father Ross, who makes pretense of relying upon logic, should surely admit that there *is* "a necessary contradiction between political freedom and religious authority" when there exists even *one* "politico-moral" question, with regard to which Rome with finality and authority forbids the American Catholic citizen to exercise his free judgment in voting *pro or con*. As a matter of fact, there are very many "politico-moral" issues and not merely "a very few."

I have dwelt at length on this Ross-Silcox incident to bring out the fact that interdenominationalism is impossible to Roman Catholics except in so far as they make pretense of it to cull favor and secure political advantage.

Were interdenominationalism good in her eyes, why should the Church legislate so severely against mixed marriages? The Church *definitely forbids them* "everywhere and with the greatest strictness" ("Casti Connubii"). They are tolerated "only occasionally on account of circumstances." Even when allowed it is foreseen by the Pope that "the Catholic party will suffer some detriment." No doubt there are thousands of mixed marriages, but their frequency is indicative rather of the avarice of priests and bishops who receive fat stipends for securing dispensations, than of any growing leniency towards heretics on the part of Rome.

Rome knows that association with heretics, as in the case of mixed marriages, leads to "deplorable defections from religion" or "headlong descent into that religious indifference which is closely allied to impiety."

Writing in the Catholic *Ecclesiastical Review*[1] an orthodox Redemptorist priest—not a priest of the Lawrason Riggs or Elliot Ross type—bewails the effect of intercourse of "our young people" with non-Catholics as tending to lessen their "doubts and fears" concerning non-Catholic religions. He says: "The constant, more intimate and more friendly inter-

[1] June, 1928.

course [of our young people] with non-Catholic friends and relatives at their social gatherings or business meetings removes all doubts and fears concerning non-Catholic religions. The transition to their easier way of living, which they cannot but notice, is only too inviting and before long the easier and wider path of life is chosen." The writer quotes from an article that had appeared in *America* to the effect that "if the Catholic Church wants to continue her success in the United States she must continue her struggle single-handed and alone, and not through aping the methods of other religionists by merging with the spirit of the times."

Everyone knows that the Church of Rome claims to be inerrant and indefectible and that she does not change her views. "Yesterday, today and forever" is her cry. What the Fathers taught and what St. Thomas taught the Roman Catholic Church still holds and teaches. Her language has become a bit more temperate, more civilized, but the thought behind the language remains the same.

What is that thought with respect to Jews and heretics? And by heretics are meant Bishop Manning, Dr. Parkes Cadman, Dr. Clinchy, Dr. Harry Emerson Fosdick and other clergyman of New York of Protestant affiliations.

What has St. Thomas to say of Judaism and of heresy? What do the Fathers say of Mgr. Lavelle's good friends of the Inter-Faith Conference? The sin of heresy, says St. Thomas, is "the greatest sin in the whole range of perversity." [1] This sin is "destructive of Christian faith." Comparing the sins of Jews and heretics, St. Thomas says: "although the Gentiles err in some things more than the Jews, and although the Jews are further removed from the true faith than heretics, yet the unbelief of the Jews is a more grievous

[1] *Catholic Encyclopedia*, "Heresy."

sin than that of the Gentiles, because they corrupt the gospel itself after having adopted and professed the same."

The teaching of the Fathers is unanimous to the effect that heretics are a bad and dangerous lot to have anything to do with. In picturesque and forcible language they say about them what they feel they ought to say.[1] "Polycarp regarded Marcion [a heretic] as the first-born of the Devil. Ignatius sees in heretics poisonous plants or animals in human form. Justin and Tertullian condemn their errors as inspirations of the Evil One. Theophilus compares them to barren and rocky islands on which ships are wrecked. Origen says that as pirates place lights on cliffs to allure and destroy vessels in quest of refuge, so the Prince of this world lights fires of false knowledge in order to destroy men. *Jerome calls the Congregations of heretics synagogues of Satan and says their communion is to be avoided like that of vipers and scorpions.*" The *Catholic Encyclopedia* adds the comforting assurance: "These primitive views of heresy have been faithfully transmitted and acted on by the Church in subsequent ages. *There is no break in the tradition from St. Peter to Pius X.*"

One speculates as to what St. Jerome would say of Mgr. Lavelle who, as Cardinal Hayes' representative, consults about moral cleanups with rabbis and Protestant divines of the "Inter-Faith Conference"? Would he have been present (as was Father Curran, the president of the International Catholic Truth Society), to compliment Rev. Dr. S. Parkes Cadman, at a luncheon tribute in honor of the latter's jubilee, and praise him for his work? And when Dr. Cadman said, "Sticking to your own group has its virtues but it is narrow, and such a person suffers from limited vision, limited thought," would the holy hermit have been pleased?

[1] *Ibid.*

Would St. Jerome, were he alive today, call congregations such as those of Grace Church or St. John the Divine "synagogues of Satan" and warn Catholics to avoid communion with Protestants as though they were "vipers and scorpions"? Frankly we believe he would! Further, we feel sure he would have violent and bitter words in plenty for Catholic interdenominationalists.

Apart, however, from what Jerome or the other Fathers said or thought about heretics, the mind of the Church on the matter of Interdenominationalism is clear and indisputable and follows as a consequence of her various dogmas of supremacy, infallibility and divine origin. She cannot yield in any matter of importance. She cannot take one step to reach an "understanding" with heretics or Jews on any disputed point. The irritation her doctrines and dogmas cause will remain forever and she will continue to glory in it. It is insincere and lacking in candor on the part of educated Catholics to "lead on" non-Catholics into the belief or hope that a *modus vivendi* with Rome is discoverable. There is nothing to be discovered but the impassable barrier which separates Catholicism from *all* other religions.

Interdenominationalism, as practiced by Catholic leaders and priests, is so insincere, so lacking in candor and honesty, so utterly "the bunk," that one has good reason to suspect that it is window-dressing with a political end in view. Its sole realizable aim is to make Catholics a little more popular for the time being with members of other creeds, and to cast a temporary veneer of liberalism and "reasonableness" over Catholicism. Real brotherhood among religions cannot be built up on lack of candor and on concealments. Rome stoops low to conquer in so far as she seeks to win a way into public esteem by the false pretense of Interdenominationalism.

CHAPTER IX

THE FIGHT AGAINST BIRTH CONTROL

"I AM beginning to feel," writes C.C.M. in the New York *World-Telegram*,[1] "that the Legion of Decency should remonstrate with Father Ignatius W. Cox S. J. These discussions of which methods of birth control are sinful or not sinful seem distasteful and quite foolish to millions of decent Americans who are self-respecting family people. The Catholic Church is just as illogical and full of special pleading as some of the Protestant Churches were on the subject of Prohibition. Anyone would think that the 'noble experiment' had shown once and for all the impossibility of imposing religious dogma on social custom. I believe that the tax-paying public will not be patient much longer with minority groups who seek to impede the giving of birth control information where it is, in all decency and common sense so urgently needed—in families on public relief."

The two points that C.C.M. raises are those which strike the average American mind. What boots it to argue as does the Catholic Church that one method of birth control is "absolutely evil and may under no circumstances be practiced," [2] while another is perfectly sinless? Why does one method lead to hell if the other leads to heaven? Why is one

[1] February 16, 1935.
[2] "Birth Control," Rev. D. Preummer O. P., p. 5.

"against natural and divine law" if the other, which pursues the same end, is in accord with both? Why, if it be wrong to frustrate growth by raking seed off good soil, is it no sin to waste seed by sowing it on barren soil? And above all, is it not, as C.C.M. says, "distasteful and quite foolish" for the Catholic Church to discuss fine theological distinctions about marital relationship in public and to expect the non-Catholic majority to submit to her conclusions?

And, to enlarge upon C.C.M.'s second point, is it not hopeless to attempt to upset the conviction in the American mind that a deep-rooted custom is impervious to priestly exorcism? If the "noble experiment," backed as it was by Protestantism, failed to uproot the drink habit of Americans, how can a plea for even more extreme asceticism prevail in the matter of birth control? Is not the Catholic Church taxing the patience of the public by her unreasonable stand, her lack of the logic of facts, her special pleading?

Protestants who feel that they have cause for irritation over the Catholic Church's fight against birth control will learn with surprise that Catholics feel like irritation over Protestant Churches' acquiescence therein. Says Father Curran, the president of the International Catholic Truth Society[1]: "The subject of birth control is one that arouses ill-feeling on the part of Catholics who consider the slimy principles and practices of birth control to be a violation of the rights of God." Which party then is justified in its irritation? The Protestant does not criticize the Catholic for regarding birth control as a sin and for abstaining from it as do the minority of Catholics, nor does he criticize the majority of Catholics who practice birth control whether in good or bad faith, but he strongly objects to the Catholic Church, in the person of Father

[1] *New York Times*, March 27, 1935.

Curran and others, describing his conduct and principles as "slimy" when he makes use of birth control hygiene. The Protestant will readily praise shining examples of conjugal felicity, fidelity and chastity in Catholic fellow countrymen, but when he finds that birth control helps him to be happy and faithful with his lawful wife, and provident for the welfare of his children, he is irritated at being told by Catholics that his conduct is "stark brutishness," "degeneracy," "race suicide," "mutual onanism" and that it is based on "pig philosophy"—all which terms are employed by Catholic clergy in reference to those who practice birth control.

Here is what the Catholic Daughters of America say (July 4, 1935) of the American Federation of Women's Clubs and The American Association of University Women who went on record as favoring birth control: "Their pronouncements are a direct insult to the rank and file of the decent and virtuous women of America. [They are] immoral and conducive to the spread of impurity. [They are] un-American, and un-patriotic, unsocial and inhuman."

The Catholic fight against birth control is difficult and complicated. It has been going on since 1921, when Cardinal Hayes sent the New York City police to raid Margaret Sanger's first clinic. The fight has spread into many fields and is pursued vigorously by the Church to the present day, but it is an impossible battle to win, and the Church's strategy might best be described as a fighting retreat. This does not mean, however, that the Church may not some time turn and reverse the trend of the battle.

Here is the Catholic "call to arms" as enunciated by Pius XI, in the encyclical "Casti Connubii" (1930) which was especially directed to America.

"The Catholic Church, to whom God has entrusted the

defense of the integrity and purity of morals, standing erect in the midst of the moral ruin which surrounds her, in order that she may preserve the chastity of the nuptial union from being defiled by this foul stain, raises her voice in token of her divine ambassadorship and through Our Mouth proclaims anew: any use whatsoever of matrimony exercised in such a way that the act is deliberately frustrated in its natural power to generate life is an offense against the law of God and of nature, and those who indulge in such are branded with the guilt of grave sin."

This clear and proud call was addressed primarily to Catholics but also it was directed to all Christians, Protestants, Methodists and the rest. It taught all that birth control "defiled the nuptial union by a foul stain" and that it was a grave sin.

Protestants refused to accept Pius' teaching and the Episcopal bishops of this country issued a counter-blast which favored birth control. They resolved [1]:

"We endorse the efforts now being made to secure for licensed physicians, hospitals and medical clinics, freedom to convey such information as is in accord with the highest principles of eugenics, and a more wholesome family life, wherein parenthood may be undertaken with due respect for the health of mothers and the welfare of their children."

The Episcopal bishops seemed to score a point or two off Pius by their references to *"wholesome* family life," *"respect* for health of mothers," and "welfare of children." During the discussion Bishop Huston let himself go and snapped at the Pope and Catholic clergy: "I submit, gentlemen, that we cannot find out the necessity for such action [on birth control] by looking through stained glass windows. We must go into

[1] Atlantic City, New Jersey, October 20, 1934.

the streets and into the homes of the poor. We have had a lot of pious twaddle from celebate clergymen who are about as far removed from knowledge of the realities of life as the man in the moon. The under-privileged should have access to information which others can so readily obtain."

And so the issue is knit between Peter and Martin on the matter of birth control. Peter puts the womb as an organ above the belly. Martin puts the belly first in importance. Peter would have the womb full, even though the belly be empty. Martin says (quoting Peter against himself): *"Primum est vivere* (our first duty is to live). It is more important to preserve life that is, than to produce life that is not. You cannot live on an empty belly, even though the womb be full." Peter rejoins: "Let the womb be full and God will provide!" Martin tells Peter that it is wrong to tempt God, to challenge Him to work miracles! "Look at our unemployed and hungry in America," adds Martin. "Look at all our empty bellies! There's many a man with an empty belly who would be tempted to kill himself if his wife became pregnant as things now are in our country!" Peter can only reply through the lips of Pius XI [1]: "We are deeply touched by the sufferings of those parents who, in extreme want, experience great difficulty in rearing their children . . . however . . . they should take care lest the calamitous state of external affairs should be the occasion for a much more calamitous error. No difficulty can arise that justifies the putting aside the law of God which forbids all acts intrinsically evil."

Martin has the last word. "No difficulty can arise which justifies putting aside the law of God? Is that what you say, Peter? Well, didn't Moses 'put aside the law of God' and

[1] Encyclical "Casti Connubii."

permit bills of divorce? And is it not true that charity is above the law? Don't you yourself teach that a hungry man can burn, rob and slay in order to get food for himself and his little ones? You're looking at life through stained glass windows, Peter!"

Protestants, therefore, refuse to accept the teaching of Pius XI on birth control. Catholics accept his teaching, but do they obey it?

There is no effort made on the part of Catholic apologists to pretend that Catholics abstain from the use of contraceptives. Already in 1928 a Catholic paper admitted: "Catholics practice 'race suicide' in the same manner and nearly to the same extent as non-Catholics." [1] This admission has been repeated in a hundred forms by Catholic preachers and by the Catholic Press. The stationary condition of the number of Catholics in this country in recent years is taken as a clear indication that Catholics in vast numbers are practicing birth control. Writes a correspondent to the *Commonweal* [2]: "Another proof of these pessimistic statements [which the correspondent was contributing] is onanism or birth control. The very figures you quote of the [paltry] increase in the number of Catholics prove beyond doubt its prevalence among Catholics. Either nature in its biological effects has suddenly become very niggardly, or else many, many Catholics are making a mockery of matrimony. That they should follow the precepts of the Church in the matter of matrimony they consider impractical; they claim it is too expensive and too hard on the women. Yet they go to the sacraments—of course! They think they can 'eat their cake and have it too' or attain heaven by doing as they please on earth."

[1] *Echo*, Buffalo, August 23, 1928.
[2] June 15, 1934.

Father Pruemmer, in his booklet on birth control, admits the contention of this letter, that Catholics make sacrilegious confessions, and hide the fact that they are practicing birth control. "That the number [of such] is enormous every pastor can testify," writes Father Pruemmer. He is less frank, however, than Pius XI who hints in his encyclical that there are priests who connive at the practice of hiding this sin, by "guilty silence." Pius XI would not have referred to such practice among priests were it not exceedingly common in America.

This lack of obedience and loyalty among priests and laity to the teaching of the Church in the matter of birth control makes the Church's fight all the more difficult. So to say, she cannot depend on the loyalty of her troops when she orders them to fire on Margaret Sanger. They are not openly mutinous or rebellious but they have no heart in the fight against contraception. Catholics who are themselves "onanistic," to use the Scriptural expression, must needs be thoroughgoing hypocrites to condemn "onanism" in others and to deprive them of its facilities. According to a well-founded theory of abnormal psychology, it is those most addicted to a practice which they consider blameworthy who are the first to condemn it in others. And laymen and laywomen who go out of their way to attack birth control on every possible occasion naturally excite suspicion as regards the motives of their behavior.

Perhaps the greatest difficulty that the Church faces in making her own and others anti-contraception-minded arises from the publicity given to "hard luck" stories of married mothers: stories which describe the awful plight in which some women find themselves when they obey to the letter the laws of nature and of the Church. As an example of such a story I take the following from the "Voice of the People" column of the New York *Daily News*[1]: "Yes, indeed, Mrs. Cohen, if I had only known about birth control I could have kept my health ten years longer. I am a sick woman from having children without proper medical attention. All I need is a good push into a coffin—but my husband wants yet more children. Enough is enough and a girl ought to stop child-bearing when she has done enough. I have the following: (1) one healthy husband; (2) a sickly self; (3) and eight weakling children." It was signed "Oversupplied." The Editor of the *Daily News* facetiously placed over the letter the caption: "Wants a Vacation."

It may interest readers to hear the official papal view of such a case as that of "Oversupplied." It is contained in "Casti Connubii." To say the least, from the human angle, it offers her cold comfort. Here it is:

> Holy Mother Church very well understands and clearly appreciates all that is said regarding the health of the mother and the danger to her life. And who would not grieve to think of these things? Who is not filled with the greatest admiration when he sees a mother risking her life with heroic fortitude that she may preserve the life of the offspring which she has conceived? God alone . . . can reward her for the fulfillment of the office allotted to her by nature, and will assuredly repay her in a measure full to overflowing.

Holy Mother Church can, of course, have no sympathy with "Oversupplied's" unwillingness to go on bearing children. Should her husband insist on his "rights," she is bound by natural and divine law, according to Holy Mother Church, to go on bearing another dozen children or more.

Incidentally we are reminded by Father Pruemmer that

[1] November 30, 1934.

"it is easier to raise six children well than to raise one"—
easier therefore, we gather, to raise twelve well than two;
easier to raise eighteen well than three; and easier to raise
twenty-four, as many valiant women have done, than four!

There are, of course, dangers, very real and terrible, in the
popularization of birth control and in unrestrained freedom
in acquiring contraceptives. For one thing, self-indulgence is
facilitated and self-control becomes a rare virtue. It is indisputable that the moral fiber of an individual and of a
nation is impaired by excessive self-indulgence. Every individual and every nation that pretends to real greatness
needs strength of will, the power to dominate passion, the
indispensable quality of self-control. Every psychologist
knows that the sex passion is liable to develop into an abnormal destructive force unless it is held in check. It should
and must be subject to repression if man is to live as a
civilized being and as a Christian. It seems that in the popularization of birth control many will find a temptation to
disregard moral restraint and become conscienceless sex fiends.
There is also the appalling danger of birth control habits
spreading among the young to the detriment of their youth,
health and happiness. Lately in Roosevelt, Mineola (Long
Island) [1] thirteen children, seven boys and six girls, all under
fourteen years were found in possession of contraceptives
and were discovered to be guilty of immoral and perverted
practices. In the children's lockers in the school supplies of
contraceptives were found. This case is perhaps a little exceptional inasmuch as the children were very young, but it
is well known that among high school boys and girls the
possession of contraceptives is common.

No sane, decent American can feel anything but alarm and

[1] *New York Times*, April 4, 1935.

horror at this outcome of the birth control movement. If anything can justify the Catholic Church's stand against allowing contraceptives to be sold, and against allowing the dissemination of birth control information, it is precisely the danger which the Mineola case represents.

As becomes the character of the American Catholic, the fight against birth control in this country is aggressive, noisy and violent. *It is not in accord with the suggestion thrown out by Pius XI.* Pius did not suggest breaking drugstore windows or raiding clinics in order to war down birth control. He took the wiser, more long-headed view that the fight should be fought on moral lines, namely, by force of example and persuasion. He said ("Casti Connubii"): "Oppose error by truth; vice by the excellent dignity of chastity; the slavery of covetousness by the liberty of the sons of God; the disastrous ease in obtaining divorce by an enduring love in the bond of marriage and by the inviolate pledge of fidelity given even to death."

Such opposition everyone should admit to be fair, unexceptional. But such is *not* the kind of opposition that the American Catholic Church offers to the birth control movement. In the public Press (January 19, 1935) it was reported that a spinster, aged 49, named Adelaide Kenna was arrested in Ridgefield, New Jersey, for smashing a drugstore window with an axe. In the window there was a feminc hygiene exhibit to which she objected. When an officer approached her she said: "Are you a Catholic? Come with me! I'm looking for more windows like this one!" Miss Kenna was medically examined and declared "of sound mind and body."

Following the incident Catholic papers commented, among others the *Commonweal*.[1] The editor condoned, not the act

[1] February 1, 1935.

but the spirit of the Ridgefield Joan of Arc, and suggested a way of dealing with the basic issue. "We ourselves feel that the best approach to this particular aspect of a greater problem [birth control] lies through an organization of Catholic pharmacists and their friends, operating without publicity and under wise guidance. We think also that in most cities large and social-minded advertisers could be brought together for an effort to induce papers not to use copy supplied by those firms at least whose products are laughed at by the medical profession."

In plain language this means that papers should be threatened with the loss of their best advertisements if they take copy from businesses selling "feminine hygiene" apparatus.

The editor continued: "It is wholly unlikely that any Catholic has a right to smash pharmacy windows but it is just as clear that *the Catholic group must seek to use its power effectively against practices of which it justifiably disapproves*" (italics ours). In the last sentence Mr. Williams, the lay leader of the Catholic intelligenzia, reveals what he considers to be the duty of Catholics as well as their right: "to use their power effectively" against birth control of which "they justifiably disapprove."

The implication of this principle is that none have the right to use or enjoy undisturbed anything that Catholics "justifiably" disapprove of. This implication, however, does not distress him or other Catholics.

Brooklyn Public School No. 129 was, like Ridgefield, the scene of characteristic Catholic effort against birth control. On March 5th, the Parents and Teachers Association met in the school to hear a lecture from Marie L. Warner on birth control. The parents and teachers were free American citizens and adults, but that fact did not affect Father Curran, the president of the International Catholic Truth Society. He heard of the proposed lecture and tried to have it stopped. In this he did not succeed, but he arranged for a stenographer to be present to take notes of the lecture and to act as a spy. Then he publicly denounced the principal of School No. 129 and demanded that he be punished for allowing the lecture to take place. *"The lecture in Public School No. 129,"* he said, *"was a crime against decency. The Catholic tax-payers of that district and the Catholic tax-payers of the entire city are opposed to such vile and un-American use of the Public Schools."* Father Curran[1] gave notice to the Board of Education of New York that he intended to carry to a showdown his fight against the use of public schools for the dissemination of birth control information through lectures. Thanks, as it seems, to the advocacy of the Parents and Teachers Association's rights by the New York *World-Telegram,* the Board of Education summoned sufficient courage to face Father Curran, and endorse the Association. Then Father Ignatius Cox S.J. entered the fray and in a Lenten sermon attacked the New York Press for its sympathy with birth control. He threatened to start a boycott of certain "liberal" papers, or as he put it "to exercise the right of non-cooperation" with them. "Is it logical," he asked,[2] "or even fitting for Catholic parents to introduce into the sanctuary of the home newspapers which by their editorial policy, their news emphasis and news selection, and their columnists aim repeated, insidious, and deadly blows at the Christian doctrine and ideals which are dearer to the Catholic than life itself?"

Father Cox charged that the Associated Press had without

[1] *New York Times,* March 21, 1935.
[2] *New York Times,* March 27, 1935.

due regard for facts, and seemingly under the influence of
birth control propaganda, issued a statement headed: "High
Birth Rates worry FERA Heads," to the effect that a disproportionately great percentage of babies were being born
to the unemployed. Father Cox charged that the United Press
was also an organ of birth control propaganda. The Associated
Press replied: "Nowhere in the story did the A.P. say that
the FERA was 'worried.' . . . A careful recheck has shown
that all figures quoted are correct as carried in the public
record."

The battle shifted again and in *America* [1] the connection
between FERA and birth control was discussed. The editor
stated that "he had before him an affidavit from a woman on
relief in Ohio who had to undergo an abortion [2] by advice of
two case workers." The implication of the article was that
FERA was encouraging its relief officers to disseminate birth
control information. It concluded: "A Congressional investigation should be made on the statement by the Birth Control
League that several administrators used relief funds for birth
control purposes. Let us know their names!"

Through Catholic activity the affidavit in question was
placed before Governor Davey of Ohio. Its truth was denied.
It had, however, the effect of bringing about a regulation
whereby it became grounds for dismissal for case workers in
Ohio to disseminate birth control information to clients.

In the larger matter of blocking the Pierce Birth Control
Bill, which would have legalized dissemination of contraceptive information through doctors and clinics, the Church
triumphed. The House Judiciary Committee at Washington

[1] April 13, 1935.

[2] Father Parsons might have known that *abortion* is discountenanced by
birth controllers.

shelved the Pierce Bill by a 15-8 vote. Mrs. Margaret Sanger attributed this defeat to Father Coughlin who testified against the measure. She was not discouraged by the defeat and stated: "The fact that there were eight men on the Committee with sufficient vision, intelligence and courage to stand out against the growing insidious influence of dogma encourages me to continue our fight until we win." [1]

It is impossible to touch upon all the incidents and phases of the Catholic fight against birth control. We find a Puerto Rican woman, Ana Alfonso de Colon, in Washington, who represents Puerto Rican Catholic opposition to a birth control measure, attacking Mrs. Dorothy Bourne, a friend of Mrs. Franklin D. Roosevelt, for sponsoring the measure against the wishes of the Catholic women of her country. We find Catholics imputing openly against birth controllers that they are mercenary agents in a racket to sell to the public worthless "remedies."

There is, of course, an immense amount of money involved in the manufacture of feminine hygienic products and such like. *Time* (February 18, 1935) calls it "big business" and records that "five makers of one device sold $35,000,000 worth last year," and that "three 'feminine hygiene' manufacturers last year spent $250,000 advertising in general magazines alone." But it also records that Mrs. Sanger refused $250,000 as fee for giving five minute radio talks to push the trade.

The lure of good money may influence the zeal of many advocates of birth control, but does it not also influence the zeal of those who oppose it? Authors anxious to run up the circulation of their books or booklets do not hesitate to authorize blurbs that are calculated to excite prurient curiosity.

[1] *New York Times*, February 6, 1935.

Here, for instance, are extracts from a blurb of a booklet by Father Martin J. Scott S.J. on *Marriage: "The frankest book on the noble and ignoble possibilities of sex* that has ever come from the pen of an authoritative Catholic writer . . . *comprehensive discussion of the dangers of sex-promiscuity, informative chapters on Birth-Control.* . . . What does it all mean? . . . *uncontrolled passion with its resultant disquiet. . . . Father Scott in his new book goes straight to the true facts; gives unflinching condemnation of modern sexual vices . . ."* etc. The Paulist Press, managed by the Paulist Fathers, publish the book and co-operate with the Jesuit author in making good money out of it. Perhaps the blurb on Father Scott's book might make a modest maiden blush as redly as if she beheld what Miss Kenna saw in the drugstore window in Ridgewood, New Jersey.

In writing to oppose birth control, priests are sometimes guilty of exaggerated as well as lurid statements. I take an example, from Father Pruemmer's booklet [1]: "In interrupted intercourse and intercourse with preventive measures *the sexual organism of the woman hardly ever reaches its natural culmination.* Consequently, inflammations of all kinds occur, and the nervous system especially is prejudicially affected."

Father Pruemmer might easily have checked the truth of this statement by inquiring of his female penitents as to their experiences. Unless his confessional clientele be very restricted or composed chiefly of elderly females, he would have discovered that he was greatly overstating his case.

Catholic reaction to the Church's campaign against birth control is not always sympathetic. In correspondence columns of the Press one sees from time to time frank letters from Catholics who disagree with the Church's activity. One such,

[1] *Birth Control,* p. 16, Paulist Press.

a striking letter, from which it is impossible to quote more than a few lines, appeared in the New York *World-Telegram*.[1] The woman gave her name as Mary R. Dillon, and said: "To get to this subject of birth control, which causes Father Cox to writhe on paper, I am sure intelligent Catholics must think that the emphasis on this one sin has been unduly heavy in the past few years. Grant birth control by contraceptives is forbidden to Catholics, so are many other transgressions of the laws of God and the Church. I did not hear a single strong and angry voice lifted against the very disgraceful actions of Tammany officeholders which perhaps caused more scandal than all the birth control. . . . If not to Catholics certainly to non-Catholics that situation must have been incongruous. . . . After all the whole birth control movement, the movement away from large families, is something like Spring. I don't think it can be stopped. . . . If Father Cox believes in large families let him say so. . . . Years ago continence and 'periodic abstention' were the only solutions the Church could offer the Catholic who for any reason wished to space or avoid children. I don't think continence is mentioned any more, certainly not as the general alternative to further pregnancy. Continence is a quite dangerous remedy. 'Periodic abstention' was something which worked satisfactorily with only a portion of the people who tried it."

We come now to the question of the Church's consistency and sincerity in fighting birth control. What exactly is the stand in the matter that the Church takes?

Five years ago,[2] in contributing an article to the *Churchman* on "Roman Catholicism and Birth Control," I took issue with a statement made by the celebrated English Jesuit,

[1] February 16, 1935.
[2] January 18, 1930.

Father Martingdale. He had said: "I think that the frightful —I repeat frightful—burden rightly laid on the average Catholic citizen by way of the Catholic doctrine concerning birth restriction tends to break down the allegiance of thousands whose shoulders are not exceptionally strong. I should not be in the least surprised to see, in a century, no Catholic country anywhere left but strong self-conscious Catholic minorities in every country."

I pointed out that Father Martingdale was overlooking or minimizing the capacity of the Church to adapt herself to inevitable conditions and added that "the average Catholic citizen does not envisage his personal problem as a dilemma between Catholicism and birth control but for the most part attempts to find a way out and to form his conscience by some subtle process of rationalizing so as to be able, while remaining 'a good Catholic' to practice birth control."

Soon after, things began to happen. Pius XI, at the end of the month in which I wrote, issued "Casti Connubii" which, while openly condemning birth control à la Sanger, gave a nod of approval to "legitimate birth control." He wrote: "Nor are those considered as acting against nature who in the married state use the right in the proper manner although on account of natural reasons either *of time* or of certain defects new life cannot be brought forth."

It may have been that His Holiness had advance information about the results of the Ogino-Knaus researches, or simply that he was once more, as a sop to the hungry, drawing attention to the old Catholic belief that there is "a safe period." Be that as it may, he prepared the Catholics for the coming of the scientific discovery and ensured their cordial reception of it. The wording of the Pope's declaration deserves careful attention with a view to what follows. It is *permissive;* and not *restrictive. It prohibits nothing.*

Placing in juxtaposition his other statement, namely, "any use whatsoever of matrimony exercised in such a way that the act is deliberately frustrated in its natural power to generate life, is an offense against the law of God," we come to the conclusion that if there be a "safe period" *during that period* (1) marital relations are lawful, and (2) since "there is no natural power in the act to generate life," *the act may be performed in any hygienic way which is desirable.*

We come now to the Ogino-Knaus teaching. In general it is to the effect that for about twenty days in the month the woman is sterile. The certainty of this fact is, of course, questioned but in such matters one opinion is possibly or probably as good as another. At any rate, the average woman can be "morally" sure that she is sterile for the twenty days. But, being a woman, she wants to be absolutely sure and would like to have the added safeguard of contraceptive precautions. Her anxiety is quite understandable.

Can she then, during the twenty days, if she be a Catholic woman, use contraceptives lawfully? Why not? As I said above, it seems probable that the encyclical "Casti Connubii" only forbids their use when there is "natural power to generate life" in the act. In the sterile period there is no such "natural power" in the act!

I am only too well aware that at the present moment Catholic theologians will describe my theological reasoning as sophistry but after a while they will come to find in it at least "a probable opinion" and will avail themselves of it in directing their penitents. I maintain that henceforth for twenty days in the month at least, the Catholic husband and Catholic wife can sinlessly practice birth control in the common way and remain orthodox Catholics. I maintain, too, that the Church is inconsistent and lacking in candor in opposing birth control so sweepingly.

To conclude this chapter on a theological key, let me instance two items of theological lore which will confirm my charge of inconsistency against the Church's attitude. The first item has to do with a woman who, against her will, is violated by force or guile. She may or may not become immediately pregnant. There is no scientific way of knowing for certain how long a time it takes, how many hours, before she becomes pregnant. At any rate, Holy Mother Church in her case allows her to have recourse to medical aid within twelve hours to make sure that she will not become pregnant or (in the event of her already being pregnant within the twelve hours), *to put an end to the pregnancy!*

A second item, which shows how the Church, perhaps unwittingly, places a premium on contraceptives. In a certain metropolitan diocese there was listed as a reserved sin *"crimen clericale,"* the sin of adultery on the part of a priest. Any priest in that diocese who committed that sin *in a natural way* —in the ordinary human way—could obtain absolution for it only from privileged confessors who had been given special "faculties" by the archbishop. So to say, it was "hard" to get absolution for it. But, if the priest was sufficiently sophisticated to make use of a contraceptive when sinning, any ordinary priest could absolve him. It was no longer "hard" to obtain absolution; on the contrary, it was quite easy. If he was a votary of birth control, the priest did not "incur the reserve"!

CHAPTER X

THE CHURCH'S AIM IN POLITICS

THERE are some who say that the Catholic Church in America is not in politics. Quite recently in a radio address[1] General Hugh S. Johnson referred to Mr. Alfred E. Smith as "going from Coast to Coast in 1928 proudly declaring that the Catholic Church and the priesthood kept out of politics," and added, "he was sincere and he was right." The more common view is that the Catholic Church in every country, and particularly in America, is "up to her ears" in politics, and that Mr. Smith was neither sincere nor accurate in pretending that it is not so.

A church keeps out of politics when she pursues purely spiritual aims by purely spiritual means, such as prayer and fasting and edification. But what church of today pursues spiritual ends alone and those only by spiritual means? What church acts up to the belief that mountains can be moved by prayer? That doors can be opened merely by knocking at them? That souls can be saved without recourse to district captains? It may be that a few of the "little religions," such as the Theosophists and Rosicrucians, have such faith and steer clear of politics in following their aims, but such is not the case with any of the "big religions" and least of all with Catholicism. Every considerable church in America is in poli-

[1] March 5, 1935.

145

tics though not all in the same degree nor in the same manner. The Episcopal Board of Bishops [1] stated openly: "Our Christian faith has not divorced us from our obligations as citizens of the State or members of society. Our discipleship relates us to the just and Christian solution of economic, social and political problems. Nothing that is of human interest can be foreign to us." Then it gave its majority opinion on several political reform measures. Other churches in like manner propounded their political majority opinions and their demands for legislative enactments, often after bitter controversy among their members. Methodists, Presbyterians, Baptists, Jews, Lutherans, all have political programs and sometimes indulge "as churches" in active lobbying. At election times, as recently in the Sinclair candidacy in California, their clergy use their spiritual influence to control votes. No wonder that Will Rogers should write[2]: "This is Monday and I have been sitting here [Beverly Hills] reading sermons delivered yesterday. On Sundays politics is transferred from the platform to the rostrum. . . . It's awful hard for a sinner in search of spiritual advice to drop into a church and receive any of it."

All the churhces offer the same pretext as the Holy Father, and affirm that they indulge in politics only when "it is a matter of common good." This pretext befits the politician as well as the priest. He has, *professionally*, "the common good" at heart and is, professedly, only active when "the common good" is at stake. He will never openly admit that he concerns himself about his own or other private interests. He rejoices to have the support of the clergy of his constituency, and if there be some clergyman, like Father Cough-

[1] Atlantic City, October 23, 1934.
[2] *New York Times*, October 16, 1934.

lin, who is in the opposite camp to his, he is the first to cry out that the priest should keep to his altar!

"Catholic Action," declares Pius XI, "is in its very nature like the Catholic Church, in that it keeps itself aloof and outside of any political party." The inference that the simple-minded are supposed to make is that since the Church keeps aloof from party it keeps aloof from politics.

Father Coughlin, who plagiarizes the subtleties of Pius, announces[1]: "N.U.S.J., while repudiating any effort on its part to establish a third, fourth or fifth party, nevertheless is supremely interested in politics in so far as politics happens to be the expression of moral principles and of social justice."

This "non-party" attitude is as much politics as is a pro-party attitude. It may be politics of a higher and more independent kind but it is essentially politics. Every legislative measure has "moral repercussions" of some kind or other and is an expression of moral principles. If, then, the Coughlin-Pius idea is to be followed out we find that it justifies the Catholic Church in being in politics all the time and one hundred *per cent.*

Writes the editor of the *Commonweal* [2]: "The effort to banish clergymen from active participation in politics" is "at bottom part and parcel of the modern spirit of materialistic secularism which is striving mightily to destroy the public influence of the clergy. . . . What politics and social life in general . . . needs . . . is more religion applied in practice and not merely preached in platitudes." In so far as Mr. Williams represents the Church, he cries: "All honor and glory to our political Catholic priests!"

The topic "The Church and Politics" has of late, apropos

[1] Cleveland, May 8, 1935.
[2] March 22, 1935.

of Father Coughlin, been touched upon in many editorials among which that of the *New York Times*[1] is perhaps the most interesting. According to the *Times*, "our custom is to keep the churches, purely as churches, out of politics." When members of a church "vote together for men or causes" there must be "nothing official about it, no suspicion of ecclesiastical endorsement open or tacit."

Has this "custom" if it is a custom, been well observed? What of the Baptist and Methodist churches in the days when the eighteenth amendment was being voted upon? What of the Smith election and the sending of nuns to the polling booths by their bishops?

The *Times* dreading the danger of a Coughlin Third Party, took occasion to warn the Catholic hierarchy that "it would never do to give color to the charge that the Catholic Church as such was forming or backing a new party."

The answer of the Church is the answer of Father Coughlin, "no new party is needed." The Church and Father Coughlin can perfectly well attain their ends by "forcing every Representative or Senator . . . to commit himself irrevocably to the principles of social justice." [2] As though he were a bishop and head of the hierarchy at that, Father Coughlin proclaims of his N.U.S.J., "We are above politics and politicians." [3] The effect of Father Coughlin's use of the ecclesiastical pretext of being "above politics" is to reduce it to its native and naked absurdity. Like Holy Mother Church in America, he is "up to his ears" in politics.

Nothing in the world is easier for the Church than to justify her participation in political agitation, whether in Spain,

[1] April 29, 1935.
[2] Detroit, May 5, 1935, radio address of Father Coughlin.
[3] *Ibid.*

France, Germany, Ireland, Mexico or here among us. She
has only to say, as Bishop Gallagher said [1] in justifying his
subject, Father Coughlin: "What I do fear is the just persecution that results when the laws of God are flouted; when
priests fail to speak without raising their voices in protest
against man's inhumanity to his fellowman. How can priests
keep silent? With wealth concentrated in the hands of a little
group of selfish men, the teeming masses of the people are
living in dire and abject poverty."

One wonders then why the Church is unwilling to call a
spade a spade and Catholic Action "political action"? Does
"political action" cease to be "political" when it is directed
towards the interests of the Church? When the Church secured tax exemption for the Knights of Columbus Hotel
through Tammany, was it not politics, even though the
Knights are "the standard-bearers of Catholic Action"? And
when honest citizens in thousands of every creed (except
Catholicism) were condemning the iniquities of Tammany,
and voting in a Fusionist administration, was it not politics
on the part of the Church to remain loyal to Tammany and
oppose its enemies?

The Church, of course, at various times uses various names
for her activities. Under Philip II she was not afraid to call
the Inquisition by its right name and she had no wish to disown it or to dub her devout bishops and theologians who conducted it "politicians." But now it suits her best to disown
the Inquisition and so she calls it "a political institution."
"Fair-minded students of history," says Father Professor
Steck,[2] of the Catholic University, "are now conceding that
the Spanish Inquisition *in the homeland as well as in the*

[1] *New York Times*, April 22, 1935.
[2] *New York Times*, March 3, 1935.

colony was no ecclesiastical institution at all but a political institution." If we are going to admit that the Church is and always has been outside and above politics, then we might as well also admit that the Church had nothing to do with the Inquisition.

A phase of present-day Catholic Action is the urging of Catholics to throw themselves into politics. At Catholic group meetings of almost every kind speakers urge political activity on their audiences. Often the plea is the crying need to fight radicalism, or the necessity of sharing with the world the treasures of Catholic social wisdom. Thus, speaking to the New York convention of Newman Clubs[1] last March, Professor Ross S. Hoffman, of New York University, said: "It is now time for us to bestir our minds. There is a crying need for us to think politically. We have in our ancient treasury of tradition, doctrine, and experience a great deal of valuable wisdom applicable to the political order of life and the world today is badly in need of it." Shortly after we find the New York "Holy Name" Society of Firemen addressed by Lieut. Gov. William Bray at a Communion Breakfast at the Hotel Astor [2] and urged "to participate more actively in politics by setting up a militant opposition to the spread of un-American doctrines."

Catholic leaders, in urging on Catholics more activity in politics and "militant opposition to un-American doctrines," do not advocate the setting up of a separate Catholic party. This expedient is considered dangerous and undesirable by the Church, and is resorted to only as a desperate measure. The Church prefers to control legislators rather than parties and to avoid the odium and the expense of running a dis-

[1] *New York Times*, March 3, 1935.
[2] April 28, 1935.

tinct organization. But the Church wants plenty of high offices for her children. The outspoken Father Curran charges that President Roosevelt "has not recognized the Catholic population in the United States" and demands that more Catholics should be elected governors and that *there should be more than one Catholic on the Bench of the Supreme Court.*[1]

The genre and intensity of Catholic political activity in the United States is best exemplified in the Knights of Columbus organization. This body is, perhaps, the most active political instrument in the country. Its members belong to all parties although it is preponderantly Democratic. It is nation-wide, permanent, rich and influential. It is in a special sense "the Pope's baby." "We have every advantage," declared Supreme Knight Carmody.[2] "The hierarchy has been with us from the start. The reverend clergy are working with us. Distinguished Catholic laymen in all walks of life have raised their voices in our behalf." The Knights of Columbus line up all or virtually all Catholic political officeholders, judges, attorney generals, senators, Congressional members, surveyors, taxing officials as well as officers of the army and navy, and every kind of business executive. They have certain secret understandings and engagements to one another, but of course no such pledge as the so-called "Bogus Oath."

The Knights, like the Church herself, disown the idea that they constitute a political body, and point to their excellent welfare work as proof to the contrary. But, the fact that they engage in and support charitable undertakings does not constitute them a benevolent organization, when they are even more active in other directions. Tammany, be it said to its

[1] *New York Times,* February 6, 1935.
[2] *New York Times,* March 17, 1935.

credit, never failed to lend generous support to the cause of charity, but who, for that reason, would deny that Tammany is political?

Speaking at the nation-wide broadcast at the commencement of the Knights' recent "mobilization," [1] the Supreme Knight thus outlined the significance of the move: "We are engaging in an intensive effort to gather up and unify all our forces and resources not for the purpose of display nor for what gratification we might gain from the contemplation of our own magnitude but rather that the Knights of Columbus may have the strength, the man power worthily *to discharge the multitude of obligations which the demands of the times place upon it.*" Amplifying the latent idea, Attorney J. W. Hilly said: "*It is necessary that our public authorities should realize that we are a very potent body of citizens under the banner of the Catholic Church.*"

Catholics maintain, as Father Curran puts it, that "one of the most important reasons for the breakdown of modern civilization in this country is that graduates of non-sectarian colleges have been in control for the past twenty-five years or more." [2] And some, follow the view, ascribed in the Public Press to Father Curran, "that Catholic teachers *in public schools* have a God-given right to teach religion to their non-Catholic classes no matter what the regulations of Boards of Education may be." [3]

Be that as it may, it is evident from various hints dropped by Catholic leaders of late that the Church meditates a vigorous campaign, with the help of the Knights of Columbus, to force the various State Legislatures to endow Catholic

[1] *New York Times*, March 18, 1935.
[2] *New York Times*, February 6, 1935.
[3] *Ibid.*, March 11th.

schools. The Constitution notwithstanding, the Catholics are determined to get the money, and it will be difficult to withstand their efforts.

The most sensational use of political power to force a Church issue, for many years, was that of Archbishop Curley when he threatened the present administration, and President Roosevelt in particular, with chastisement at the polls for delaying to interfere in the Mexican imbroglio. The *New York Times* captions [1] told the story briefly: "Archbishop Curley assails Roosevelt—He charges President killed the Borah Resolution for an inquiry into Mexico—Hints at rebuke at Polls—Prelate says 20,000,000 votes of American Catholics may provide answer."

Archbishop Curley's language as well as his gesture were so violent, as well as so obviously political, that the editor of the *New York World Telegram* took occasion to remind him that when he and other clergymen like him "speaking as citizens" "attack other citizens with force and vigor they can expect to be taken at their word and treated as citizens." [2]

If Archbishop Curley had appealed to his subjects to pray that the heart of the President might be moved by divine grace and his mind enlightened by the Holy Spirit so that he might see and do what was best, in God's eyes, as regards Mexico, no one could reasonably complain. His action would not have been political. But when he took it upon himself to tell the President what he should do, and to threaten him with political extinction if he did otherwise, then Archbishop Curley was acting not merely as an ordinary politician but as a political dictator.

Archbishop Curley, as head of the "Confederation for

[1] *Ibid.*, March 26th.
[2] March 27, 1935.

Religious Liberty in Mexico," represented the Catholic hierarchy and the Church in his attack on the Administration. He demonstrated the inanity of the *Times* remark about "our custom of keeping the Churches out of politics."

A month later, a Catholic layman, Judge Martin T. Manton, spoke at a conference of the Catholic Association for International Peace and remarked that the Borah Resolution "was surcharged with tremendous possibilities for mischief" and expressed the opinion that it was "unwise to provoke our Government into interfering in the Mexican situation." He advocated an appeal to Permanent Court of International Relations for an advisory opinion on the Mexican question as the action that Catholics should take.

Judge Manton was at once subjected to a series of attacks from Father La Farge S.J., Father Thorning S.J., and finally from Archbishop Curley himself who called him "a New York lawyer" and accused him of ignorance of what was going on in Mexico and of the precedents for United States intervention there. It was evident that nothing less than active and direct political pressure on the present Administration was acceptable to the clergy and bishops.

The Catholic bishops' agitation against the Child Labor Amendment has already been referred to. Their opposition does not take the form of an appeal to reason but of suborning legislators and politicians to sidetrack the Amendment. In an appeal to reason they would fare badly, for one of their ablest economists, Mgr. John A. Ryan, is in favor of the measure. To the plain man the Church's opposition is unintelligible. It seems wholly desirable that the young should be protected by Federal law and by the Constitution against the danger of exploitation. But the Church puts the interests of the young second to her own anxiety lest the Federal Government should be able to claim the right as a result of the passing of the Amendment to interfere with the authority of priests and parents over Catholic children and endanger the prosperity of the parochial schools. Already sixteen states have rejected the Amendment this year, thanks largely to Catholic opposition, and the ultimate ratification becomes increasingly improbable.

It is not without significance that many Catholic bishops of America surround themselves with politicians and invite them to propound Catholic doctrine at religious-social gatherings. It is seldom that a "Holy Name Society" function of the police, the firemen, the post office or customs officials, or any other city or Federal department takes place without prominent politicians to address to them a few words of sound advice. In his day Mayor Walker often officiated at "Communion Breakfasts" and performed this religious duty to the edification of all. No doubt there is something to be said for the practice of speechmaking at breakfast parties, and admittedly politicians are fluent speakers, but, on the other hand, when the parties are given by the Church and the speakers are invited by the Church, one would expect to find less favoritism shown towards political orators, especially towards men of questionable civic virtue.

It seems to be the policy of the Church here to maintain intimate relations with politicians, and with State employees. As regards the latter, the police are first in favor with the Church. "There is," said Mgr. McIntyre of New York,[1] "a very close friendship between the clergy and policemen and that is due I feel to the fact that both are public servants.

[1] *Catholic News*, May 4, 1935.

There is a nobility to service!" The Church's policy to which I refer—that of keeping in well with "public servants," especially those in uniform—might lend color to the idea that the Church is preparing well ahead for the day when, as chief power in the country, she will have to rely on their fidelity to her in service. It may mean nothing more, however, than that the Church appreciates the thousand and one *little services* that her devoted children in uniform render her, and that having them in their thousands in her tow she can all the more easily *command* politicians.

What Dante, who was no less skilled in theology than in the art of poetry, wrote six centuries ago in *Il Purgatorio* is true today: "The Church of Rome by confounding two powers in herself falls into the mire and fouls herself and her burden." Dante was no less a good Catholic or truthful historian for stating the fact as he saw it. He recognized the impossibility of reconciling pure religion with impure politics, and the inevitable trend of the Church into the morass. He foresaw that when faith would fail the Church would employ the poisoned cup or the bribed rabble according as customs varied or evolved, to protect or expand her interests.

Today there are no deeds of violence, and there is no distribution of gold pieces, but there pass among the people glib-tongued emissaries, promising favors and rallying men to the banner of the Church. In America the Church's janissaries are the alumni of her law schools.

As against the foregoing opinions, that the Church meddles a great deal in politics, cherishes many political aims and fights for certain privileges denied her by the Constitution, we have a confident assertion to the contrary from the dean of the American hierarchy, that in all fairness should be quoted. "Americans," says Cardinal O'Connell,[1] "whatever their creed, know and acknowledge the power for good that is exerted in season and out of season by the Catholic priests and bishops of the country who, *abstaining from any meddling interference in the political world,* being as they are outside and above all mere parties, love their country with an absolutely unselfish love, *desiring no privilege for themselves or their Church,* but the freedom which the fathers and founders of this nation guaranteed to them from the beginning."

Thus His Eminence pleads "not guilty" to the charges made above!

[1] At the Catholic University, Washington, D. C., November 14, 1934. We shall refer again to this statement of His Eminence.

CHAPTER XI

THE STRANGE CASE OF FATHER NORMAN

THE story of Father Norman will serve as a concrete illustration of the evils which follow when a church exercises influence over politicians, and it will serve as a substantiation of opinions expressed in the preceding chapter. It is a story which should intrigue three classes of citizens: those interested in the phenomena of religion; those interested in "detective stories" in which district attorneys and modern "sleuths" figure; and those who pay taxes and are concerned about the manner in which their taxes are expended. By these three classes of citizens, especially should they be citizens of our Empire State, the name of Raymond J. Norman will not soon be forgotten.

Father Norman, in the late fall of 1930, was the pastor of St. Peter's Mission situated at 429 East 14th Street, New York City. He was a validly ordained priest thirty years of age. The church to which he adhered was not the "Roman" but the "Old," or "Orthodox" Catholic Church. This church, which claims to antedate the "Roman" church, is held by the latter to be schismatical, but the validity of its sacraments is generally admitted. To put the matter in plain language, an "Old Catholic" priest could, equally well as a "Roman Catholic" priest, absolve from sin a Roman Catholic in circumstances of danger when no "Roman Catholic" priest was available. But between the two Catholic Churches great enmity has existed, and the Roman hierarchy for excellent reasons of its own has taken great pains to discredit the "Old Catholic" Church and to put every possible obstacle in the way of its expansion in this country. Being infinitely more powerful than its puny rival, the Roman Catholic Church has almost succeeded in smothering it out of existence. Father Norman, the subject of this story, was the victim of this profound and disedifying ill-will.

Attached to Father Norman's mission in East 14th Street, was a relief station or cafeteria at which, with the aid of several assistants, he distributed free meals to the poor and unemployed. He received many gifts of food, clothing and money, in alms, from those who admired his work, and usually he was enabled to distribute a thousand free meals a week. However, as times grew worse he had to cast about him for a further means of getting funds to carry on. He hit upon the idea of a big dinner-dance at the Commodore Hotel. He arranged with the proprietors, on October 20th (1930), to have the dinner-dance on January 28th following. His contract was in writing and duly signed. He had tickets printed and his assistants proceeded to sell them. The tickets were sold at $15 per couple. Apparently the sales progressed favorably. So far all was in order. He was doing a most Christian and Catholic thing in arranging the dinner-dance, as there were but few Roman Catholic pastors in the whole country who had not, at some time or other, organized such events. It was no sin for Father Norman to sell the tickets nor was it a sin for his followers and friends to buy them. Neither was it a crime for him to sell them, nor for purchasers to buy them. Most likely it was a virtuous and good deed on both sides as the proceeds of the dinner-dance were to be devoted entirely to the giving of free meals to the hungry poor of the East Side.

Meanwhile, however, on the opposite side of East 14th Street, facing (or frowning at) the schismatic mission was the Roman Catholic Church of the Immaculate Conception. The pastor of this church was Father Thaddeus Tierney, a man who had a sense of proprietary right over all his parishioners, and apparently over all "Catholics" of whatever kind in his parish. Father Tierney noticed with dismay that St. Peter's across the street was flourishing. He saw with horror some of his own poor parishioners entering the cafeteria for free meals. He believed that their souls were being endangered by Father Norman's influence. And when, at length he either discovered or suspected that from the pocketbooks of some of his parshioners good Catholic bills of $10 and $5 denominations were being exchanged for Father Norman's dance tickets his anger knew no bounds. Early in December he strode across 14th Street, entered the mission and accosted Father Norman, demanding of him that he close down both St. Peter's Mission and the relief station, and that if he did not do so he (Father Tierney) would close them himself. Father Norman refused to be intimidated.

From the moment Father Norman resisted Father Tierney *there was no power in New York City that could save him.* There was no law sacred enough, and no judge strong enough, to protect him from his religious enemies.

It now became Father Tierney's duty, according to customary ecclesiastical procedure, to lay the situation before his spiritual superior, H. E. Cardinal Hayes, and consult him as to what had best be done. Cardinal Hayes was at once a citizen of vast experience and immense political power. St. Patrick's was known familiarly in Tammany circles as "the power house" and *hints* emanating from it were virtual commands. In many matters the wishes of St. Patrick's were anticipated by City Offices and Departments and it was unnecessary for St. Patrick's to convey intimations. Among others, the office of the District Attorney and the Department of Public Welfare were obsequious in their respect to the will of the Church. Be that as it may, shortly after the Tierney-Norman rencontre, District Attorney Thomas C. T. Crain, and Public Welfare Officer James W. Kelly became suddenly and mysteriously interested in Father Norman. They sent for him and subjected him to minute questioning into his affairs, into the operation of the Mission, and particularly into the matter of the sale of the dinner-dance tickets. When the inquisition was finished they suffered him to return to St. Peter's but he was not to be left there in peace for long. Out of a hitherto clear sky there broke upon him such a flood of "official" blackguardism as has seldom been equalled in New York City.

On December 30th two charming if plump "society" ladies interested in charitable enterprises visited the mission and one of them purchased a dinner-dance ticket from Father Norman. While he was putting the $15 into his pocket one of the ladies whistled or signaled with her handkerchief and with a whoop and howl into the mission poured a squad of police followed by a crowd of newspaper reporters and Press photographers who had been tipped off by Welfare Officer Kelly with the object of giving the utmost possible publicity to the capture of the schismatic Father Norman.

The "society" ladies, Winifred O'Neil and Bertha Conwell, policewomen in disguise, together with Detectives Charles Kane and Ronayne Sullivan, all devout Catholics, set about seizing all the books and papers and records they could lay hands upon. They "frisked" Father Norman of the fifteen dollars he had just received. They smashed and battered and despoiled. They had no warrants of arrest nor warrants of law of any kind, but what did that matter? They carried off Norman and his staff of eight clerks to 13th Precinct Police Station where they were booked as criminals and imprisoned. There were no hesitations about procedure as there had been when the police were sent to raid Margaret Sanger's Birth Control Clinic in 1921. Norman and five of his staff were held in bail of $1,000 each to appear for examination. The policewomen swore complaints of petty larceny against Father Norman and his assistants. The case was due to come up on January 7th (1931) before Magistrate August Dreyer, a Jew, in the Magistrate's Court.

The fact that Magistrate Dreyer was a Jew did not in the least diminish the hopes and expectations of Father Tierney. When Jews fall under the influence of the Catholics of Tammany, they are usually more Roman than the Romans themselves, so far as readiness to serve the Church goes. Father Tierney knew he could rely on the Jew Dreyer as much as on the Irishman Kelly.

The eve of the hearing of the case was the great and triumphant feast of Holy Church, the Epiphany and the mystically-minded will be interested in the fact that the Norman case was, so to say, punctuated by other great feasts of the Church. It was on no less a significant and important feast than that of the Holy Innocents, that Father Norman was finally condemned to a convict's cell. However, we are anticipating.

On January 6th, Father Tierney no doubt celebrated the Epiphany with brother priests in his comfortable parochial house and discussed with them the nefarious conduct of "that blackguard Norman" who had set up a schismatic mission so near his church. In the eyes of Catholic priests, the gravamen against Norman, was not that he was teaching heresy, but that he was competing against them in business and taking Catholic money that *should* have come to them.

The feast that saw Father Tierney full of joy was a sorrowful one for Father Norman. He saw himself ruined. He knew now that he was "in their clutches" and that nothing could save him. Perhaps he regretted his rashness in attempting to withstand the Roman Church. What a fool he had been! He realized that his dinner-dance was wrecked; no one would buy any more tickets for it and it would collapse. He would have to return the money received—but that would be difficult. Agents had taken their commissions for selling tickets; some of the money had already been expended on the mission; more of it would be taken by lawyers for defending him. Naturally enough, the young Orthodox Catholic priest felt in despair.

On January 7th, Magistrate August Dreyer discharged his duty—to the Church. He dismissed the case against the assistants of Father Norman, but he held Father Norman himself for trial in the Court of Special Sessions in the exorbitant bail of $10,000! Father Norman was, of course, unable to procure this enormous amount and in default of it he was committed to the Tombs.

District Attorney Crain now filed information (Jan. 9th) against Father Norman in the Court of Special Sessions. He did all he could to trump up a plausible charge. Catholic policemen and policewomen co-operated to the best of their ability and we fear to the detriment of their consciences, but the case against Father Norman was so utterly bogus, ground-less and dishonest that when the Court of Special Sessions met on January 19th, the defendant was duly and unani-mously and on the merits of the charge found and adjudged not guilty and acquitted. *The justices decided that Father Norman was not guilty of the crime of petit larceny for sell-ing a ticket for the Commodore dinner-dance.*

Father Norman had now but eight days in which to make good his arrangements for the dinner-dance on the 28th, or to have it postponed. He tried in vain to arrange a postpone-ment. The Commodore people refused to give him another date unless he put up in cash, and at once, $1,500.

Policewomen O'Neil and Conwell, with the other officers of law, had carried off his records and he had neither the names nor the addresses of those who had purchased tickets. He recalled some twenty names and he arranged a substitute dinner-dance at the Hotel Breslin for March 18th. About twenty came to it—and as it proceeded there arrived the two Catholic detectives who had been in the raid on St. Peter's. They were Charles Kane and Ronayne Sullivan. These de-tectives, who were working for the Public Welfare Officer James W. Kelly, did not bother to secure or bring warrants. They were sure it was Norman who was holding this dinner-dance—that was enough. They arrested him and threw him into the 13th Precinct jail, booking him on a charge of "felony of grand larceny!" Kane and Sullivan had absolutely noth-ing to go on. As alleged in subsequent legal proceedings, Kane forged the charge—in the name of a lady as complaining witness—a lady who at the time the charge was made was in Florida and who, of course, did not appear against Father Norman. The charge, thus fabricated, was, however, good enough for the purpose of holding Father Norman on bail until something else turned up.

Magistrate Dreyer was to hear the case on March 26th. By a stroke of luck on March 24th Kane and Sullivan found a man, Hugh M. Hughes, a good Catholic, who had bought a ticket for the original Commodore dinner-dance and who was prepared to swear that he had been tricked by Father Norman into purchasing it. Hughes consented to swear a complaint against him.

On March 26th the tragic comedy recommenced. When "the felony of grand larceny" charge was called against Father Norman before Magistrate Dreyer *no complainant appeared, no evidence was produced, and Dreyer had to discharge Father Norman.* But before he left the court and while still in Dreyer's presence, up comes Detective Kane and arrests him again without any warrant of arrest or authority of law and without a lawful complaint lodged against him! Kane brought Father Norman to the same old jail (13th Precinct) and later on, the same day, arraigned him before Magistrate Dreyer on another charge of petit larceny. Magistrate Dreyer fixed bail this time at $500 and held Father Norman for another trial at the Court of Special Sessions *on the same charge as the one on which he had already been acquitted!*

At this point we take a couple of paragraphs from Father Norman's "Complaint" which has since been presented in a suit before the Supreme Court to recover damages against certain defendants about whom more anon. Referring to March 26th (1931), it reads:

> That the said defendant Dreyer, . . . well knew that plaintiff had previously been acquitted of the same alleged crime of petit

larceny by the said Court of Special Sessions; and well knew that
he could not legally be again charged with or held for trial for
the same alleged crime; and well knew that the said complaint or
affidavit of the defendant Hughes did not charge a crime against
plaintiff [Father Norman]; and well knew that plaintiff was
not guilty of the said alleged crime of petit larceny; notwithstanding which said facts and knowledge, the said defendant
Dreyer, Magistrate, in furtherance of said conspiracy of the
defendants, unlawfully, maliciously and in willful disregard and
abuse and in excess of his lawful authority, forced plaintiff again
to be held and put to trial for the same illegal crime in violation
of his plain legal and constitutional rights. . . .

That the said defendant Crain . . . upon receiving said
affidavit of the defendant Hughes and other records in the case,
and knowing that said affidavit or complaint did not charge a
crime, willfully and maliciously and in furtherance of the said
conspiracy, altered the true and insufficient allegations of the
same, and prepared and filed in said Court of Special Sessions on
July 27, 1931, an information against plaintiff artfully and
falsely so framed as to charge plaintiff with the crime of petit
larceny by alleging in substance that plaintiff had fraudulently
and falsely represented to the said Hughes that "plaintiff prior
to 27 October, 1930, made arrangements" with the Hotel Commodore for the said dinner and dance "whereas in truth and in
fact . . . he had not made any arrangements whatever" with the
said Hotel Commodore.

Since a great deal of the subsequent events turned upon
this affidavit of Hugh M. Hughes, it may be well for clarity's
sake to explain it.

On October 27th (1930) an unknown man had indeed
sold Hugh M. Hughes a ticket for Father Norman's dinner-
dance. The check for the ticket was subsequently endorsed

by Father Norman. The dinner-dance, as we know, was never held. District Attorney Crain, although he knew he was falsifying facts, pretended that the sale of the ticket was fraudulent. He pretended that at the time of the sale *no arrangements had been made* to hold the dinner-dance, and Father Norman never seriously intended to hold one! Actually, at the first trial before the Court of Special Sessions, *the banquet officials of the Commodore swore that arrangements for the dinner-dance had been made*, and in Father Norman's possession there was the written contract for it, and it was presented in evidence!

The State well knew that Father Norman had already been acquitted on the false charge of selling tickets for the dinner-dance, and that it was unlawful to charge him again on the same count. But what did law or justice matter in the case?

The trial before the Court of Special Sessions (December 21, 1931) was a mockery of law; "an amazing abortion of justice" it is called in his brief on appeal, to be mentioned later. As Father Norman complained, *it was not prosecution but persecution.* To quote again from the complaint before the Supreme Court referred to above:

> As the record of the said trial shows, and as the fact is, as the defendant Crain and the other defendants herein well knew, there was no evidence against the plaintiff upon the said trial to justify or sustain his conviction of the said false and illegal charge and the said judgment and sentence were and are in violation of the legal and constitutional rights of plaintiff to one fair trial, and the same were illegal and null and void.

Father Raymond had at this trial no lawyer and no witnesses present on his behalf nor any documentary evidence to produce in court in his defense. *He asked for an adjournment which was refused after five adjournments had been granted to the District Attorney.* The Court appointed Mr. Mark Wolf as his lawyer. The State's chief witness was Detective Kane, who told of arresting Father Norman at the Hotel Breslin and described an imaginary conversation with him. He put the words "what the hell" into the priest's mouth.

> Mr. Justice Rayfiel: You mean to tell us that this clergyman used the expression "what the hell"?
>
> Detective Kane (witness): Yes, Sir. He used worse than that, Your Honor, which I wouldn't wish to express.

The justices cross-questioned Father Raymond as to his ordination and early employment. They had been primed to inquire if he had worked on a railway, and extracted an admission that he had worked for a few months on a railway. They extracted the further admission that he had sung a few times as an extra in a chorus at the Metropolitan Opera.

They badgered him and then found him guilty of petit larceny and when Attorney Wolf applied on Father Norman's behalf that he should be allowed out on bail to fulfill his clerical offices for Christmas, the presiding justice, Charles Pope Caldwell, refused, saying: "I do not know whether the Community would be benefited by a man *who has been convicted of this kind of crime.* . . . It seems to me the request is not well founded . . . remanded for sentence on December 28th." His Eminence Cardinal Hayes and Father Thaddeus Tierney no doubt spent Christmas, 1931, preaching mercy and love and justice and good-will and forgiveness, and feasting themselves and their friends and rejoicing in the triumphs of Holy Mother Church.

Father Norman spent Christmas in the Tombs—an innocent, helpless victim of Catholic Action!

On December 28th (the Feast of the Holy Innocents), Father Norman was brought up for sentence before Presiding Justice Daniel Direnzo, the admirable Catholic, who had acquitted him previously (Jan. 19, 1931) on the same charge for the same offense.

When interrogated by Justice Direnzo, Norman said: "You yourself are very familiar with my case! This is only a repetition of the same case." Justice Direnzo answered: *"This is evidently different. You were acquitted on that occasion. You were found guilty on this one."*

Justice Direnzo sentenced Father Norman forthwith to an indeterminate term of up to three years in the City Penitentiary on Welfare Island where his term of imprisonment was later assessed and fixed by the Board of Parole at the exorbitant term of two years of penal servitude.

Father Norman was now—where in the view of Holy Mother Church he belonged—a convict among convicts in the New York State and City prison on Welfare Island. He had been arrested three times, always without a warrant. He had seen the inside of the Tombs and precinct prisons. His mission was closed. His name and reputation were befouled. Twice the charges against him had been dismissed as utterly groundless and unsupported by any kind of credible evidence. But the third attempt was lucky. It brought a glorious conviction!

All this had cost the city a fair amount of money, but was it not well spent? Was it not an admirable achievement for

religion and morality to prevent the hungry poor from receiving free meals from the contaminating hands of an
"Orthodox" Catholic priest?

The day following the Feast of the Annunciation of the
Birth of Christ in Norman's first year as a convict—
March 26, 1932—an attorney who in the eyes of religious-
minded folk is a thoroughly wicked man, came into the case.
Major Joseph Wheless, a freethinker, an atheist, and the
author of such blasphemous works as *Is it God's Word* and
Forgery of Christianity, had heard of Father Norman's difficulties and offered his services. On the date mentioned he
was substituted as attorney for Father Norman, and took up
the defense of the convict.

Major Wheless at once set in motion an appeal to the
Appellate Division of the Supreme Court from the conviction
of the Court of Special Sessions. On May 20, 1932, the appeal was heard. Major Wheless discovered that neither fact,
nor reason, nor law, could prevail in New York City against
the authority of Holy Mother Church. He made a little
progress, indeed, and converted two of the five justices to
recognize the innocence of Father Norman. But the three remaining judges could not be moved. They sustained the
conviction.

One of the dissenting justices granted to Father Norman
an appeal to the Court of Appeals, and a certificate of reasonable doubt. Thereupon, on July 13, 1932, after seven months
of convict life, Father Norman was released from imprisonment in bail of $500, pending his further appeal.

The appeal was heard in the Court of Appeals in Albany
at the October Term of 1932. On October 18th the seven
justices of that court *unanimously* reversed the affirmance of
the Appellate Division and the judgment of conviction of

the Court of Special Sessions, and discharged Father Norman. Major Wheless was not suffered by the justices to finish his argument. The plain facts that he put before them, even before finishing his argument, so astonished and shocked them that they interrupted him, enquired of the District Attorney if the facts as stated were true and on his confessing that they were, the Court announced its written decision, all the justices concurring.[1]

Had Major Wheless been a religious-minded man, he would no doubt have counseled his client to proceed no further and to attribute whatever injuries he had suffered to a pardonable excess of religious zeal on the part of Mother Church. But unfortunately Major Wheless was bereft of piety and reverence and he counseled his client to institute proceedings against the chief agents in his persecution for conspiracy, in malicious prosecution and to demand judgment against them in $500,000 actual and punitive damages.

On October 20, 1932, in the Supreme Court, Bronx County, began the action of Raymond J. Norman, plaintiff, by summons and complaint for damage for malicious prosecution against Patrick Joseph Hayes, individually and as Cardinal Archbishop of the Roman Catholic Archdiocese of New York; Thaddeus Tierney; James W. Kelly, Ronayne Sullivan, August Dreyer, Thomas C. T. Crain, Hugh M. Hughes, and Charles Kane, defendants.

It is not yet three years since the action began and the defendants through various legal expediencies have been able to keep ahead of pursuit. But the pursuit has not slackened and will not slacken.

The complaint, as filed on October 20th, by Major Joseph Wheless, contains accusations of a grave character against the

[1] The decision is found in New York Reports, vol. 260, p. 75.

defendants, Pars. III and VI, having to do with the motives
that impelled them to their conspiracy.

Par. III. On information and belief, that all of the defendants
above named, with the exception of the defendant Crain, were
and are members of the said, so-called Holy Roman Apostolic
Catholic Church, and acted in the matters herein complained of
as and because of being members of the said Roman Catholic
Church and in its interest and behalf, and at the instance
and direction of the defendant Hayes; and the defendant Crain
acted herein by and through an assistant appointed by him, who
is a member of the said Catholic Church and acted in the same
interest and behalf.[1]

Par. VI. Upon information and belief, that the several defendants above named concerted and conspired together to
commit and they did at the several times hereinafter mentioned
commit against the plaintiff the several unlawful and malicious
acts below set forth, for the purpose and with the intention of
damaging and ruining plaintiff in his person, property, and
repute, and of putting plaintiff and said Mission out of business
in alleged competition with the said Holy Roman Apostolic Catholic Church and said Church of the Immaculate Conception conducted by the defendant Tierney; and that to that end the defendant Tierney procured the consent and authorization of the
defendant Hayes to force plaintiff to close said St. Peter's Mission and its relief station, and to enlist official aid of the other
defendants for that purpose.

Thoughtful men will see in this "Complaint" filed in the
Supreme Court a challenge, a daring and historic challenge,

[1] Through an oversight Magistrate Dreyer is incorrectly referred to as a
Roman Catholic in this section.

made to the Catholic Church to justify its alliance with the political arm. It exposes what virtually amounts to a *Union of Church and State* in the City of New York; *it indicates corrupt Tammany as the secular arm of the Church.* Never before perhaps, in a court record, did a Complaint in this manner defy both Church and State; never before was such a Complaint of such deadly necessity. Those—and they are many—who have at heart the best interests of this great Empire City will eagerly await a verdict which will end forever the ruination of law and order through ecclesiastical "malfeasance." For as the Complaint asserts (Par. XXIX): "all the injuries and damages have been inflicted upon [Father Norman] by the defendants willfully, maliciously, lawlessly, and corruptly."

The first move to delay the action was made when the attorneys of Hayes, Tierney, and Crain served motions to dismiss the complaint on the grounds that it did not state facts sufficient to constitute a cause of action as against them. *These motions to dismiss were granted on February 24, 1933, by a Roman Catholic justice.*

In due course Major Wheless appealed from the judgments dismissing the complaint against the parties named. Many legal obstacles and delays were put in his path but the judgments were at length unanimously reversed by the Appellate Division. At the time of writing Major Wheless is preparing to present his case to the Supreme Court for trial of the original action for conspiracy and malicious prosecution.

The general public will await with interest to hear the argument in which Major Wheless will endeavor to link up H. E. Cardinal Hayes with the alleged conspiracy. No doubt he will base his plea on principles of Canon Law and attribute to the Cardinal responsibility for the actions of the Pastors of his diocese. How far his argument will influence a New York City jury remains to be seen. Neither Cardinal Hayes, nor indeed Father Tierney came out into the open in the campaign against Father Norman, but this fact is not a proof that they were not in it. To stand back from a fight for the Catholic Cause and allow lay Catholics (and their henchmen) to deliver the blows is in perfect accord with clerical tactics in Catholic Action.

By way of conclusion to this tragic story of Father Norman let me point out, and I do it with deep sympathy for those concerned, that Catholic judges, jurors and lawyers find themselves in a terrible quandary when a case against a priest or bishop crops up. They know that the Church does not recognize the jurisdiction of the civil or criminal courts over her ecclesiastics. Canon Law insists that ecclesiastics can be lawfully and justly tried only by ecclesiastical courts, except in so far as the Church expressly hands over the culprits to the secular arm.[1]

The Catholic judge who tries a Bishop of Albany (Noonan case) or a Cardinal Hayes knows that in the eyes of his Church and in the light of his Faith he has no true jurisdiction over them. The same holds for Catholic jurors. It should be their duty to escape from their difficult position, if possible, by having the accused handed over to their religious superiors.

Americans have reason to question the suitability of Catholic judges and jurors in cases that involve Canon Law or the interests of the Catholic Church. Americans are right in as-

[1] Cf. *Codex Juris Canonici, Lib. Quartus, Pars Prima.*

suming that the consciences of Catholic judges and Catholic jurors are fettered in such cases.

The sincere and orthodox Catholic sees only one satisfactory and final solution of this problem, namely, that America yield to Rome and **recognize the jurisdiction of ecclesiastical courts.**

CHAPTER XII

THE JESUITS AND THE JEWS

IT IS idle to deny the existence of a certain amount of anti-Semitism among American Catholics, especially among those in whom the European tradition persists. In Catholic countries across the water hair-raising tales of Jewish wickedness and Jewish plotting against the Church are part of the ordinary education of the Catholic youth. They are taught that all the misfortunes that have befallen and still befall the Jews are evidences of God's anger against them. The firmer the Catholic's faith in Providence, the stronger for him is the proof that Judaism is accursed of God.

American Catholics are naturally not so benighted as regards the Jews as are their European fellow Catholics, nor are they prone to believe "the hideous accusations so often hurled against the Jew by foreign Catholics whose anti-Semitism makes them as hysterical when the Jew is mentioned as the craziest A.P.A. or K.K.K. in our land could be at fancied machinations of Rome." [1] But though they are warned against excessive receptivity to "hideous accusations," they are also warned not to shut their ears to what is said "in reason" against the Jews.

The Catholic Church has never succeeded in either converting or dominating the Jewish intellect, and never will.

[1] *Commonweal*, February 1, 1935.

Intellectual independence, or as the Church would call it, intellectual arrogance and obstinacy, is too dear to the Jew and too much part of his nature and heritage to forsake. The Jew has often been robbed of civil liberty, but never of his freedom of thought. While the Catholic, and especially the Jesuit, can easily surrender his will and judgment and submit his mind to belief in "unbelievable" dogmas, and rest happy and content in such mental slavery, the Jew could never do so. He cannot tame his mind; he cannot be a Catholic.

The Catholic Church in America, looking ahead, foresees a serious clash with the Jews. The Jews represent the only permanent, powerful and closely welded group that can block or delay her march. Ku Klux and A.P.A. groups arise, flourish for a while and disappear. They are never deeply rooted nor long-lived and the Church has no fear of them. But it is a different matter with the Jews. She knows they are, and will continue to be, strong enough to challenge her pretensions and challenge them resolutely.

While there are several Catholic leaders, Alfred E. Smith, Michael Williams, Cardinal O'Connell, etc., who openly and sincerely profess the necessity and the desirability of Catholic-Jewish harmony, there are others who take the opposite view and who prefer to be dissociated from the Jews.

Sometimes the Jews are lacking in tact as regards Catholic sensibilities. For instance, as regards the Mexican situation, the Jews have not wept and howled as they perhaps should have done over the plight of Mexican Catholics. The Catholic Press has been hurt by this want of sympathy. "We Catholics cannot help wondering how men like Rabbi Wise and President Bernard S. Deutsch of the Board of Aldermen not only keep silent on anti-religious conditions in Mexico but as in the case of Mr. Deutsch utter words of commendation for the Mexican Government. The Jews in Germany have not suffered half the wrongs of the Catholics in Mexico yet our public men do not erupt with one quarter of the vigor in the case of Calles as with Hitler. There is an inconsistency here that we have never been able to understand." [1]

When Father Coughlin, in a radio talk last March, attacked a group of bankers, five out of six of whom were Jews, an alarmist group of Jews took offense and interpreted his remarks as a call to arms of the anti-Semitist forces. Rabbi Wise at once denounced Father Coughlin and the Jewish *Daily Bulletin* followed suit in a strong editorial. "One cannot be so naive," it said, "as to think that Father Coughlin in just picking the names of a few Jewish financiers did not realize that he was spreading anti-Semitism in his radio speech. Father Coughlin is a schooled politician. He knows what to emphasize and when. He, more than others, knows that by mentioning the names of just the few Jewish bankers and by emphasizing again and again that Mr. Baruch's middle name is Manasses, he sows anti-Jewish poison." [2]

The incident disclosed clearly how sensitive are the relations between American Catholics and American Jews. Father Coughlin answered the attack by saying that his N.U.S.J. would be "not worthy to exist" did it not embrace Catholic, Jew and Gentile alike in its membership. "Because I attack a Catholic," he asked, "should I be called anti-Catholic? Or if I attack a Jew should I be called anti-Jewish?" But the harm was done, and in the Press correspondence columns there appeared several bitter letters anent the matter. The Jewish correspondents called Father Coughlin a fanatic and a Fascist; the Catholic correspondents pointed out that it was

[1] March 9, 1935.
[2] March 14, 1935.

impolitic on the part of Rabbi Wise and others to raise the question of anti-Semitism. One said: "What good purpose does it serve to advise all and sundry that they [the Jews] are disliked by some? What is the natural reaction of the individual non-Jew? He pulls the next Jew he meets literally to pieces to see what makes him tick."

Rabbi Wise made, as it seems, a tactical blunder in finding fault with Father Coughlin for attacking Jewish bankers. Father Coughlin did not attack them because they were Jews but because of their banking. He was expressing a common feeling of distrust. Every race has its failings: the Germans are distrusted for their warlike propensities; the Irish, when in control of the political machine of a city, excite distrust as grafters; the Jewish bankers, with their propensity to gamble and speculate, are distrusted when their control of finance is excessive. Who would like to live in a continent where the Germans were supreme in military affairs; the Irish in political affairs, and the Jews in financial affairs? Father Coughlin may be much more anti-Semitic than is ordinarily suspected or, possibly, he may be pro-Semitic. But whether pro or anti, he has no doubt good reason for suspecting Jewish bankers as much as, if not more than, other bankers.

In any case the kind of anti-Semitism that is to be discovered in Father Coughlin's radio talks is innocent enough when compared with the more serious form of anti-Semitism which is the subject of this chapter, namely, the anti-Semitism of the great Jesuit Order.

The Jesuits, as is well known, exercise immense influence in the government of the Church and the formation of its policies and doctrines. They stand ever at the Pope's right hand—his intellectual and spiritual bodyguard—the mighty "defenders of the Faith." They are, as a body, changeless as the Church herself. Only in a slightly lesser degree than the Church do they lay claim to divine protection, divine inspiration, and infallibility.

Owing to an early experience of a painful kind, which was all but disastrous to the Order, and which was due to a group of Spanish Jesuits of Jewish descent, who threatened to dismember the Order, the Jesuits as a body have conceived and fostered an intense animosity against the Jews. Never since the days of "the great storm," as the Cardinal Toletus revolt was called, has anyone of Jewish blood or descent been admitted into the Order. Never since that day has the Order ceased to pursue vindictively the Jews. The spirit of the Order can be gleaned from the extraordinary prayer of the greatest of Jesuit saints, Francis Xavier: "Put me some place where there are no Jews or Moslems," cried Francis. The present writer, who spent twenty years in the Jesuit Order, can recall no single occasion on which a word of praise for Jewish achievement or a word of sympathy for Jewish suffering was uttered by a Jesuit.

When Pius IX, who was liberally disposed until he fell under the influence of the Jesuits, relaxed something of the severity of the laws of the Papal States, the Jesuits were disgusted. Writing later, Father Hammerstein S.J. declared: "We consider it a misfortune that in the delirium for freedom in 1848 and the following years complete civil rights were bestowed upon the Jews." When the Order was suppressed by Clement XIV in 1773 it was believed among the Jesuits that the suppression was largely engineered by Masons and Jews working on the weaknesses and fears of the Bourbons. This suspicion did not tend to lessen their obsessional phobia of Judaism.

The Jesuits, in the days when they controlled every Catholic court in Europe, and when as an Order they were swollen with pride, were challenged by a like pride and a like intellectual intolerance by the Jew. They could not break or bend the Jew. They could convert, or seemingly convert, every type of human from Japanese to profligate Parisian, but they could make no headway in leading Israel into the fold of Mother Church. They ceased to look upon the Jew as "a lost sheep," and identified him with an incarnate devil, the sworn enemy of the Catholic. They hated the Jews because the Jews did not bow in homage before them.

This tradition of hate and ill-will has lasted through three centuries. In great part the Catholic ill-will against the Jew in Catholic European countries is due to Jesuit education. Every movement against the Church, every development of Freemasonry, and Socialism, every doctrine of heretical philosophy that has weaned intellectual Catholics from the true Faith has been ascribed to Jewish machinations. This tradition is still latent in Jesuit teaching, even in this country. Naturally it is not often announced in blatant terms in the United States, but it is steadily and constantly insinuated. Once in a while—and twice recently, as we shall presently see—all the full volume of Jesuit anti-Semitism is poured forth. So long as Jesuitism flourishes in this country there will prevail among Catholics distrust and animosity against the Jews. And were it not that Jesuit influence among Catholics in America is more limited than it is among Catholics of European countries, the distrust and animosity would be infinitely more serious and disturbing.

In substantiating these statements I will confine myself to two recent writings of two prominent Jesuits, Father Francis Xavier Murphy and Father Laurence K. Patterson. Both writings were censored and passed by Jesuit superiors, and being such, bear the watermark of the authority of the Order. Further, the first and more important of the two writings was, before being published, read as an address before a convention of Jesuits at Manresa Island, Connecticut. Had it therefore represented doctrines that were not thoroughly "Jesuit," it would have been denounced to Jesuit superiors and would never have been allowed to be given to the general public in its present cheap and popular form.[1]

Here then is the Jesuit teaching about the Jew. The words that I write between quotation marks are from Father Murphy's article.

The Jew is ubiquitous. "Like Chaucer's Friar he 'entremets himself everywhere.' "

He is a troublemaker. "Where he is there is trouble." Father Murphy's heart sometimes feels pity for the Jew even when his intellect tells him that the Jew is getting what was coming to him. "My feeling is not always against the Jew; no man can read his past history without feeling deeply for him even where his reason may tell him that the Jew is simply bearing the human or Divine retribution of his acts." Jews may be divided into four classes: Orthodox, Conservative, Liberal and Radical. Some of the Orthodox are good to the Goyim, "others maintain the fiercest spirit of hostility towards the Goyim." Conservatives may be friendly, unfriendly or bitterly hostile towards Christians. Some Radicals even after they have repudiated Judaism as a religion, "seem to manifest a racial if not a religious rancor toward what they consider their ancient foe."

Historians have conspired to whitewash the Jew and to blacken the Church for her attitude towards him. "Prot-

[1] *The Catholic Mind*, October 22, 1934, published by The America Press.

estantism has done much to foster this notion of the Jew as a poor unoffending creature shrinking humbly from Catholic arrogance, bigotry, truculence." "The concept of the Jew as an innocent victim of Christian malice down the ages is an untrue and an unhistoric one." The Jews are so blind to their own faults that they resent any imputations against their past. "Any reference to historic fact that tells against them, any suggestion that they could be in the wrong, is rejected as a Christian lie and an additional proof of Christian hate. That is, the vast majority of them so think; that is the idea sedulously inculcated into them from earliest childhood."

Father Murphy finds proof in the Bible that the Jews were "fierce, truculent, coarse, sensual, crafty, cruel" and rises "from the perusal of the Sacred Text with an unfavorable notion of the Jews." He adds: "What the Jew was in Holy Writ we may justly expect to find him down the ages" . . . namely, "fierce and sensual beyond the Aryan."

Father Murphy reprobates the Jews for their "intense clannishness" and affirms that since Judaism is at once a religion and a race "of their very nature they are exclusive." This he considers a factor making for hostility against them. "There is unmistakably a deep gulf fixed between the Jew and Gentile. . . . With the Jew most men feel there is an unbridgeable gap . . . only when the Christian has lost his Christianity and become an anti-clerical does he feel that he can perfectly fraternize with the Hebrews and often then he doesn't."

Father Murphy is mystified over the business acumen of the Jew. "Today he seems to possess an uncanny power of acquiring an undue amount of wealth and that often in the most surprisingly short time. . . . And when as they so often do, the Jews acquire an undue amount of the wealth, the honorable positions and the power of a land, sooner or later murmurs are heard at the monopoly which the stranger has acquired." There follows the Jesuit theory as to how the Jews make good in commerce. "The Jew seems everywhere able to take advantage of the established commercial and industrial habits or customs of a land in such a way as to get, so it is claimed, an unfair advantage over the native who does keep to established rules of the commercial game." The result of Jewish practices and successes in business has been "his economic strangulation of every land he was allowed his freedom in." The Jewish problem hinges on this "supersuccessful accomplishment in annexing such disproportionately large amounts of the national wealth."

The Jesuit professor continues his criticism of the Jews with the intent of finding fault with them for winning the honors and rewards of their intellectual energy and ability; for "obtaining the profits that spring from gifts of intellect." Although the Jew in Germany numbered only one per cent of the population, he held fifteen per cent of the professorial and professional posts that were lucrative. Talking of the Jesuit University at Fordham, Father Murphy adds: "Fordham is a splendid example of Jewish earnestness and Christian apathy in university and college life." The implication seems to be that the Jews are not "playing the game" by studying hard and acquiring knowledge when their Catholic fellow students prefer to be slack. In fact, it is positively mean and avaricious of them to pass the examinations that others fail to pass!

Hear what follows: *"We may yet hear of a Jewish problem in our own America, and that it may become a genuine one we may conjecture from the different ethical outlook of the Hebrew.*" Father Coughlin, in his attack on Jewish bankers, spoke only for himself, but Father Murphy, in dropping such ominous if vague warnings, spoke for an enormously rich and powerful Order, or at least, if he did not speak for it, he disclosed what is its common feeling and thought.

The Jews, according to Father Murphy, teach "sane selfishness" in place of Christ's neighbor-love; they support philosophies that run counter to Christian doctrine; they aid and abet anti-clericals; they formulate subversive social theories and lead subversive movements. Witness Engels, Lassalle, Marx, Most, and Emma Goldman! They undermine morals. "Everywhere we see the unbridled lust for gain inducing them to prostitute agencies in themselves capable of a vast amount of good for mankind into instruments for debasing the taste if not the morals of the multitude."

The Jesuit, as though fearful or ashamed of the violence of his attack on the Jews, concludes his article under cover of Latin. He writes. "In Europe you may safely say they are *aut Socialistae, aut Masones, semper autem anti-Catholicae.*" ("In Europe you may safely say they are either Socialists, or Masons, always moreover they are anti-Catholic.")

So far as the writer knows this recent Jesuit diatribe against the Jews, written though it was in the midst of the various interfaith and good-will conferences and movements between Catholics, Protestants and Jews, did not provoke any protest on the part of a Catholic. One writer, a Jew, Louis Minsky, protested strongly[1] but his article was in turn subjected to criticism, for giving "a grossly distorted impression of what the distinguished Jesuit historian Reverend J. F. X. Murphy

[1] *Commonweal,* December 28, 1934.

said about the Jews" in his "calm and eminently fair exposition of an extremely controversial theme." [1]

The second Jesuit piece against the Jews is brief and pungent. It is contained in a review [2] written by a distinguished Jesuit of the younger school, Father Laurence K. Patterson. The review which he made the vehicle of his remarks was of Herman Bernstein's *The Truth about "The Protocols of Zion."*

Father Patterson is less outspoken, if even more insidious, than Father Murphy. He belongs perhaps "to that type of anti-Semite who says he has nothing against the Jews but at the same time poisons the American air with anti-Jewish insinuations and with well-manipulated hidden anti-Jewish propaganda." [3] In a brief, condensed paragraph which we shall quote in full Father Patterson endorses all the bitterest accusations made against the Jews—that they direct Communism—that they influence Latin Freemasonry (against the Church)—that they never "amalgamate"—that radical Jews are a menace to Christian ideals—that Jews are disproportionately powerful in finance, in the Press and in various occupations thanks to "other causes" (namely, some secret understandings with one another?).

Father Patterson takes as his text Mr. Bernstein's statement that "Israel's dream is still of peace, of justice and of human brotherhood" and writes:

"The reviewer [Father Patterson] does not doubt the sincerity of this statement; he believes that most Jews can endorse it. But Mr. Bernstein seems to assume that all anti-Semitic feeling is utterly baseless. Is it? Can he deny that

[1] *Ibid.*, February 1, 1935.
[2] *America*, March 23, 1935.
[3] *Jewish Daily Bulletin*, March 14, 1935.

Jews largely direct Communism? Can he fail to show that Jews are influential in Latin Freemasonry? The Jewish question requires frank and charitable ventilation. To deny the existence of a Jewish problem is to become an ostrich. The Hebrew nation (for it is a nation) is never really amalgamated by the peoples among whom it dwells. The apostate Jew who has renounced the God of Israel and the Code of Sinai is a menace to Christian ideals. Candid Hebrews realize this. Again it cannot be denied that in both high finance and in the Third International, in the press, and in the theater and cinema, in education and at the Bar, Jews exert a power out of proportion to their numbers. This is due in part to the natural talents and indomitable energy of the race. *But it is also attributable to other causes.* The leaders of the Jewish people should examine their conscience and see how far *certain elements in their race give reason for distrust*" (italics ours).

Father Patterson concludes his review by praising Belloc's *The Jews* as brilliant, frank, charitable and sincere!

Many Jews, students of law and medicine, attend the Jesuit Colleges of this country, and enjoy friendly relations with individual Jesuits. These young Jews have no means of knowing of the existence of the three-century-old Jesuit animosity against their race and religion. They may find it hard to credit its existence. But it is there and will be there until the end. The mind of the Jesuit Order never changes. The heart of the Jesuit Order will never open or soften into brotherly feeling for the Jew.

If we turn now to glance at authentic records of Jesuit history, we find that there is hardly an accusation that the Jesuits make against the Jews but is strangely out of place in their mouths. The Jesuits accuse the Jews of being "meddlers" and "troublemakers." The Jesuits were suppressed by Pope Clement XIV because they had meddled in every conceivable business from trade to politics, and their suppression was necessary "to restore tranquillity to the Church." Clement XIV said: "It was almost and indeed absolutely impossible for the Church to enjoy a true and solid peace while this Order existed," and referred (in his brief "Dominus ac Redemptor") to "grave dissensions and quarrels rashly provoked by its members not without the risk of loss of souls and to the great scandal of the nations, against the bishops, the religious Orders, and about places consecrated to piety and also with communities of every kind in Europe, Asia and America." The Jesuits accuse the Jews of lowering the moral tone of nations. Clement XIV complained that Jesuits employed "the use and interpretation of maxims which the Holy See deemed to be scandalous and evidently harmful to morality." The Jesuits accuse the Jews of "an uncanny power of acquiring an undue amount of wealth." Clement XIV condemned the Jesuits as "everywhere reproached with too much avidity and eagerness for earthly goods," which greed "exasperated many rulers of nations against it." [1] The saintly Mexican bishop, the Venerable Palafox, had to complain to a previous Pope, Innocent X, about "the extraordinary skill with which the Jesuits make use of and increase their superabundant wealth. They maintain public warehouses, cattlefairs, butcher-stalls and shops. They lend out their money to usury and thus cause the greatest loss and injury to others."

The Jesuits attack the Jews for being clannish, aloof and for not amalgamating. Throughout their history the Jesuits have been notorious for their exclusiveness and for highhatting other Orders and "mere secular" priests. In fine, as

[1] Cf. *The Jesuit Enigma*, Chapter X, by E. Boyd Barrett.

against the various accusations that Jesuits make in an attempt to defame the Jews, we find the Pope writing: *"There is scarcely any kind of grave accusation that has not been brought against the Society [of Jesus]. . . . Numberless complaints backed by the authority of Kings and Rulers have been urged against these religious [the Jesuits] at the tribunals of Paul IV, Pius V, and Sixtus V.* Thus Philip II, King of Spain, laid before Sixtus V not only the urgent and grave personal reasons which prompted his action in this matter but also the protest of the Spanish Inquisition against the excessive privileges of the Society."

On the whole it comes badly from the Jesuits to attempt to promulgate anti-Semitism on the basis of charges that have been not only officially made but believed and acted upon by the Supreme and Infallible Pontiff of the Roman Catholic Church when made against themselves. People in glass houses are foolish to throw stones.

Even though the Jesuits foresee that the Jew will stand opposed to the excessive aggrandizement of the Church in this country, they should try to understand that the Jew may be proving himself a sober, wise and courageous American citizen in so doing.

CHAPTER XIII

THE CATHOLIC CHURCH AND COMMUNISM

IT IS unnecessary to tell readers that the Catholic Church fears and loathes Communism, and that Communists recognize the Catholic Church as an implacable foe. American Catholics, as I have already stated, foresee a war in this country between the Church and Communism. "A decisive conflict," says Cardinal Hayes, "must be fought between Christianity [Catholicism] and Communism. Communism by its very nature hates the Church." [1]

Catholics are warned against the Red Peril wherever and whenever they congregate. They are urged to be on the watch, to be ready to combat the evil. Their fears are played upon by preachers and orators. They are told that "Communism is knocking at the Gates"; that the devilish horde of Reds is preparing to throw the country into chaos; that the safety of the nation is at stake; that they, the Catholics, alone can avert the disaster. "Communism is a real menace. It is no bugaboo, or scarecrow; no laughing matter and no mere occasion for brilliant epigrammatic debate. We had better look to it." [2]

The Catholic case against Communism is stated by Pope Pius XI in his encyclical "Quadragesimo Anno." He declares

[1] Pastoral Letter, 1935.
[2] Father James M. Gillis, in the *Catholic News*, February 9, 1935.

that the aims of Communism are twofold: "merciless class warfare and complete abolition of private ownership." He says that Communists "shrink from nothing and fear nothing" to attain these aims. When Communists win to power "it is unbelievable how cruel and inhuman they show themselves to be." Pius evidences "the ghastly destruction and ruin with which they have laid waste immense tracts of Eastern Europe and Asia." He points to their deeds as proof of "their antagonism and open hostility to Holy Church and to God·Himself." They are "impious and nefarious." He has no good word, no praise whatever, for either the Communists themselves or their theories.

Back of the Pope's condemnation of the men and methods that make up Communism is the fact that Communistic philosophy is the direct contradictory of Catholic philosophy. The former is rationalistic; the latter is authoritarian; the former is materialistic, the latter is spiritualistic; the former is fatalistic, the latter is based on belief in Providence. In Communism the State is deified; in Catholicism the State is looked upon as the mere handmaid of the Church. There seems no point of contact between the two systems of thought, save the elusive fact that both systems are idealistic and apostolic.

When Pius XI charges Communism with aiming at class warfare he astutely employs the adjective "merciless." Bloody or merciless class warfare is, of course, an aim that he can with consistency and justice condemn. But in itself class warfare is not irreconcilable with Catholic doctrine. The whole Catholic dichotomy—the division between the saved (*the predestined*) and the lost; the Christian and the Pagan; the orthodox and the heretic; the cleric and the mere layman —suggests and engenders class warfare of a varying degree of intensity. The Church, in recognizing and teaching the existence of "sacred" as opposed to "profane" classes of humans and in upholding the former as privileged against the latter, lays a broad basis for class warfare and religious strife.

The second aim of the Communists, as stated by Pius, namely, that of "completely abolishing private ownership," is in the eyes of the Church hateful and damnable. The Church in every land holds valuable properties that if once taken over by the State would be lost forever. In modern times the Church could not recoup her losses. To destroy "private ownership" would hamstring the Church forever. Never, never will the Church consent to the theory of State ownership, or to any other theory that would jeopardize her wealth.

The most serious of all the accusations that Pius makes against the Communist is that he is "hostile to Holy Church," in other words, anti-clerical. Here we have the real reason why the bishops of this country are so exceedingly angry over the manifestations of Communism in schools and universities. They know how easy it is to raise a laugh at the expense of the clergy and how easy it is to stir up contempt of their hypocrisy. In their eyes anything said to the discredit of "the cloth" constitutes a "subversive doctrine" and is, therefore, so they argue, Communism.

When we turn to examine how the Church is fighting Communism we notice: a varied and intensive anti-Communist propaganda (some of it Gilbertian); two schools of Catholic Action designed to defeat the Reds; a tremendous effort to win the Negro. On each of these points we shall dwell.

First, as regards anti-Communist propaganda, throughout the length and breadth of the land there is one great Catholic howl of horror over the nefarious conduct of "Mexican Com-

munists" (as the Mexican Government is called) in respect
of the Church. Next there is a loud and vociferous declaration that Catholic youth is loyal to the Constitution whereas
non-Catholic youth, as educated in the godless state schools,
is lapsing into disloyalty. "You will find no picketing, no
communistic rebellions on the campuses of Fordham or Notre
Dame Universities." [1]

At every rally of Catholic societies emphasis is laid on the
"good citizenship" of Catholics as contrasted with the evil
and subversive conduct of the radicals, and the ills of modern
times are attributed to the fact that for the most part the
government has been staffed by the product of the State
schools, a youth brought up without religious training. The
recent troubles at New York University and Columbia University are dwelt upon as evidences of what non-Catholic
training leads to. "Only yesterday," said Corporation Counsel Arthur J. W. Hilly at a Knights of Columbus rally
(May 12, 1935), "we read stories in the newspapers of a
great educational institution in this city [New York], where
the spread of communism and socialism has made such headway that the *alumni* of that University are withdrawing their
support. Radical thoughts and tendencies have advanced far
beyond the soap-box stage which we knew twenty years ago."

The emphasis on the patriotism and good citizenship of
Catholics, old as well as young, the promotion of the idea
of war-preparedness as opposed to pacifism, the support of the
forces of law and order and of the forces that are curtailing
our civil liberties, are all aspects of the Church's campaign
against Communism.

Sometimes the boosting of the "solidity" as citizens of a

[1] Father Callahan (June 10, 1935) at rally of five thousand Holy Name
Members, at Convent Avenue, New York City.

Catholic group becomes laughable. Thus, at the Knights of Columbus rally just referred to when Mr. Hilly concluded his address with the words: "Thank God I say for the Knights of Columbus," ex-Mayor John P. O'Brien delivered himself of the following: "In the close to 1,000,000 members [of the Knights] we have on this continent we have the bulwark to combat Communism. We need not fear those who by their machinations are trying to strike at the very foundations of the Republic. *As long as we have the Knights of Columbus and its like our country is safe!*"

A speech of that kind, however childish or adolescent it seem to the non-Catholic, and however Gilbertian it really is, serves the purpose of spreading the idea among Catholics that they are the backbone of the nation and that "Catholic Action is American Action." It fans the flame of hate against Communists.

The Catholic argument against the Communist idea of a State governed and ordered on economic principles and without any regard for religion is a flat denial that such a system could work. "No new social and economic structure," says Cardinal Hayes, "can be built without religious principles. . . . A new structure, social and economic, that would justify its existence cannot be built without the cornerstone of Christ's own charity."

Catholics attach enormous importance to having God mentioned in some way or other in the Constitutions. So long as his name is to be found in the index at the back of the big book of the basic laws of a State all is well. They do not seem to realize that a casual mention of God in a book in which he does not really belong is as much an insult as an honor. No State in the world draws up its laws with a view to expressing "the holy will of God." Laws today express only the political interests of the majority party in the Legislature. The Soviet Republic is not at all exceptional in its elimination of God from practical politics.

Catholic propagandists against Communism do not fail to trace the evil back to the old enemy, Martin Luther. The individualism that he started is in the eyes of Catholic thinkers the source of the trouble. That individualism engendered economic liberalism, which in turn begot sovietism and the deification of the economic law. In St. Patrick's Cathedral [1] Father Fulton Sheen, one of the great spokesmen of the American Catholic Church, developed this thought before an immense audience. He called Communism a religion—the religion of Antichrist—the true offspring of Protestantism. He conceded that its disciples displayed more zeal in proselytizing than did Catholics. He wound up by warning his audience that only one choice lay before them, the choice be-. tween "the brotherhood of Christ and the comradeship of Antichrist."

With good, old-fashioned religious frankness the Jesuit, Father Talbot, writes[2]: "There are two straight roads leading out from this world into the next, the road to heaven and the road to hell. . . . The straight road to heaven is Catholic . . . Communism [is] the other straight road out of this world."

The chief Catholic organ directed against Communism in New York is the *Catholic Worker* already referred to. It treats more intelligently of the subject, and more understandingly, than the clerical Catholic Press. While aggressively Catholic, it seeks to be fair and not to exaggerate the "errors" of its opponents.

In the February (1935) issue it listed under the heading

[1] March 24, 1935.
[2] *America*, July 6, 1935.

"Easy Essays" statements of the beliefs of Communists, Fascists and Catholics. It made the subtle distinction in sub-captions, "What the Communists *say* they believe" and "What the Catholic Worker believes." We quote the statements:

Communists believe that the Capitalist system has reached the point when it does no longer work. Communists believe that when the workers come to the realization of the downfall of Capitalism they will no longer tolerate it. Communists believe that the Capitalist class will resort to all means that may be in their power to maintain its existence. Communists believe that the Communist party knows how to assure the production and distribution in an orderly manner according to a predesigned plan.

As against this we have the following very poetic description of the faith of the Catholic worker:

The Catholic worker believes in the gentle personalism of traditional Catholicism. The Catholic worker believes in the personal obligation of looking after the needs of our brother. The Catholic worker believes in the daily practice of the works of mercy. The Catholic worker believes in Houses of Hospitality for the immediate relief of those who are in need. The Catholic worker believes in the establishment of farming communes where each one works according to his capacity and gets according to his need. The Catholic worker believes in creating a new society within the shell of the old with the philosophy of the new.

The *Catholic Worker* has rapidly increased its circulation. This increase is due to its popularity among others than Catholic workers and Communists. It is unlikely to stem the spread of Communistic philosophy. At most it will serve as a check to its spread among Catholic high school students.

In fighting Communism the Church is suffering from divided counsels. On one side there is the Pius-Coughlin theory; on the other, that of old-timers like Cardinal O'Connell. The prescription of Pius XI, as contained in "Quadragesimo Anno," called for sacrifices on the part of employers. He said: "Even more severely must be condemned the foolhardiness of those who neglect to remove or modify such conditions as exasperate the minds of the people and so prepare the way for the overthrow and ruin of the social order." In following out this advice, Father Coughlin calls for higher wages and a better distribution of wealth so as to decrease the poverty of the lower and middles classes. Father Coughlin keeps in line with the Pope's views about Communism.

But, on the other hand, we find Cardinal O'Connell decrying the "hysterical, disturbing voice" of Father Coughlin and laying down the principle that the poor should be taught to be patient and submissive and content with their lot. "The office of the priest," he said,[1] "and of the Bishop of the Catholic Church is to continue to love poverty, to love the poor, to respect the poor and to teach them, to help them, and to guide them, not to ill-gotten wealth or anarchy or discontent in their lives, but to bring them through the grace of God, the word of God and the sacraments, peace and happiness *in whatever condition of life they may happen to be*. That is the true Catholic principle of life and no other." Continuing, he said: "We all come from hard-working people, people who have faced great difficulties during their lives. What lesson would they teach us today? Would it be

[1] Boston, May 23, 1935.

this lesson of discontent and howling and shrieking for more money?"

Does it ever occur to the rich prelate of the type of Cardinal O'Connell that the American Catholic worker is no longer a terrified and ignorant peasant? Does it never occur to him that the American Catholic worker has learned to think and to ask the question: "What love of poverty does Cardinal O'Connell show?"

Cardinal O'Connell chides the worker for being discontented and seeking more money. Cardinal O'Connell and his like enjoy the best material things of life, and find fault with the poor for desiring to have the same things. Why do they do so? Are they afraid that if the poor start grabbing good things there will be nothing left for themselves?

The bishops, unless they are all high-grade morons, must know that unctuous advice bestowed upon the poor does not enable the latter to pay rent or purchase a meal or see a football game. The bishops must know that a father who has children whom he cannot feed or clothe has fierce and envious feelings in his heart that will not be assuaged by pious palaver.

In the Catholic worker's mind the seed of suspicion is sown that the Catholic Church in this country is the great mainstay of the capitalist system, and that the clergy who profess to lead him to heaven are helping to keep him in hell. "If the bishops and priests want to keep us in the Church," they say, "let them give us a lead! Let them help us to better our standard of living! It is with our money that they have built themselves fine houses, bought fine cars, and live well! We don't object to their having a good time but we also want to have a good time! Why not? Let them give us a hand now! Let them all, bishops and priests, come out and fight with us! Else we'll know they're double-crossers as well as hypocrites!"

Writing in *America* apropos of a discussion of Father Coughlin's activities, a Catholic "man in the street" said: "Do you not believe that it is the duty of the Church and its priests to help the common people in a material as well as in a spiritual way? A Mass by itself is merely a lot of words and music. It never filled an empty stomach or put a pair of shoes on a barefoot boy. It may have given him hope but that is all. Do you not think that it would have been better to have turned public opinion against conditions that leave many hungry and poorly clothed? If the Catholic clergy would only get solidly behind Father Coughlin we would have a new and prosperous America in a very short time. . . . This letter will let you know how the man in the street feels. I have talked to many who feel the same as I do. Is it any wonder that the people of Russia and Mexico have turned against the Church? They found no help there from conditions that oppressed them. I should hate to see the American people turn the same way but I am afraid that unless the Churches decide that it is their duty to lead in a material as well as in a spiritual way that it is a peril they will have to face before many years." [1]

Actually, as Pius XI admits with sorrow, there is a drift of Catholic workers into the Communist Party. In this country the activities of Father Coughlin have, for a moment, stemmed the tide. But up to the moment of writing there is no sign of that happening which the writer of the letter called for, namely, that "the Catholic clergy should get solidly behind Father Coughlin."

The bitterness of the feelings of the Catholic followers of

[1] *America*, June 15, 1935.

Father Coughlin against the bishops and priests who oppose him, or who fail to support his efforts, was well brought out by an analysis of the letters (such as the one given above) that reached *America* after the series of articles referred to. Father Parsons, the editor and author of the articles,[1] conceded that the letters were "a fair cross-section of the Catholic opinion which is behind Father Coughlin," yet they showed "a terrible hatred of the clergy and Hierarchy." He says: "Over and over again the letters, particularly the anonymous ones, attack the priests and Bishops for callous and cruel neglect of the poor."

We come now to describe the most active and important sector of the Catholic front in its campaign against Communism in this country. It is the Negro sector. The Church is frankly and avowedly in terror of the Negro going Communist. She is also amazingly frank about her past neglect of the Negro, which neglect she now realizes has brought about the present dangerous situation.

Out of about 18,000,000 Negroes in this country there are only 250,000 Catholics. Until recently there was no Negro priest, and no seminary for training Negroes for the priesthood. Many Catholic colleges excluded Negro students, and in the majority of Catholic churches Negroes were discriminated against. Mr. Michael Williams, of the *Commonweal*, has been among the most outspoken in describing the situation: "That American Catholics have lamentably neglected—or perhaps it would be truer to say have not even seen—their duties towards the Negro is a fact so notorious that now it stands as the chief stumblingblock in the path of the small minority of white Catholics who not only see but recognize and seek to perform those duties. As a body white

[1] *America*, June 29, 1935.

Catholics have been callous and cold and indifferent. It is not only true we have disregarded the Negro's own claims—worse than that we have disregarded the teachings of our own Church." [1]

A year later, referring to the pastoral of the bishops which year by year, for fifty years, has been read in every parish in the United States, urgently asking the faithful to contribute to the Indian and Negro missions, Mr. Williams remarked: "We can say that this appeal from the hierarchy is treated with an indifference which is most saddening, indeed it is alarming . . . there seems something almost contemptuous in the lack of practical response."

A generation back Archbishop Ireland had protested against "the shame and scandal of putting colored people into corners and lofts of Catholic Churches," but his protest was disregarded and Negroes are still insulted and snubbed when they seek to enjoy equality with the whites in the so-called "houses of God." A recent instance of Catholic snobbery is described in a letter written by a Negress, Mrs. Ruth Coffie, which has already appeared in the Press, but which is so appealing and important that it merits the utmost possible publicity. Her story belongs to Cardinal Mundelein's diocese, and has to do with the Catholic Legion of Decency move in Chicago. She wrote:

I am writing in reference to the big "parade of decency" held recently as a protest against the production of immoral films, and want to say that there was plenty of prejudice shown my little girl who is a student of a Catholic High School. These students were the only colored in the parade; they had to pay

[1] June 1, 1934.

ten cents and got a dollar's worth of insults, some of them being called "niggers."

One of our boys asked a white student where they should go to get in the parade and the latter said they had no right to be there. They were finally put in the back of the line where they had no music to march by. It really hurt me to know there is so much prejudice when we are trying our best to raise our children and educate them. My girl goes to St. Elizabeth's High School and a number of the children and their mothers were talking about how they had been insulted by the whites. All the colored citizens were neatly dressed and looked as good as the others but they were put at the end of the parade and grossly humiliated. It should have been called "the parade of prejudice."

The story of Mrs. Ruth Coffie is appealing for its very simplicity, and for the significance of the little incident it revealed.

Cardinal O'Connell says of his fellow Catholics, "we all come from hardworking people," and the implication is that the last generation of Catholics had to labor on roads, and in mines, and in building dams side by side with the Negro. The present generation of Catholics, forgetting the past, are too snobbish to have any truck with the Negro.

Dr. Hudson Oliver, a highly educated Catholic Negro, in an address delivered at a convention of the International Federation of Catholic Alumnae,[1] told how "the Negroes were being attracted to Communism by false lures held out by Communistic propagandists and that these lures were so calculated as to be in striking contrast with the attitude of certain people holding themselves out to be good Catholics." He told of the snubs that Catholics put upon Negroes and how Negroes complained that when they went to Catholic schools "they were not accepted in the best white circles." He

[1] February 9, 1935, at New Rochelle, New York.

roundly accused his fellow Catholic whites of refusing social
equality to the Negro and added that the best preventive
against Negro Communism was to accord such social equality.

Almost as hurting as outspoken jeers to Negro sensibility
is the condescending attitude of Catholics. They discuss the
Negro as though he were a strange animal. Having come,
thanks to the wisdom and guidance of Mother Church, to
recognize him as a human being, they decide that it is right
and proper to treat him as such. Had the resolution, which I
shall presently quote, of the Sacred Heart Alumnae of Manhattanville, been adopted four centuries ago it might have
been called "enlightened," but today it stands as a perfect
example of priggishness. The convent students resolved: *"to
maintain that the Negro as a human being and as a citizen is
entitled to the rights of life, liberty and the pursuit of happiness,* and to the essential opportunities of life and the full
measure of social justice." No doubt the Sacred Heart nuns
thought it would flatter and please the Negro to know that
they and the girls they educate at Manhattanville were prepared to admit that the Negro was a human and "entitled
to the rights of life." The Negro might be assured, therefore,
that if he came within the sacred precincts of Manhattanville
he would not be shot down as a wild animal!

The Harlem riots came as a reminder to Cardinal Hayes
and Mgr. Lavelle of the disgraceful neglect of the district
by the Catholic administrators of Tammany. How many
Catholic mayors and aldermen and borough presidents have
come and gone and sought advice from the occupants of the
Episcopal Palace of St. Patrick's! The Catholic Church is
more responsible for conditions prevailing there than any
other factor in the city. "When the Negro first moved into
Harlem and began expanding Catholic people resented his
very presence and even tried to prevent his attendance in

parish schools . . . when the Negro came to worship in the House of God he was shunned, became the center of hostile glances. . . . If the attitude of the Catholic had been really Catholic at that time Harlem would probably be Catholic now." [1] But the Catholics not only ostracized the Harlem Negro in those days, but have ever since refused him civic aid. Hylan, Walker, O'Brien and the Catholic mayors that preceded them had plenty of time for attending Catholic festivities and vindicating Catholic contributions to citizenship in their speeches, but seemingly they had no time to attend to the welfare of the Negro in Harlem. "It should be irrational," says Pius XI, "to neglect one portion of the citizens and favor another."

In sharp contrast to the Catholic attitude towards the Negro who comes to the House of God, is that shown by the Protestants, as when the funeral took place [2] in St. John the Divine of Richard Berry Harrison, the old Negro actor who had played in *The Green Pastures* for five years. Seven thousand, mostly colored, thronged the cathedral and under the blessing of Bishop Manning let themselves go in their hymns, and demonstrations of sorrow. "This service," said the preacher, "is the simple Christian tribute of an adoring populace to a man who walked upon the earth and touched men like himself in a mystic way that made them feel that they had been with God."

The Catholic Church has at last begun to move. In every Negro district she has her teachers and preachers striving by hook or crook to propagandize Catholicism. In some places, notably in Newark, she is having some success. She sees that it is vital to her interests to win the Negro to her side so that he may be a friend rather than an enemy; so that, if possible,

[1] *America*, April 6, 1935.
[2] March 17, 1935.

his vote may be won for the Catholic Cause. Were she so fortunate as to capture even half the Negro vote, she would be assured of her political ambitions. On the other hand, should the 18,000,000 Negroes side with the Communists her Cause would be lost.

The Church bitterly deplores her inaction in the past. "It may be too late [now]," writes Father LaFarge S. J.,[1] "to achieve results that could have been accomplished twenty-five years ago. But if another ten, another five years of inaction and neglect ensue, we may find that the Negro will have passed for ever from our spiritual ken."

Father LaFarge imagines that if, even now, the Catholic clergy and laity could be brought to envisage the Negro as a human much could be achieved. "Once the white Catholics of the United States have thoroughly acquired *the view of the Negro as a human being* like themselves, with the same duties, needs, and responsibilities, that they themselves possess, the door will be open to the conversion of the great body of the Negro race to the Catholic Faith." We doubt, however, that the mere fact—or if you will, the singular privilege—of being regarded as humans by American Catholics would so overwhelm Negroes as to make them embrace Catholicism.

Be that as it may, the Church *must* have the Negro, not so much for his soul, for hitherto she cared little about that as her admissions reveal, but for his vote and to prevent the Communist's getting him. One may expect before long a papal encyclical for the benefit of the colored masses. To conquer them Rome will stoop to flattery, and cajolery.[2]

[1] *Commonweal*, July 5, 1935.

[2] Since this was written it is announced that Pius XI intends to canonize a Negro saint!

CHAPTER XIV

THE RELIGION OF THE AMERICAN CATHOLIC

WE HAVE studied Catholic Action in America in many
of its phases. We have seen it assaulting "indecency" and "Neo-
Paganism" and opposing birth control and sterilization. We
have observed how it has built up a new Press and strength-
ened its organizations. We have watched it stirring up trouble
with the Mexican Government and playing at the heretical
game of "interdenominationalism." We have heard its large
demands for more political power and more high offices for
Catholics, and for State aid for its institutions. We have seen
its efforts to secure material aggrandizement and to dominate
the social mind of the nation. It remains for us to ask how all
these activities, which the American Catholic pursues in the
name of religion, are going to help on the cause of religion.
In other words, how far is this great Catholic campaign, this
Catholic revolt against the *status quo*, in accord with fundamental religious principles?

Catholic Action is daring, restless, ambitious and voracious.
It embraces, as we have seen, every kind of activity, from
knitting socks to smashing windows, from lauding Dr. Parkes
Cadman to insulting and harrying the President. It builds
schools, it stages enormous demonstrations, it houses orphans
and smuggles arms, it clothes the poor and tears to pieces the
reputations of enemies, it boasts of infallible guidance and

206

takes shelter behind false and soft conceptions of "offensive" doctrines of the Church. Inside the Church it praises Christ's Sermon on the Mount, outside on the piazza it issues blood-curdling threats. It proclaims the blessings of peace and keeps aflame the spirit of strife. What is the religious motive behind these diverse policies? Is it holy zeal? Is it love of truth and righteousness? Is it enthusiasm for the spiritual and the mystical? Is it ardor for personal perfection? Is it tender love for a paternal merciful God?

Is not religion supposed to be essentially spiritual? Is not its source man's longing to decipher the riddle of life, and understand the purpose of his being? Is it not, in short, the expression of man's need to identify himself with the great spirit or spirits of the beyond and offer the worship of his mind and heart?

But how is this need of union with the divine power or powers, which is the core of religion, exemplified in such Catholic Action as we have seen in the Raymond Norman case? How is it fostered by melodramatic Catholic morons announcing to the public, "As long as we have the Knights of Columbus our country is safe?" If Catholic Actionists in this country stand by Catholic Action as the outpouring of the religion that is within them, then this religion of theirs is something at variance with traditional ideas—certainly with the traditional ideas of the Old Masters.

Catholics, of course, take their faith for granted. They also take for granted that what they do in the name of and under the guidance of the Church is above reproach and criticism. As religionists they are egocentric, incapable of getting outside themselves and looking critically and impartially at their own conduct. They are hurt and amazed when they discover that there are some who do not see eye to eye with them. Those who differ from them and disapprove of what they are doing are dubbed bigots. Catholics are unconscious of the reactions that they provoke and of the thoughts that are harbored about Catholic Action.

Mr. Williams, in a passage which I have already quoted, betrays this carefree ingenuousness of the Catholic mind as he holds up for admiration Catholic Action in America: "All Catholics with even a modicum of imagination cannot fail to be thrilled with the vision of the vast Catholic force which gleams through the calm figures of the [Catholic Year Book] Directory—the force of the Church in action, permeating the national life, the leaven in its mass; uplifting its ideals, directing its way toward the only road which is consonant with humanity's true nature; the road of Christian civilization."

Does the Catholic Church of America "uplift the ideals" of the mass of the nation? Is it the spiritual "leaven" of America? Catholicism in America is far from being an inward, a mystical expression of union with God. It shrinks from mysticism, asceticism and the cultivation of that calm reserve of soul, that cloistered repression of human instincts, which high sanctity calls for. American Catholicism pours its energy into movement and external affairs. It fights, it mixes in the world, it beats the air, it prays aloud, it must be forever doing, talking, moving, making changes, traveling hither and thither to conventions and parades. "Those who travel much abroad seldom become holy," says À Kempis. "Let not the right hand know what the left hand is doing," says Christ. But how is American Catholicism to be described? "We have," wrote a contributor to the *Catholic Charities Review*, "a great amount of spread-eagleism in Catholic work in the United States. We have been too much inclined to measure

THE RELIGION OF THE AMERICAN CATHOLIC 209

our spiritual progress on the basis of material progress."
American Catholicism is not spiritually "uplifting" nor is it
a spiritual "leaven," because it is more of a big business than
a school of mysticism, it is more of a fancy dress ball, a
splendid noisy show, a holy fireworks display, a tournament
where motives of sordid ambition as well as of chivalry excite
the champions, than a hall of prayer and noiseless contemplation.

When Cardinal O'Connell laid down what he called "the
true Catholic principle of life," [1] he painted a picture of
bishops and priests *who loved poverty* and who loved the
poor, laboring to shepherd the poor through lessons in Christian perfection. His "true Catholic principle of life" was in
deadly opposition to "all those disturbing voices, the shout-
ing, yelling, screaming." *"The Christian principle,"* he said,
*"is not to fight with our neighbors and call names and stir
uprisings."* When saying these things, he was unconsciously
administering a severe rebuke to American Catholicism.

To confirm the views expressed above, I quote a few
paragraphs from a thoughtful letter which appeared in the
Commonweal. [2]

The writer, Mr. G. B. Neale, was discussing an editorial
entitled "Progress of the Church" which had appeared in a
previous issue of the same review. He said:

Material success amongst Catholics of the present and prior
generations and the great god "keeping up with the Joneses."
have made Catholicism a mere formality with many of those who
profess the faith. They go to the sacraments but it is mainly a
matter of routine and quite perfunctory. They are good Cath-

[1] *New York Times*, May 24, 1935, already quoted.
[2] June 15, 1934.

olics statistically but poor Catholics in the deep spiritual meaning of the word. . . . The Catholic who practises any kind of asceticism is indeed rare. Naturally asceticism is not an advertised habit but it must necessarily be accompanied by piety. What is the evidence in this regard? Observe those who go to Communion. They crowd up to the rail like a mob getting on a subway train and they rush out of the church as soon as the priest leaves the altar. Asceticism? The average Catholic does not know what it means.

(You ask) Is the mystical element in religion appealing more or less to American Catholics? . . . To the great mass of Catholics mysticism is practically unknown—even repudiated. "Let us be practical" is their attitude.

(You ask) Is the practise of prayer increasing? Again the answer is "No." About the only time that really fervent prayer is resorted to by the great majority is when some material boon is sadly needed. . . . Asceticism, mysticism, prayer and liturgy can only be appreciated by those who "know God"—through humility and simplicity of faith.

Mr. Neale apparently shares the opinion of the author that American Catholicism, as a religion, is "something at variance with traditional ideas" in fine, that it is very seriously lacking in "inwardness" however impressive its external forms and its statistical soundness.

The decay of the religious sense among American Catholics is due in great measure to the lack of spiritual guidance. There are priests, 30,000 of them, as well as 124,000 nuns, but one has to suspect that they either cannot or do not choose to attempt to cultivate a religious sense in the people.

The American Catholic priest is essentially a businessman, who builds schools, manages the affairs of his parish, organizes Catholic clubs, mixes with the important political people of his parish and looks upon mysticism as tomfoolery. He is relatively as ignorant, if not relatively more ignorant, of Catholic doctrine, and the history of the Church, than the laity. He is, for the most part, astoundingly indifferent to the philosophy of Catholicism. Probably not a fourth part of the Catholic priests of America read either of the great encyclicals of Pius XI, "Casti Connubii" and "Quadragesimo Anno." The average American priest would scoff at papal encyclicals as "highbrow stuff." "What the h ——," he would say, "how d'ye think I'd have time to read that junk?" Of course, at the Communion Breakfast he would praise such encyclicals to the skies!

The average Catholic priest regards preaching as a bore and takes no pains to prepare his sermons, with the result that if one attends a Catholic last-Mass on Sunday, one may be pretty certain of hearing a third-rate sermon— empty of doctrine, bereft of any thought to stimulate either the mind or the heart.

In business matters the priest gives a lead. He is a go-getter so far as money matters are involved. We take the following from the pen of Mgr. Belford[1] it is a straight talk to his parishioners who are growing stingy during hard times: *"There is no doubt that many Catholics will go to hell because they have not done their share to support the Church.* Then think of the base ingratitude! We cannot reach God directly with gifts or expressions of appreciation. But we can reach him through the poor, the sick, the orphan, the aged. We can reach him by building and *maintaining churches* and schools in which religion will be taught and worship conducted."

Mgr. Belford introduces God, the poor, the sick, the

[1] The *Mentor* (Mgr. Belford's parish paper), January, 1935.

orphan and the aged into his appeal, which, however, as a previous paragraph shows, is solely for a better plate collection on Sundays. "About 4,000 people attend mass here every Sunday. Of these about 3,000 are adults. Usually we receive one $10, two $5 bills, and about thirty one-dollar bills. Twelve hundred give a quarter, and less than one hundred a dime. *This is not only unjust it is shameful and sinful.*"

In spite of the fact that the priests drive them hard and help them little in spiritual matters, the Catholic laity are on the whole devoted to them. In the big cities the priests mix like the laity; all are on the same level; priests from the altars announce dances, bridge parties, radio parties and all other Catholic social functions and work hard to make them successes. Religion and social life merge. The church is in a general way a fraternity house, a club where the "bunch" get together on Sundays. A new homogeneity between the sacred and the profane has been discovered by the American priest and the old rigorous division between "God's anointed" and the mere layman tends to disappear. The Church in this country has become a breeding-ground for solid Knights of Columbus and sturdy, fighting Catholic Actionists, rather than a nursery of saints and ascetes. What Leo XIII feared, and warned against, has come to pass: that the American priest should create "another kind of Church" than the old European type.

The shortcomings of priests, the hurried, undignified manner in which they say the Church prayers at services—"streamlined praying," as it is called—is, of course, excused by devout Catholics. Apropos of "streamlined masses" a correspondent of *America*[1] writes: "Perhaps there were parish

[1] May 25, 1935.

duties waiting; a sick call, a sodality meeting, a St. Vincent de Paul Conference. An apostle must have a sense of values; must be able to separate gist from chaff." Priests can "get away with murder" as far as the devout are concerned. The correspondent, Marie Duff, reserves her criticism for non-Catholics and concludes her letter: "Form, form! Yes, it is perfect in non-Catholic rendering. Why shouldn't it be? *What else have they?*"

To justify Catholic Action, as it obtains in America, Catholics say, "You get nothing without fighting," meaning that "unless you fight you can't get on top." "Organize," says the Catholic, "organize and show your teeth! High-hat the haters! Do the Joan of Arc thing!" As a Jesuit Father (of West 16th Street, New York City) put it to his lady sodalists: "You must fight for the Church as that little girl Joan d'Arc fought for France."

The Catholic mind is easily inflamed. There is in it a mysterious sensitivity. It is intensely touchy where the interests of the Church are at stake, or where the honor of the Faith is involved. The clergy, instead of allaying this proneness to take offense and to quarrel, seem to encourage it. Said Father Hogan [1] at a large rally of the Holy Name Society in the Bronx: "More than ever what we need is men with warm blood and courage in their veins." Said Father McGirr [2]: "Very shortly the Catholic Church is to become much more militant than it has been heretofore." Catholics like to give a military veneer to their doings—they "mobilize" under generals and Knight Commanders—they have their colors and flags and camps and posts and troops and brigades and guards of honor and reviews, and so forth. They

[1] June 17, 1934.
[2] *Catholic News,* February 16, 1935.

conceive of Catholic Action as a war, of religion as fighting! The American Catholic never dreams of *praying for the "heretic."* He knocks him down if he can—if he is unable to do that, he calls him names or writes him an abusive letter.

Neither the Protestant nor the Jew conceives of religion in this peculiar way. Both will fight to defend their homes and their business interests and their freedom of conscience. They will not fight an aggressive war to force their religious views upon others or to chastise others for criticizing the tenets of their religions.

The Protestant mind does not associate religion with fighting; the Catholic mind does. Protestantism can prosper under conditions of peace in the absence of controversy; Catholicism fares ill unless it be opposed or unless it be achieving some new conquests. Unless Catholics be kept in fighting trim, primed for a fight, they grow lax, "take it easy," and fade out as Catholics. A Catholic M.D. is approached by a salesman of birth control merchandise. He says, "I am a Catholic," and being a big man, he pitches the salesman out of his office. Then with a glorified ego he writes naïvely to tell readers of *America*[1] how he deals with the matter, adding: "The *military training* at St. Joe's has been a help to me in life." Fine! But has this "military training" which enabled him to knock out a smaller and unoffending man helped on in any way the cause of religion? Has it increased "the love of God"? Let us add that this virtuous M.D. endeavors to make a little material capital for himself out of his prowess by advocating in his letter a salutary habit for Catholics, namely, that *of choosing Catholic M.D.'s for their physicians!* Notice how the mind of this American Catholic M.D.

[1] June 1, 1935.

worked: (a) here is an insult to the Church's teaching; (b) here goes for a good blow and a kick; (c) now, let me make a bit of publicity and money out of the incident. In the whole mental (and physical) process there is no thought of prayer or of Christian love!

One doubts if there be much promise for the future of religion in Catholic Action of the type just described.

Aggressive fighting tactics are not confined to the Catholic laity, nor to the lower ranks of the clergy. High and low, all alike, from bishops to bootblacks, Catholics are ready for a scrap. We have seen how Archbishop Curley took it upon himself to challenge and threaten President Roosevelt over the Mexican question; in a similar vein Mr. Patrick Scanlan, editor of the *Brooklyn Tablet*, delivered an assault on Governor Lehman because he vetoed the Kelly-Corbett Transportation Bill. Father Curran (president of the International Catholic Truth Society) wrote to the editor of the New York *World-Telegram*[1] anent a birth control controversy, taking exception to an offending editorial, and concluded his letter as follows: "Since your editorial is not based on facts and since it is an insult to Catholic readers and to Catholic advertisers, I propose to bring it to the attention of our numerous Catholic population in the greater City of New York and to all Catholic business men *unless you make fitting reparation on the editorial page of your newspaper!*" The editor had the good sense to publish Father Curran's threat and he had the rare courage to subjoin the remark: "If this is a democracy let us act as if it were a democracy and not resort to dictatorial procedure."

As is well known, when an editor in this country ventures to publish an article critical of Catholicism or Catholic Ac-

[1] March 20, 1935.

tion he is inundated with abusive letters and excoriated in
the Catholic Press. Supposedly high-standing Catholic journals, as for instance the *Commonweal*, resort to the language of the gutter in order to express loathing and detesta-
tion of the indignity done the Church. When last March
(1935) the *American Mercury* published an article entitled
"The Troubles of American Catholics," in which in a temperate way certain idiosyncrasies of Catholics were alluded
to, the editor of the *Commonweal* published[1] an open letter
to the editor of the *American Mercury* in which the following
remarks were to be found: "No more superficial or sillier
or out-of-date article on the subject" [of Catholicism] than
this "shallow, this provincial, this weakly vicious performance" . . . has appeared for thirty years. "A maundering,
vacuous, spineless thing . . . stupid if not mendacious." The
author "stands revealed an old-fashioned liberal" . . . one of
the liberals "who now amazed and angered at the striding
power of the Catholic Church are exerting all their vicious
enmity to check her resurgent movement throughout the
world."

Recently Heywood Broun ventured to criticize Father
Coughlin and the mail he received as a consequence made
him declare: "I think no columnist can possibly know what
it is to be bawled out until he has said something derogatory
about Father Coughlin." Heywood Broun gave a few extracts from the mail in question: "Dear Sir, You smell on
rye bread"; "You are to put it mildly a skunk while your
column was, to put it in a mediocre manner, lousy."

The present writer had the temerity to accede to a request
for an article on convent life—"The Sociology of Nunneries"
—which appeared in the *American Mercury* (February,

[1] March 15th.

1935). The article kept close to facts, was mildly critical and eschewed references to many serious scandals that the author knew about. It was an article, however, which touched Catholic Actionists on a sore spot, as was amply proved by the mail which forthcame. The letters were for the most part anonymous—they were abusive—insulting—and some of them filthy. If Mr. Michael Williams of the *Commonweal* were to read these productions of the Catholic mind he would not be so cocksure that Catholicism is "the leaven of the nation" and that it "uplifts its ideals." I append a typical letter:

Lusus Naturae[1]:—

Judas, you know, did not sell Christ for thirty pieces of silver— 'twas himself he sold. So shall it be down through the ages—as long as there are traitors and cowards to crawl, and money to pay them for their slimy efforts. If you got thirty pieces of silver you should have given back some change, for I think thirty cents would be *ad valorem* in your case. You claim you have been a priest—a Jesuit. Perhaps you were—so was Judas; but if you ever had the presumption to put S.J. after your name you should have added in parentheses Sic Judas, which in your anomalous case would be more fitting than the Blessed Name which makes the dying live.

Your slimy attack upon the ladies in Convents is as reliable as you are—unprincipled and base beyond words. No doubt you dress in man's clothes; but it is hard to picture you as a man, attacking defenceless ladies—ladies whose clear eyes and clean hands your vile suggestive lines could never reach. If Convents did nothing else in God's beautiful world but protect clean lives from coming face to face with such an article as yours in the Mercury, they are priceless in the cause of humanity.

[1] Latin for "freak of nature."

You seem very much perturbed over the number of ladies who enter convents. Statistics show that great numbers enter every year. Thank God the same statistics do not give such proportions to your species. Most cowards at least have respect for women—not you—surely your mother must have been a woman, or was it a case of another Miss X. you so picturesquely feature in your Mercury ramble. X always marks the spot you know! This start may account for your depravity and your non compis mentis, lies beyond your control. Since you left your own country and came to America where, it is well known, only dangerous lunatics are locked up, you should at least respect those on a higher level, who live on higher standards, and whose lives should be spared the contamination such as you breed. Reptile like, you create your own slime . . . scorpion like, you are stinging your way through life.

Because you found yourself locked out of the Monastery, you whined. All "undesirables" whine at the atmosphere they find themselves in. Do not for one moment think that you are the first dog to bark at the serenely shining moon—Maria Monk has preceded you in licentious strides. Joseph McCabe, another genius from across the seas has polluted our press, and I would suggest that you have your photo, get one of Joe McCabe and between your two repulsive countenances place Maria Monk's, then send the trio to Ripley for his "Believe it or not" strip, and label it "Three of a kind"—as you may know, three of a kind beat two pairs. . . .

You do most of your thinking in quotation marks, your ramble in the Mercury proves this beyond a doubt. Herein also you display all the ear marks of Judas—even to the "kiss" featured. All you need to complete the picture is the piece of rope. Why hesitate? Rope is so cheap! In the meantime, use a good strong mouth-wash, thereby rendering to those who have to inhale the same air, at least some service.

One can imagine the gloating smile upon the sensual face as you grasped the money that paid you for the slimy attack upon the convents; but your line will be carried on by your kind as long as the right kind of bait is dangled before your garbage collecting hands. It is just such vile lines as yours in the Mercury, that give stimulus to those of us who merely belong to the rank and file of the countless thousands who would give their lives for the cause you so cowardly try to defile. Your tactics are as readily seen through as a screen door and ten to one there is another Miss X in the offing.

I will not sign my name to this, nor would I write you by any other means than by machine. I respect my name too much to even have you trace it in lead pencil and I would not waste ink on such a poor specimen of homo.

Momento mori; but Don't forget the piece of rope—the sooner you invest, the better for clean living and humanity.

This letter, with its Latinity and scholasticism, was quite obviously written by a priest. Further, it is not improbable that it was written by a Jesuit priest. It shows signs in its composition of Father Rodriguez' *Christian and Religious Perfection*, the spiritual treatise on which young Jesuits are nurtured.

However, what is important to our purpose is to note that it is a typical Catholic letter. It harmonizes line for line, thought for thought, with a hundred other such letters coming from Catholics. It does not lack the salient note of "mother-baiting." "Let's insult his mother! That's the way to get him! Have at it, boys! Throw mud and dirt at her! Who says Catholics are not good Americans?" No mawkish sense of chivalry, nor silly sentiment of decency, restrains the pen that drips with the honest ink of Rome!

Besides the fighting, truculent ingredient of the religion

of the American Catholic, there is another ingredient that should be described as lack of candor. The American Catholic is afraid to face facts. He is afraid to admit the faults and shortcomings of the Church. He is unwilling to discuss matters in an intelligent, impartial manner. When recently the Nazis in Germany sentenced Sister Wernera to five years in prison for violating the laws governing the transfer of money abroad, the Catholic Press dubbed the affair "Persecution of Nuns in Germany." Sister Wernera had done wrong and she admitted it in court. "Of course it was not right," she said. Her sentence may have been severe but in what sense is it "persecution" for the State to punish the guilty? [1]

When Governor Lehman vetoed the Kelly-Corbett Bill, already referred to, because "it contravened a definite policy which the State has always followed," namely, that of refusing to appropriate State funds to the succor of "private schools," the Catholic Press attacked him with violence instead of admitting that his veto was justified by precedent. The bill was most probably unconstitutional although Governor Lehman avoided giving his decision on that point. Catholics, who boast of their citizenship, are not honest and candid in acknowledging the good citizenship of those who happen to be in the right in opposing their will.

In an interesting letter to *America*[2] a correspondent from Barcelona, Spain, points out that "those charged with the government of the Church in Spain (as in Mexico) have their share of responsibility for the undoubted injustices from which the Church in those countries suffer," and goes on

---

[1] Some German Catholic bishops have since dissociated themselves from the money-smuggling nuns and priests. Cf. *New York Times*, June 6, 1935.

[2] March 9, 1935.

to ask: "Why cannot the Church have the courage to face all the facts?" The matter is particularly important as regards Mexico. The eyes of all, Catholic and non-Catholic alike, are open to the defects and misconduct of the Church in Mexico but no official admission of such defects of misconduct can be wrung from the American Catholic Church. American Catholics would have this country intervene on behalf of a religion that is largely pagan and a clergy that is largely ignorant and corrupt. The whole Catholic propaganda on behalf of the Mexican Church is rank with *suppressio veri*.

The late Arthur Preuss, who edited the now defunct *Fortnightly Review*, of St. Louis, Missouri, was one of the few American Catholics who believed in a brave policy of candor. He is now esteemed by Catholics as "one of the greatest literary lights of the day"[1] and his loss to the Catholic cause is felt. Reviewing one of my articles which appeared in the *American Mercury* (January, 1929) in which I criticized American Catholicism, he wrote: "We wish the article would be reprinted in pamphlet form and sent to every bishop, priest and educated Catholic layman in the country with the exhortation to ponder the charges it makes, to consider to what extent they are well-founded, and to devise ways and means of combating the terrible blight of "Americanism" which is slowly destroying the vitality of the Catholic faith in the midst of seeming prosperity."[2]

Arthur Preuss was, of course, bitterly attacked by other sections of the Catholic Press for this frank admission of the weight of the "vile vituperations of a fallen-away priest." Even he could not awaken courage in the Church "to face all the facts." Only too well he knew that the American

[1] *America*, March 9, 1935.
[2] *Fortnightly Review*, January 15, 1929.

Catholic prefers to live in a world of make-believe as regards the true state of Catholicism in this country.

As confirmation of the point I have made that the energy of Catholics goes into the material, external side of religion rather than into the spiritual side, it is interesting to study the wretched showing that is made in respect of converts to the faith. Taking the figures for 1933-34,[1] the Methodists, who number less than half the Catholics, made 213,662 converts; the Baptists, also less in number than half the Catholics, m Je 193,571 converts; the Lutherans, less than one-fourth the Catholics, made 65,782 converts; and the Catholics, whose numbers almost equal the combined totals of Methodists, Baptists and Lutherans, and who as a consequence, had they like zeal, should have made about 470,000 converts, made only 53,426. This figure—53,426—means either that it takes one priest plus two nuns twelve months to persuade a non-Catholic American to become a Catholic, or else that the vast majority of priests and nuns are completely without zeal in that direction. As everyone knows, a large percentage of people in this country are easily attracted to some new religious experience and they would be drawn into the bosom of Mother Church if Catholics were zealous in proselytizing, as they should be according to the tenets of their religion. But Catholic Action is too busy in other directions and the souls of all these thousands are allowed to wander in the desert of heresy.

One finds less evidences of the eccentricities of piety in the religion of the American Catholic today than heretofore. It was significant that when the stigmatized woman of Hempstead, Long Island, Mrs. Mary F. Connors, sat in state with a nun by her side in her cottage which she named

[1] *Literary Digest,* June 2, 1934.

"Little Flower Cottage" to tell all and sundry how "she walked with Jesus in a dream" only a thousand or so visited her.[1] Had the "miracle" happened a decade back the number of visitors would have reached the hundred thousand mark. At Our Lady of Lourdes Church, Broadway (Brooklyn), which is decorated with crutches and braces "testifying to the cures which have taken place in America through its influence,"[2] although a "special" new relic of St. Bernadette was acquired for the occasion, only a paltry four or five thousand Catholics visited the shrine each day of the recent "special" triduum. American Catholics are apparently souring on the more exotic forms of piety.

In one such practice they are, however, still faithful. It is the practice that symbolizes their belief in the synthesis of politics and religion—the devotion of hanging a picture of Al Smith (or, failing him, Father Coughlin) between the pictures of the Sacred Heart and the Blessed Virgin in the "holy corner" of the family kitchen.

[1] *New York World-Telegram*, April 26, 1935.
[2] *New York Times*, April 26, 1935.

CHAPTER XV

CATHOLIC LEADERS:

(*A*) FATHER CHARLES E. COUGHLIN

OPINIONS will differ as to the propriety of calling Father Charles E. Coughlin a Catholic leader. Opinions differ as to everything in his regard. Some claim that he has done more for Catholicism in America than anyone ever did and that he has given Americans a new and better idea of the faith. Others, as for instance Dr. Nicholas Murray Butler, affirm[1] that "he has already done more harm to the Church which he professes to serve than all the attacks made through a generation by the K.K.K. and their bigoted followers."

As Catholic Leader, for we deem he deserves the title, Father Coughlin is not recognized by the Catholic hierarchy, the *official* leaders of the Church. Only one of them, Dr. Gallagher, openly supports and favors him, the rest for the most part are opposed "to him personally or to his doctrines or to his methods." The dean of them all, Cardinal O'Connell, is his sworn enemy, as well as his rival in actual leadership. But among the younger clergy and among the vast mass of the laity, Father Coughlin represents "the Catholic hope." Furthermore, if we read events correctly, Father

[1]Columbia University, Graduating Exercises, June 4, 1935.

Coughlin has the support and backing of the Holy Father—is in fact "the Pope's man" in America.

In the ranks of the Catholic laity there is, of course, one distinguished American who until recently had an enormous following of Catholics, priests and people: "the Happy Warrior," Alfred E. Smith. He has been honored by various Catholic colleges with medals—the Laetare Medal of Notre Dame and the Bonaventure Medal of St. Bonaventure's—as "the Catholic whose activities on behalf of the Church are considered the most outstanding." In 1928 he was the standard-bearer of Catholicism and was acclaimed as such by his fellow religionists. But for all that Alfred E. Smith never deserved the title of Catholic Leader. Ever and always he put his own political career first. He even subordinated his faith to the interests of that career. In no sense was he a "defender of the faith" or an active agent of the Pope. In fact, as we have seen, he preferred not to exalt the prerogatives of the Pope lest he should, in so doing, lose valuable votes. It is true he never denied or hid the fact that he was a Catholic "born and reared" but, on the other hand, he never put himself out to teach and promulgate Catholicism in public. As a Catholic he was "poor fish."

Never, until the appearance of Father Charles E. Coughlin, has there appeared on the American stage a man who is heard from coast to coast praising the Pope and promulgating his teaching. There is none of the old "forget the Pope" spirit of the American Catholic about the Detroit priest. He is not ashamed of his allegiance to the Pope. He does not hide it. When attacked by his own fellow Catholic clergy, his invariable defense—that he makes public to the world—is: "I am teaching papal doctrine by the order of the Pope."

Until the coming of Father Coughlin there was not a

single Catholic bishop or cardinal who had the courage to be outspoken about his relations with Rome. Their boast has always been that of not kowtowing to the Pope. As Cardinal O'Connell puts it in diplomatic language: "The Prelates of America while maintaining always the strictest loyalty to the Holy See have rarely *be it said to their credit* stooped to the attitude of a sycophant or a cringer." Whatever sycophancy they may have shown in private, in public speech in America they have always made pretense of being independent of papal interference.

It is something new, therefore, to Catholic ears to hear a priest proclaiming the glory of a Pope of Rome as Father Coughlin does, and Pius XI, who as an executive is singularly modern-minded, appreciates the invaluable publicity which accrues to him through Father Coughlin. Pius XI also is well aware that the Catholic Press of this country, which of course expresses his views and is "his voice," reaches only a Catholic audience, whereas his other voice, Father Coughlin, reaches Protestants and Catholics alike. Indeed, it is only through Father Coughlin that the Pope can secure a nation-wide, attentive audience in America.

I have already pointed out that Father Coughlin preaches the papal industrial and political doctrines, and preaches them almost to the letter. He sees eye to eye with the Pope on everything—or else pretends to do so. Like Pius XI, he is anti-labor, anti-Communist and pro-Fascist. Like Pius, he is, indirectly at least, anti-Semitic. In creating his "new voice of the people" he has adopted the most up-to-date political strategy favored by Rome. It is not difficult therefore to understand how deaf the Pope's ears are to criticisms uttered against him. Indeed, it would be hard to find fault with

Father Coughlin's doctrines without finding fault with
"Quadragesimo Anno" and "Casti Connubii."

Father Coughlin has played up to His Holiness in many
ways: for example, he has attacked the Mexican Government; he has opposed successfully the Pierce Birth Control
Bill; he has pursued Communists venomously; and lastly,
he has tiraded against militarism. With his enormous following and his nation-wide influence he is an invaluable asset
for the Pope and it is hardly likely that the Pope would
think of lessening the value of this asset by relegating him
to another sphere of activity than that which he occupies.
When the time comes, as it soon will come, for the Pope to
bargain with the Republicans or the Democrats as a party, his
chief bargaining power will derive from the eminence of
Father Coughlin.

American Catholics are not blind to these facts. They see
quite clearly—those at least whose eyes are not blinded by
jealousy—that Father Coughlin has enhanced enormously
the power of the Catholic Church. They like to think of a
priest occupying so important a position as does Father
Coughlin, and they are all the more pleased because of the
fact that he makes a boast of his Catholic priesthood. "I
glory in the fact," he says, "that I am a simple priest endeavoring to inject Christianity into the fabric of an economic system woven on the loom of greed. . . . While
always a priest I carry to you the fundamental doctrines of
social justice." Catholics are reassured by the endorsement
of Father Coughlin by his bishop. "I pronounce Father
Coughlin sound in doctrine, able in its application and interpretation. . . . He preaches the doctrines laid down for all
priests and bishops to preach, by the Popes."

"Here then is a man, a priest," say the Catholics, "who has the warm approval of his bishop, who courageously preaches the papal doctrine, who has such an audience as no man ever had in the history of the world, and who is showing all America what fine things there are in the old Catholic Church!"

The feelings of his more devoted Catholic followers are such as were the feelings of those Irish of the early nineteenth century who listened to the eloquent stentorian voice of Daniel O'Connell. He, the great Tribune of the People, the Irish Demosthenes, held spellbound vast audiences, "monster meetings" that sometimes numbered three to four hundred thousand. He was, like Father Coughlin, vituperative, flamboyant and passionate. He swayed the emotions of his followers; he won them by the mysterious thrill of his voice. He was a Catholic leader who appealed to Catholic followers on account of his devotion to Rome. Like Father Coughlin, he had to cross swords with bishops. The Irish bishops whom O'Connell fought were preparing to hand over to the English Crown the papal prerogative of appointing bishops to vacant sees. The American bishops whom Father Coughlin is secretly fighting are those who are obstructing the developments of papal policy in this country. Even though Coughlin be charged as Daniel O'Connell was with "using the cloak of religion to seek political power," such a charge is too general to have much weight with a devoted following.

Father Coughlin, like his great predecessor, is full of self-assurance, arrogant, dogmatic and autocratic. But these characteristics endear a leader to people of Irish blood. The Irish, who at a guess number half of Father Coughlin's followers, admire a mail-fisted ruler—one who on his own responsibility leads strongly and strikes hard. Parnell was adored in Ireland because he had such a mentality. In other respects Parnell and Coughlin differ; the former was reserved and silent; an aristocrat and a highbrow, while Coughlin is a talker and a plebeian.

Father Coughlin's clerical enemies, both Catholic and Protestant, are singularly unfortunate in their criticisms of their big brother. Mgr. Belford, who has the reputation of being a political oracle and who talks much politics from his own pulpit, sided with General Johnson against Father Coughlin, saying: "I liked particularly what General Johnson said about Father Coughlin leaving the priesthood or politics." If all the American priests and bishops who play politics were to quit their clerical state, not many would be left to care for the parishes. Father Parsons S.J., who dabbles as much in economics as in religion, declares it "a shame that Father Coughlin with his power over the popular mind has not restricted himself to the reformation of this mind." Father Lawrence Riggs, whose cuffs are faultlessly ironed for tête-à-têtes with Daughters of the American Revolution and who runs the utterly un-Roman-Catholic interconfessional stunt, bewails the fact that Father Coughlin does not make clear how far the opinions he expresses are his own, and how far they are those of the Church. A lot of regard Father Riggs shows for *real Roman doctrine!*

On the Protestant side we have Dr. Norman Peale likening Father Coughlin to Barnum whom he calls "America's first great faker," and Dr. John Haynes Holmes complaining of his "insufferable arrogance" and "appalling ignorance."

It is not necessary here to tabulate the criticisms of Father Coughlin and his theories that are made by the general public. It is fairly obvious that he constitutes a menace to the *status quo* and that he is "a potential leader of an active Fascist movement." General Hugh S. Johnson translates this into "Ulster" language by hinting that "Father Coughlin is an agent of the Pope trying to upset this Protestant country in the interests of Rome." General Johnson went on to accuse Father Coughlin of various minor crimes but found, as he admitted, that "as a cracker-down Father Coughlin has me backed off the boards."

Father Coughlin won his spurs as a new leader of Catholics by facing Cardinal O'Connell and, so to say, "telling him where he got off." "He ripped the shirt off the Cardinal's back," says General Johnson. The Cardinal had made every effort to discredit Father Coughlin with his people by telling them that his talks were "hysterical harangues" and that he was "humbugging the world." "It's wrong," said His Eminence, "to humbug the world." When the Cardinal [1] participated in an International Broadcast *for universal peace* he seized the occasion to have a good lunge at his old enemy: "We have heard through the air the loud voices of those proclaiming the universal panacea that was to cure the ills of poverty but no one who has listened intently could fail to detect in many of them the note of self-assurance and inexperience." Father Coughlin's chief attack was delivered last December (1934) when he said: "For forty years William Cardinal O'Connell has been more notorious for his silence on social justice than for any contribution which he may have given either in practice or in doctrine toward the decentralization of wealth and toward the elimination of those glaring injustices which permitted the plutocrats of the nation to wax fat at the expense of the poor." He accused the Cardinal of neglecting to obey the papal encyclicals which called on all

[1] April 21, 1935.

prelates and priests to do their uttermost to rectify social conditions and concluded by challenging the Cardinal in a significant sentence to discuss his (Father Coughlin's) conduct *"in private with the proper authorities."* In this clause he revealed the fact that the Papal Nuncio in Washington was behind him.

Father Coughlin was within his rights in refusing to accept direction from the bishop of another diocese than his own, and Cardinal O'Connell, in spite of his red hat and his deanship of the American hierarchy, had absolutely no authority to reprimand Father Coughlin. Father Coughlin won out in the conflict and, in spite of the disedification which the scrap caused, raised himself mightily in the esteem of his Catholic followers.

If the open breach with Cardinal O'Connell indicated pretty clearly that Father Coughlin can rely on the backing of Rome, his subsequent conduct in speaking at Madison Square Garden without the permission of Cardinal Hayes confirms the same conclusion. There can be no doubt about the fact that according to the New Code of Canon Law, Father Coughlin was bound to seek Cardinal Hayes' approval and permission before delivering his address. Yet he did not do so, and Cardinal Hayes made no protest. The incident was extremely significant. Father Coughlin seeks and receives the *imprimatur* of his own bishop when speaking in Detroit, and *a fortiori* should seek and receive the *imprimatur* of the bishop of another diocese when speaking in that diocese. Why did he not do so? The inference is too obvious to need elaboration. By the Pope's orders Father Coughlin is not to be interfered with! For the time being at any rate he is *ex lex* as regards the Canon Law of censorship in places where it would be refused.

Needless to say, Rome will never admit to the general public that she has dispensed Father Coughlin from Church Law, but is there not the evidence of fact that she has done so? If Rome wished to trip up Father Coughlin on his theology or his conduct, she could do so without much difficulty. In his article in *Today*[1] he rather flagrantly misquoted and misinterpreted the Pope but nothing was said about it. His dealings in silver and his stock speculations were on the face of it uncanonical. Yet he was not reproved. His financial ventures in hiring nation-wide hook-ups are so colossal that it is doubtful that his own bishop has authority to permit them without reference to Rome. Yet they have not been checked, much less forbidden. His great campaign is so venturesome from the point of view of its possible effects on the destiny of the American Catholic Church as a whole that it is far from likely that Dr. Gallagher would have permitted it without the definite approval of His Holiness the Pope. As a matter of fact, when Dr. Gallagher made public his endorsement of Father Coughlin he added the signficant proviso that it would endure only so long as it was not overridden by the supreme authority, namely, by the Pope. Only the Pope could override Dr. Gallagher—*and the Pope has not done so!* When Protestants ask, "Why don't *they* stop Father Coughlin?" they should be informed that there is no *they* but the Pope, and that he has good reasons of his own for not stopping him.

We have said that the bishops are the official leaders of the American Catholics, but this only means that each bishop is the official leader within the confines of his own diocese. No bishop has extra-territorial authority to lead. Only Father

[1] December 29, 1934.

Coughlin, of all the Catholic clergy, is extra-diocesan in his leadership. In this, his position is unique.

The loyalty of Father Coughlin's followers was evidenced at the Madison Square Garden meeting. The Press admitted the enthusiasm of the enormous audience that greeted him. The Press was hostile but it could not conceal so obvious a fact as the adoration of Coughlinites for Coughlin. When the *New York Times* refers to him as "a would-be political tyrant" and to the "moral terrorism" he exercises by means of "the irresistible power of a vast radio audience," [1] it confesses implicitly that Father Coughlin's followers are not only strong but loyal to him. "Do not chide Father Coughlin," writes a Columbia University Catholic to his fellow religionists. [2] "Raise up twenty Coughlins. Instead of one fighting priest let us have twenty fighting bishops. That is what Catholicism means today."

Father Coughlin has been astute in making his N.U.S.J. a non-sectarian organization and in proclaiming that it would not be worthy of its name unless it embraced Protestants, Jews and Catholics alike. He has been careful to make his appeal on a non-confessional basis, and as an American citizen. "I am an American citizen," he says, "privileged as such to speak to American citizens." But he has been equally careful to keep all the power in his own hands. He is quoted as assuming a dictatorial stand: "The ideas will come from the top! There will be no attempt made to get ideas from members. Meetings have been outmoded by the radio!" In Mr. A. B. Magil's book, [3] it is stated that at a lecture delivered

[1] March 6, 1935.
[2] *New York World-Telegram*, June 5, 1935.
[3] *The Truth about Father Coughlin*, p. 35.

January 22, 1935, somebody in the audience asked Father Coughlin, "How shall we know how to vote in the elections?" His reply was: "That's my job to tell you!"

No one has so far called the N.U.S.J. a "Catholic Organization," but can there be any doubt but that it will be such before long? More and more Catholics will join up; Catholics at the present hour are ripe for such a leader. Those who quit the N.U.S.J. will be Jews and Protestants, *not* Catholics.

The oncoming of this new feature of American politics is a threat to the maintenance of the spirit of tolerance. The mere fact of a priest with strong Fascist leanings, one who is so wholeheartedly identified with papal policy and papal doctrines, being in absolute control of a mighty body will awaken stark fear and hate in the hearts of millions of Americans. "If this thing spreads in this country," cried General Johnson, "there may well be a persecution." The General did not, however, say who he thought would be the victims of the persecution.

Father Coughlin replied with spirit that bigotry and the idea of religious persecution and intolerance was all on the General's side, not on his. "Away," he said, "with that prostituted bigotry which at one time has been the poisoned rapier of arrant cowards and at another the butcher's cleaving axe wielded to destroy a national unity."

If religious excitement grows to fever-pitch around the central figure of the priest-demagogue, who are likely to be the first victims? Would Father Coughlin, carried away by passion and ambition, stir up anti-Semitism so as to consolidate his following?

Rabbi Wise and many others apparently think that he would and that already he is preparing the way for an anti-Semitic drive. "Do you think," asked Rabbi Wise of Father

Coughlin, on the occasion of the latter's reply to General
Johnson in which he accused him of being a tool of Baruch
and other bankers, "Do you think it fair, Christian, priestly
to name six international banking firms and make it appear
that five are Jewish? Do you want to evoke anti-Semitism?"
Father Coughlin did not answer the rabbi's question frankly.
He hedged and said: "When I attack a Catholic, am I to be
accused of being anti-Catholic? When I attack a Jew, am I
to be considered anti-Jewish?" Of course, there is no parity
between Father Coughlin's attack on, say, Al Smith, and
his attack on a class, namely, international bankers, who are
identified in the Catholic mind as being the core of Jewish
power. To avoid the appalling danger of religious strife it
is, of course, incumbent on Father Coughlin to dissociate himself in the clearest and most emphatic manner from every
form of religious intolerance. "If Father Coughlin looses
the latent bigotry of this land all will suffer. Reason is the
only thing that can lead us as a nation out of this great distress. If intolerance comes in, reason flies out the window." [1]

The Fascist traits and leanings of Father Coughlin have
been so widely publicized that there is no occasion to dwell
upon them here. Our business is to study the radio priest
from the angle of his leadership of Catholics. His idea is to
gather all the Catholics of the country under his banner and
to unite them into one massive voice that will be so loud and
imperious and threatening (with real threats back of it) that
it will have its way. When he has this voice functioning according to his plans he will set in motion a new program, one
no doubt that will be drawn up in consultation with His
Holiness the Pope.

It is not too much to say that the destiny of the Catholic

[1] Editorial, *New York World-Telegram*, May 10, 1935.

Church in this country lies in the hands of Father Coughlin. He can make or mar her fortunes for a generation or more. The Church will falter and stumble if Father Coughlin fails. She will rise to new heights of glory if he uses his skill and power on her behalf. No other American Catholic could as an individual do much harm to the Church, nor indeed for that matter do much to enhance her prestige. If Cardinal O'Connell betook himself to a life of penance and wore sackcloth and rubbed ashes over his head, it would have little effect. On the other hand, were he to abandon his episcopacy and become a Unitarian, it would not matter enormously. But were Father Coughlin to become a Peter the Hermit and preach a crusade or were he to lapse into heresy and raise the standard of revolt against a Catholic dogma, the very pillars of St. Peter's would be shaken. He is now a momentous figure in both Church and State.

If the Pope owes much to Father Coughlin, Father Coughlin owes his greatness to the Pope. It was the Pope who gave Father Coughlin to America. Father Coughlin is the Pope's present to this nation. Out of the pages of "Quadragesimo Anno," Pius XI's fateful encyclical, he sprang. Like an elf out of a mighty pie at a stag dinner, Father Coughlin arose from the platitudes and aphorisms and moral hectorings and political lucubrations of the Pope's little book. He personified the dynamite that was hidden beneath the text. The words and thoughts, the excited denunciations, fitted his hungry tongue. He was ready waiting to explode; and when he did explode his flash and roaring thunder were consecrated in advance.

Father Coughlin synchronized with two great needs: the need of Pius XI for a sounding-board in America, and the need of American Catholics for a popular orator to advertise their growing power and to stir them up to a larger revolt.

Father Coughlin has filled the two roles admirably. He is almost all that the Pope wants; he is peculiarly adapted to publicize, inflame and lead American Catholics. He is tough, he is wary, he is brave and persistent, he is resourceful and he is daring. He has the right to discount the complaint made against him that he is causing trouble and a nuisance; already the land was full to the neck of trouble and overrun with human and economic nuisances before his coming.

Americans—and they are many—who have no Catholic affiliations, and who nourish a deep-rooted distrust of the Scarlet Woman, resent the fact that Father Coughlin represents in his person a tremendous effort "to upset this Protestant country in the interests of Rome." They see in him the one among all the chiefs of the Church who is most likely to succeed in leading the Catholic legions to the victory of their dreams. They tell themselves that his power and position are ephemeral and that something will soon turn up to discredit him and alienate his following, but there is no sign on the horizon to justify this comforting self-deception.

Father Coughlin is consolidating his power as the weeks go by. The fact that discontented Catholics have joined his camp, and mingle therein with Catholics that are utterly loyal to the Church, has increased Father Coughlin's strength vis-à-vis of the American hierarchy. The fact that the Administration in its efforts to tax the rich is adopting Father Coughlin's doctrine enhances his prestige in the mind of the general public. If the Administration fails to advance its leftist program, many millions will look to the radio priest for his leadership in achieving that aim. The decisions of the Supreme Court have emphasized the need of Father Coughlin. While the Pope continues to back him an extraordinary career, and one of infinite moment for this country, lies before him.

CHAPTER XVI

CATHOLIC LEADERS:

(*B*) CARDINAL O'CONNELL

UP TO a short time ago William O'Connell, Cardinal-Archbishop of Boston, dean of the American Catholic hierarchy, held undisputed sway as leader of the Catholics, lay and clerical, of this country. His long and prosperous career as a churchman, his wide experience of business and political as well as of ecclesiastical affairs, his high repute for prudence and sagacity, his wealth, his domineering character, and the public esteem which he enjoyed seemed to entitle him to a life-tenancy of this position. He was the strong man among the bishops, and the one whose knowledge of and influence in Rome was unequaled. He had been the friend of many Presidents of the United States, and he numbered among his acquaintances many of the richest and most influential of his fellow countrymen. When, last November, he celebrated in his seventy-fifth year the golden jubilee of his priesthood at the Catholic University (Washington, D. C.), the hall was crowded with ambassadors, senators, nobles and statesmen. Attorney General Cummings lauded him as "a great churchman, an eminent citizen and an ardent patriot." In reply he modestly stated: "No greater honor can come to any man than has come to me."

As long as the eldest among us can remember Boston's haughty prelate has been faithfully served by the Press, his every journey duly reported, his every pungent remark headlined, his opinion sought on every important occasion. He has enjoyed as much if not more publicity than any other American; he has had better opportunities than any other living American to influence public opinion and to educate his fellow countrymen in nobler and humaner modes of thought and conduct. As archbishop for almost thirty years, and cardinal for twenty-four years, he has had a unique opportunity of leading American Catholics in the direction of a purer and more Christian religion and a more liberal social outlook. For all these years he has been virtually Pope of America and with the steady Catholicizing of Boston he has reigned over a city that was more loyal to the Church than Rome. Nothing was wanting to him, neither opportunity nor power, to display Christian leadership, to improve the condition of the poor and to espouse the cause of the oppressed, but Cardinal O'Connell betrayed his trust and his responsibility. He failed his fellow Catholics; he failed America. His heart was too narrow; his mind was too obtuse; his prejudices in favor of the rich and the respectable were too deeply rooted; his outlook was too bourgeois; his pride of place was too stubborn; his enjoyment of the good things of life was too keen to allow him to "waste his time" on matters that really counted. Today he makes a weak defense for himself by attacking Social Justice and proclaiming: "The priest's mission is to preach the word of God and not to arouse animosities and feelings of partisanship especially in the fields of economics or what might be called economic politics."

It is a significant comment on his wasted years and fruitless career that when, on the occasion of his jubilee, the present

keen-witted Pope wrote to felicitate him he singled out for
comment (and praise!) the Cardinal's business ability, saying:
"In these later years when the whole world was faced with
economic peril you had such great prudence that the flock
committed to you hardly felt the stress of the times." The
President with sly humor wrote to felicitate him "on the
*affectionate place you hold in the hearts of your fellow-
citizens.*" Good for you, Mr. President!

William O'Connell, the last of eleven children, was born
of Irish immigrants in Lowell, Massachusetts, in 1859. He
attended public school in Lowell and suffered from the puri-
tanical and anti-Irish attitude of his teachers. At the age of
eleven he entered a cotton mill, but a few hours' work there
sufficed to convince him that millwork was not his vocation.
When the bell rang at midday he said to his companions:
"Boys, I'm going home I can never stand this."

At seventeen William O'Connell entered a seminary in
Maryland to begin his training for the priesthood. He states
that while there he "never received the slightest reprimand."
From the seminary he went to Boston College where the
famous Jesuit Father Fulton received him and introduced
him to his class saying: "I have brought you a new companion.
His name is William. And, boys! look to your laurels."
William proved more than a match for the young Bostonians
and captured all the prizes.

From Boston College he was sent by Archbishop Williams
(whom he later succeeded) to study in the American College
in Rome. There he was ordained priest in 1884.

We next find him working as a curate in Boston and working with fellow priests whom he considered slack, ignorant
and inclined to overeat. He tells us in his autobiography: "It
was a time when everybody [among the clergy] ate far too

much for his health and this was true not only of the occasional banquet but also at the daily meal in the parish house."
Many of the priests "dug their graves with their teeth."
Father O'Connell soon made a name for himself by his devotion to his duties, and the care with which he prepared his
sermons, all of which he wrote out in full and committed to
memory. He tells us: "I learned by practice and by dint of
hard work to preach rather well. I could handle the English
language by this time fairly well." He published several
volumes of sermons and read standard works of literature.
Of those days he says: "I am not holding myself up as a
model but I can say honestly that I have never consciously
shirked a single duty."

In 1895 he was called to Rome to become Rector of his old
seminary there. He threw himself into the work of organizing its finances and increasing the number of its students and
he received the congratulations of Pope Leo XIII. Meanwhile he stepped out socially in Rome and cultivated the
acquaintanceship of the Cardinals and the best families. Many
socially prominent people visited Rome or lived there for
periods. Mgr. O'Connell made a point of meeting them all.
He was charmed and thrilled. "In all my delightful and intimate intercourse with many of the highest nobles I have
never found," he tells us, "the slightest trace of that vulgarity
of soul which is called snobbishness." Mgr. O'Connell broke
into royal circles—Prince Ludwig Ferdinand's family and
Prince von Bülow's family—and records: "Knowing what I
did of them and many others of royal lineage I became thoroughly convinced that there is something noble in blood like
theirs." Already the Irish peasant priest had a fixation on
Norman blood and the *"je ne sais quoi"* of the wealthy.

Leo XIII appointed our Beau Brummel ecclesiastic to the

See of Portland in 1901. The beneficiary protests that he studiously avoided "soliciting and petitioning for advancement" and Church politics of every sort. But we dare to suspect that his noble friends pulled a few wires on his behalf. As Bishop of Portland he lunched with Theodore Roosevelt and delivered to him as President of the United States a profession of loyalty (which profession he never failed to repeat to subsequent Presidents). It contained the clause: "I have no favors to ask but I can and do offer now and hereafter any service in my power to the President of the United States who in his civic position represents to me an authority given by God for the welfare of all its citizens."

Bishop O'Connell thus had himself pigeonholed as a "solid citizen" and as opposed to all revolutionary madness and tomfoolery!

The accession of Pius X to the throne of Peter (in 1903) proved to be the turning point in the fortunes of Bishop O'Connell. When the two sturdy little churchmen met in Rome they embraced, recognizing each in the other a kindred spirit. Both were champions of piety for the lower classes; common sense; strict orthodoxy and financial security. Both were bitterly hostile to Socialism, modernism, and the progress of science. "Caro O'Connell," cried Pius, "la mia fiducia in voi è illimita" ("Beloved O'Connell, my confidence in you is unlimited"). On three separate occasions these words of virtual canonization fell from the pontifical lips into William O'Connell's ears—and the words were substantiated by expressions of honor and trust. In 1905, Pius X sent O'Connell to Tokyo with an autograph letter for the Emperor of Japan. This diplomatic mission netted the Bishop of Portland great publicity, the Grand Cordon of the Sacred Treasury of Japan, and the Archbishopric of Boston (1907). The story of the

mission is no less amusing than interesting, but it would take
us too far afield to describe it in detail.

As Archbishop of Boston, William O'Connell's career as a
great churchman began. It has remained the career of a
churchman and nothing more. He found the diocese in disorder. Abuses were rife. Charities were "in an incredible state
of disorganization or worse." There was no attention paid to
Canon Law. There was no adequate training for priests. The
nuns were playing fast and loose with finances. Some were
little better than rogues. Heads had to be lopped off, and the
new Archbishop was the executioner. "I went my lonely way,"
he says, "absolutely ignoring the annoyance of others and
without either fear or rancor, indeed without bothering my
head about them. . . . I have lived to see my entire program
carried out with complete success."

Archbishop O'Connell proved himself "an efficient ad-
ministrator of enormous properties" (Upton Sinclair) and a
skilled organizer of pious societies. He set up St. Luke's
Guild for Catholic doctors; St. Apollonia's Guild for Catholic dentists; St. Genesius' Guild for stenographers; the Guild
of the Presentation for "Hello-girls" and so forth. He bought
and revamped the *Pilot*. He made daily communion a general
habit. He bought real estate shrewdly. He sent millions of
dollars, collected from the poor, to Rome for the Pope's
missions. He uttered condemnations of short skirts, lipstick,
rouge, dance halls, light music, crooning, scientific research—
such as that of Professor Osborn and Professor Einstein,
labor movements and demands for higher wages, and every
other item remotely connected with human progress or the
effort to raise the standard of living. Pius X was enchanted.
In 1911 he bestowed upon Archbishop O'Connell the red
hat. "All these honors," writes the Cardinal, "came as it were

out of a blue sky and it was not for me to refuse the burdens since I had never in the slightest way invited them or indicated the slightest preference for them . . . *it was clearly God's will.*"

On his return from Rome, wearing his new red hat and mozzetta, he was accorded an official reception in Boston. The poor Irish cheered themselves hoarse and a large group of *nice* people waved their handkerchiefs. As soon as they could get him in a corner a group of twenty-five bankers and big businessmen surrounded him and presented him with a silver casket containing a check for $25,000. As "it was not for him to refuse—it being clearly God's will," the Cardinal pocketed the bankers' bribe. From that day—in 1911—to the present he has deserved the name of "the bankers' bishop."

As Bankers' Bishop, the Cardinal has discoursed a great deal on money—usually in a vein to comfort his friends. He believes in the *unequal distribution* of wealth, this being the subtle manner in which he expresses his approval of plutocracy. "If everybody was just the same," he said, "if everybody in the whole world had the same amount of money, all would be a pack of lazy-bones and nothing would be done."

He justifies plutocrats by his own peculiar Biblical exegesis. "Riches do not spoil most Americans," he says. "*The average rich American* [the ten thousand millionaires] would not have the same difficulty in entering heaven as the man of wealth in Biblical days."

He defends the plutocrats against unfair play. "It is as easy," he says, "to be unjust to the rich as to the poor." Let us not then meditate injury to the millionaires! The poor fellows! What have they, after all, to protect them save their hordes of shyster lawyers, their bodyguards of thugs, their control of the police and the minute men through politics and so forth. Sure! "It is as easy to be unjust to the rich as to the poor" who have but their bare hands and such strength as comes from empty stomachs to protect them! Cardinal O'Connell, who survived so well the depression that as the Pope testified neither he nor his "felt the stress of the times," declares on behalf of bankers that "most bankers deal honestly with money." Under his breath he added—as we suppose—"God bless 'em and God strafe Coughlin." Still discussing money, the Cardinal applies his teaching to his Catholic flock. And here his philosophy takes a peculiar twist. Like the good old-fashioned soggarth of Erin, he likes to have his flock well under his thumb. He likes to have them down and to keep them down. He wants them poor. He gets more from them when they are poor. He says. "I used to think, Oh! some time ago, that it would be a fine thing to help our Catholic people to become materially well-to-do and prosperous. I have given it up. You lose them when you do! I don't know why it should be so but it is so!" Again, he says: "*I have given up wishing any riches on Catholics!*"

His Eminence, as everyone knows, is vastly prosperous and enjoys all the luxuries that money can buy. His fellow bishops and the majority of Catholic pastors are likewise rich men, comparatively at least. How comes it that the Cardinal does not declare that riches are bad for Catholic bishops and Catholic priests? If they are bad for the laity, are they not bad for the clergy? Is clerical human nature immune from the danger that riches produce in the human nature of the laity? The matter is one on which Father Coughlin and his followers do not see eye to eye with the great Cardinal.

In this connection, it is interesting to record the observations of Upton Sinclair (in *Boston*) on the Cardinal's policy

with regard to his clergy. "The Cardinal was exiling rebellious spirits to the backwoods and raising up a generation
of young clerics who were at once preachers, politicians, and
real estate experts. You could know when one of them was
in favor by the fact that his mother and father, brothers and
sisters, cousins and aunts moved immediately into expensive
residences."

We have said above that neither the opportunity nor the
power was lacking to Cardinal O'Connell to show leadership
as a Christian. There were, among other opportunities for
displaying humane and Christian citizenship, four very important ones since his cardinalature: (1) the mill strike in
Lawrence, Massachusetts, in 1912; (2) the police strike and
riots in Boston in 1919; (3) the political scandals of the
Curley-Pelletier period (1919-1922); (4) the horror of the
Sacco-Vanzetti trial (1927).

The Cardinal who boasts that "I have never consciously
shirked a single duty" has consistently and egregiously failed
to take sides with the oppressed when his friends or his
friends' friends were the oppressors.

The 25,000 mill hands who struck in Lawrence were justified if ever strikers were justified. The conditions in the mills
and in their homes were appalling. When they struck they
were bludgeoned by order of the Irish Catholic civic authorities in Lawrence. The elite waited to see them *starved back*
to slavery in the mills. Cardinal O'Connell did not utter a
syllable to encourage or help them or to condemn the thiev-
ing, murdering mill owners. It was Ettor and Giovanni of the
I.W.W. who came to the rescue of the strikers and won the
battle for them—*not* their godly shepherd, William of
Boston.

In 1919 when Boston was thrown into disorder by the

police strike and the riots, and the blackguardism and violence of the bankers' armed thugs, Cardinal O'Connell stood aloof. By his astute silence he lent all the support he could to his real friends.

When District Attorney Joseph C. Pelletier, assisted by two other Irish Catholics, Daniel Coakley and William Corcoran, began their nefarious blackmail campaign under the mayoralty of James Michael Curley, the present Governor of Massachusetts, Cardinal O'Connell must have known, from various sources, what was afoot. Joseph C. Pelletier was a member of the Supreme Council of the Knights of Columbus; he was accorded an honorary degree by the Jesuits of Boston College; he was adorned with the papal honor of Medallion of the Order of St. George; and he was, of course, honored by the friendship of His Eminence of Boston. He was a cunning, unscrupulous blackmailer and used the political machine of the Tammany Club in his plots. Curley put business in his way, although Curley subsequently escaped prosecution. All the dirty political work of the period—or practically all—was done by "good Catholics." His Eminence was silent. He refused to condemn Boston's Tammany as his brother Cardinal in New York City has refused to condemn the parent Tammany. It was the Bar Association (1921-1922) that finally saved Boston from the Pelletier gang and not Boston's Pope.

Cardinal O'Connell has boasted of the capture of Boston by the (Irish) Catholics. "The Puritan has passed," he declared, "and the Catholic remains. The city where a century ago he came unwanted *he has made his own.*" Has the Catholic—the Catholic as led by Cardinal O'Connell—since 1907 purified Boston? Or has he besmirched its name? Hear Dr. John Haynes Holmes as he discussed Boston (December,

1925): "Boston has been dominated by Catholics and has been disgraced by them."

The story of Luigia Vanzetti's visit to Cardinal O'Connell in the fall of 1927 is well known. She came to implore him to use his influence *that justice might be done* in the case of her brother Bartolommeo. He gave her tea on the lawn of his summer home at Marblehead and commented, playfully we suppose, on the honor she was enjoying in having a Prince of Holy Church pour out her tea! He spoke platitudes to the poor woman, and when she departed and the Press arrived to hear a pronouncement from him on the famous case he confined himself to observing that "the ways of God are mysterious." Not a syllable did he utter to influence the authorities in favor of a retrial. His friends Thayer, Fuller and the bankers had to be considered first. What the radicals got was, in his eyes, good enough for them. Let Bartolommeo and Nicola burn—and to h —— with them!

But has Cardinal O'Connell given no leadership at all to the Catholics of America? To be sure, he has! When war was declared he gave what Attorney General Cummings called "outstanding leadership." He whipped up men with words of burning zeal to throw their lives away—to enrich the bankers and big businessmen. Then when the war was over he flattered the Catholics of America by publishing the astonishing lie that from 30 to 40 per cent of the A.E.F. were Catholics! Secretary Baker had to scotch the lie by stating: "There never was a religious census of the army made. In fact I refused to allow one to be made!"

Cardinal O'Connell has also given leadership to his flock in warning them against the movie theaters which he called "gilded palaces of vice"; by warning them against Einstein "with his utterly befogged notions of space and time"; by warning them against the "grotesque gullibility of so-called modern scientists"; by warning them against listening in to radio crooners, "whiners and bleaters who defile the air with their base appeal to sex emotions in the young"; by keeping Isadora Duncan out of Boston: and lastly by exhorting his flock, in season and out of season, against "the spirit of strikes" and the false promises of labor leaders. He has faithfully observed two good old Catholic episcopal practices in his so-called leadership: firstly, to denounce roundly anything that seems to endanger the holy virtue of chastity; and secondly, to condone all social injustices of the *status quo*.

Against Cardinal O'Connell the intransigent Father Coughlin hurled the accusation already quoted: "For forty years William Cardinal O'Connell has been more notorious for his silence on social justice than for any contribution which he may have given either in practice or in doctrine toward the decentralization of wealth and toward the elimination of those glaring injustices which permitted the plutocrats of the nation to wax fat at the expense of the poor."

Cardinal O'Connell, in his autobiography, tells us that he has striven "to imitate the qualities which constitute the best and noblest in life," and adds, "I have never willfully wronged anyone through motives of personal feeling. . . . I have never been accused of favoritism or injustice." These claims are large, even for a Cardinal of Holy Church to make, and they are claims that would be difficult to substantiate. Apart from the wrongs he has done by neglecting the material interests of the Catholic workers and the Catholic poor of his diocese, he has been directly responsible for the steady stream of vulgarity and abuse that has poured forth from his diocesan paper, the *Pilot*, for a quarter of a century. He is responsible, more than any other Catholic bishop, for the truculent, pugnacious spirit of the Knights of Columbus and other American Catholic societies. He has encouraged them to make noise and hit hard instead of teaching them that religion is not a matter of loud boasts and bludgeon blows, but of spiritual refinement, gentleness, truth and justice. He is responsible, too, for aligning the Church with politicians of questionable records and for introducing into her counsels bankers and real estate agents. He has helped, indeed, to build up an impressive if flamboyant façade for the American Catholic Church but he has done little or nothing to purify the interior.

If the Catholic group in America today are more than ever a menace to the peace of the nation, this is largely though unwittingly due to Cardinal O'Connell for his share in leading his flock away from the true spirit of religion into the new Catholic conception of religion as bitter fighting. If what Father Coughlin stands for is a danger; no less a danger is what Cardinal O'Connell stands for. If we call what Father Coughlin stands for "Catholic Fascism," we still know that if the great coup which we presume he meditates fails, his Fascism will wane and fade away. On the other hand, if we call what Cardinal O'Connell stands for "Catholic pugnacity," we know that it is there to endure and that it will be a trouble to the peace of America so long as there remains a considerable body of Catholics in our midst.

In spite of his hopeless failure as a leader, Cardinal O'Connell is still a remarkable figure. Sure of himself and suspicious of others, strong-willed, shrewd, with a thick skin and a good appetite, he has survived many storms. He is a typical Irish peasant-priest, dogmatic, cunning, tight-fisted, afraid a little of being laughed at but afraid of nothing else. He is a good politician and a good businessman. He has held in his hand the immense vote of the Irishry of Massachusetts for a generation. To a large extent he controls it still. He is a power in the land, a power to be reckoned with. Few fully realize how potent his word is.

But he is no longer potent in Rome. The present Pope sees in him a type that has outlived its usefulness. Pius XI, besides, has never liked him since that fateful hour, following his elevation to the Papacy, when Cardinal O'Connell burst in upon him to protest the election that was held in his absence. Cardinal O'Connell had arrived only an hour late for the Conclave's final vote—a vote that he had possibly hoped would have been cast in his own favor. For William O'Connell, Cardinal Archbishop of Boston, had undoubtedly cherished the dream of reigning as Peter over all the Catholic world.

CHAPTER XVII

POPE PIUS XI, GENERALISSIMO

IN SPITE of the greatness and zeal of the Catholic force, it would not constitute an immediate threat to the present order in America were it not directed by so able and experienced a generalissimo as His Holiness Pius XI. But in Pius XI, as few people seem fully to realize, the Catholic Church has for the first time in several centuries a leader of supreme genius, of indomitable purpose and of untiring energy.

Though the age be one of great leaders, *great*, that is, in various senses of the word, there is no one among them who can compare, in accomplishments and in what he gives promise of, with the ruler of the Vatican City. Hitler, Stalin and Mussolini are mighty figures in the eyes of their millions of devoted followers. In little Ireland, DeValera ranks among his own as a God-given hero. In Spain, Gil Robles has largely fulfilled the aspirations of Catholics. But none of these names represents the intellectual grasp, moral force, and amazing skill in dealing with diplomatic problems that the name Pius XI represents.

A great Pope is a rare phenomenon. To be such there is called for a synthesis of qualifications that few men possess. The great Pope must be an expert in the difficult science of theology; he must be steeped in the vast history and traditions of the Church and learned in justifying her immense claims; he must be a fine psychologist in religion so as to have the art to play on religious emotions; he must be the most calculating of diplomats and the most practical of executives; he must be a man of wide vision and of an understanding capable of grasping the most complex of situations; he must be inspiring in his leadership; patient; unperturbed by opposition; relentless in the pursuit of his aims. He must be, in fine, an autocrat as well as a paternal bishop; a soldier as well as a priest; an intriguer as well as a forthright statesman; an alert and polished courtier and gentleman as well as a dour intolerant fanatic.

These qualities, all of them, belong to Pius XI. They did not belong to Pius IX, nor to Leo XIII, nor to Pius X, nor to Benedict XV. Not within human memory has any Pope had the grip of affairs, or the strength in action, or the bold faith in the Church's immediate destiny that Pius XI possesses. He towers over every other figure in the Church; he subordinates his judgment to no one, not even to the astute internationalist, his Secretary of State, Cardinal Pacelli, nor to the subtle and experienced Jesuit General, Ledochowski. He takes, day by day, more and more into his own hands. He overrides bishops and patriarchs and directs in person the policies of national churches. His mind, feverishly active, but ever clear and cool as a cube of ice, busies itself with a thousand questions. He is here, there, everywhere, studying situations in minutest detail and directing Catholic Action—French, German, Austrian, Spanish and in particular American—in its every phase. In his deep brain there is a settled plan, an ambitious yet practical scheme, that, should he live to put it into effect in all its amplitude, will for a certainty revolutionize the world. In that scheme the part that the

Catholic Church in America is planned to play—and has begun to play under Pius XI's personal leadership—is momentous for the Church and for us, Americans.

To realize that the Church, under Pius XI's superb leadership has become a world power again, it is only necessary to glance over the map of Europe and to estimate fairly and frankly the status and influence of the Church in the more important countries of that Continent.

In Italy, thanks to the Lateran Treaty which Pius negotiated with Mussolini, the Church is infinitely stronger than she has been since 1870. Not only is her prestige enhanced, but her will is largely obeyed by the most arrogant of dictators. The democracy that the Popes feared has disappeared. Freemasonry and Socialism are driven underground. Canon Law is, in part at least, accepted as Civil Law. The Italian Government is now dependent upon the Church for its stability and will become more so when a less strong ruler succeeds Mussolini. The Pope is no longer a prisoner; at his court attend ambassadors from half the countries of the world.

In Austria an even more favorable situation has developed. The devout Dollfuss made over the Constitution into a Church State. When, in 1931, he had studied the Pope's encyclical "Quadragesimo Anno" and grasped its political content, he declared: "We are determined to make it [the encyclical] the basis of our Constitution." So sure of his ground is the Pope that he has withdrawn the clergy in Austria from participating in politics and dissolved Catholic political parties. In their place he has set up a Catholic League, as a school of Catholic Action. Both Starhemberg and Schuschnigg are faithful devotees. Austria is safe for the Church for a generation.

In Germany, Hitler was able to browbeat every church

except the Catholic Church. He met his match in Pius XI. Pius XI at first opposed him, and subsequently, when Hitler sent von Papen to negotiate with Pius (1932) and to agree to the papal terms for a Concordat, the Pope directed the German Catholics to relent in their opposition. The Church yielded nothing of importance; she still has her schools open, and her Catholic Associations for Catholic Action. "Permeate the people of the Reich with all the force of your love of God and for your neighbor," said Cardinal Schulte to his subjects. Hitler had to accept the papal doctrine of the mystical "extraterritoriality" of Catholics in virtue of their being *members of a universal organization.* The Pope insisted that German Catholics were his subjects and that he had the right to represent their needs. Writes Max Ascoli [1]: "The Catholic Church is so strong that she is able to make fanatical and all-pervasive dictatorships recognize her universal corporate entity. In representing Catholics who are subject to dictatorial rule she enjoys the privilege of collective bargaining *which is denied to every other national or international group.*"

So powerful is the Pope in Germany that we find his Nuncio sitting in Cardinal von Faulhaber's cathedral, to give papal sanction to the Cardinal's threats of excommunication against Hitler's officials.[2] The significance of the situation might be understood if we pictured the Nuncio here, Mgr. Almeto Giovanni Cicognani, smiling approval while Cardinal Dougherty was threatening Mr. James A. Farley, the Postmaster General with excommunication for allowing the Mexican Government the use of our mails.

In Spain, the revolution of April 12, 1931, seemed likely to lead to the destruction of Catholicism in the Peninsula.

---

[1] *Foreign Affairs,* April, 1935.
[2] *America,* February 23, 1935.

In the two years that followed the Church was disestablished, her property was confiscated and the Jesuits were exiled. But Pius XI faced the situation with courage, and excommunicated the Government. He sent Mgr. Tedeschini as Nuncio to stir the Catholics, priests and laymen, to militant activity. He supported the fury of Archbishop Goma's leadership and saw his intrigue crowned with success. Today the Church is stronger and better organized than ever and Gil Robles and his Catholic Actionists are busy consolidating her position. A weaker Pope or one with less judgment would have lost Spain to the Church.

In France, Pius' task was most difficult. He had, in order to secure the general good of the whole Church, to break with the old Royalist Catholic Party. In 1926 he placed their journal *L'Action Française* on the *Index* and through Cardinal Andrieu excommunicated the Royalists who would not submit. In order to secure the re-establishment of diplomatic relations with Paris he worked for the interest of the French Republic in Alsace, Lorraine and Syria. He carried on his negotiations with men whom he hated as infidels but whom it was necessary to serve in order to gain benefits for the Church. As usual he succeeded. "The Vatican has shown," writes George Seldes,[1] "that it can compromise to win and that it has held to its canons. It has been on the defensive when that was expedient but where it knew it was strong it has been aggressive or taken the offensive. . . . Everywhere the Vatican has tempered the intensity of its action in accordance with the strength or weakness of its adherents."

Thanks to Pius' diplomacy and his genius in striking a bargain, the Church in France has regained much that was lost and faces a brighter future.

[1] The *Commonweal*, March 1, 1935.

We cannot fail to notice, as we study Pius XI in his character as diplomat, that he has gained enormously in insisting on the internationalist character of the Catholic Church; that Catholics, no matter what other allegiance they owe, are still his subjects as members of the Universal Church. This leading principle of Pius' diplomacy, that the Church is international (and also supranational) was emphasized by his extension of the "Holy Year" Jubilee. The "Holy Year" in essence was the convening in the Vatican of a long-drawn-out meeting of Pilgrims from all the nations of the earth—the delegates came and went in tens of thousands—but the mighty International Convention remained in session, demonstrating to the whole world the internationalism of the Church.

We notice, too, in studying Pius' diplomacy and policy that he has freed the Church from the old incubus of Catholic political parties. There is no longer a "Center Party" in Germany, a "Popular Party" in Italy, a "Catholic Party" in Austria or a Catholic-Royalist bloc in France. Pius now depends for his political work on "massed Catholic opinion" as expressed in Catholic Action. This "massed Catholic opinion" is more dependable, as it is the immediate and direct expression of his own will filtering through the wills of his bishops, priests, and faithful lay folk in the various countries. It is a new, potent, political engine, like the engine that we see operating here, in the N.U.S.J. of Father Coughlin.

The third characteristic of Pius' strategy is his ability to make advantageous "adjustments" or "concordats." When he is given an inch—presently the *inch* is transmuted into an ell. He shows from St. Thomas that "the whole is contained in the part." Every ruler who made a Concordat with Pius XI came to regret it before long; to discover that he had been outwitted. Pius, who has proclaimed himself prepared to "negotiate with the devil," has shown, more clearly than any Pope who ever lived, that the Church is "an organism capable of *miraculous readjustments and transformations* in the struggle to preserve herself." [1]

It should, of course, be understood, in appraising Pius' successes as diplomat and leader, that post-war conditions have told in favor of his schemes. He could rely, first of all, on the widespread fear of Communism, to engender a favorable attitude towards the sober conservatism of the Church. The excesses of the Reds naturally enough threw timid and moderate-minded people into the arms of the Church. Then, as a consequence of the Versailles Treaty, there were many mutations of frontiers, all of which created problems of a religious and nationalistic kind. The emergence of every such problem became an occasion of appeal to the Pope and gave the Pope a fresh opportunity of bargaining, and a new bargaining power, from which he invariably derived some gain. Lastly, with the gradual disappearance of democratic forms and with the decay of the spirit of democracy, the mental habit of rationalism waned. Men's minds were too frightened to think; there was less profit in criticizing the Church and religion; the old enemies of the Papacy were reduced to silence or discredited.

For the first eight years of his Pontificate, Pius was absorbed in European affairs and unprepared as yet to take over control of the Catholic cause in this country. He was content to watch events from afar, to study American problems during such time as he could spare, and to size up the fiber and quality of American Catholicism from the visiting bishops, priests and laymen from our shores.

In 1924, in recognition of a generous response from

[1] *Foreign Affairs*, April, 1935.

America to his appeal for funds to help starving Russians, he created on the same day two Americans cardinals, the Archbishops of New York and Chicago. In conferring the honor, he said: "We have been well inspired in seeking and finding a means to demonstrate to your great people all our Paternal pleasure in honoring that people in your persons with the Sacred Roman Purple." Be it remarked that it was through no obtuseness of mind or lack of sense of proportion that Pius used the term "honoring the American people." Such is his feeling of the incomparable dignity of his spiritual Overlordship of the world that in his eyes the American people are exalted by his recognition of their existence. God-on-Earth he believes himself to be—*and means to be*. If the American people do not as yet recognize him as such, it is because they are still blinded by heresy and degraded by their semi-Pagan manners.

Though Pius has little liking for our wicked ways and our heresies, he sees in us the nation that counts for most in the world today—the nation of the future. We are rich, young, strong, and our life is before us as a nation. He would have us; he needs us; he means to have us. He believes that the destiny of the Church will be fulfilled in America and that with the spiritual conquest of America the world-dominion of the Church will be regained.

In his great scheme His Holiness is handicapped by the blundering stupidity and crassness in technique of his officers here, the bishops, priests and lay leaders of the American Catholic Church. He is fully alive to their generosity, energy and good intentions, and to their capacity for organizing, but he is also alive to their sheer inability to appreciate the delicacy of the task before them. He sees them committing tactical mistakes on every hand and beating the air like peevish children. Though a large and well-equipped army, American Catholics, in his eyes, are badly officered, by ecclesiastics who are unskilled in the fine art of religio-political strategy. But Pius XI hopes to compensate for these defects by personal leadership and constant vigilance.

I have already referred to the American Catholic Church's colossal exhibition of shortsightedness when she endorsed in 1928 Mr. Alfred E. Smith's *Credo*, "I believe in the absolute separation of Church and State," and I have recorded the words of Pius XI wherewith he damned that heresy and re-oriented the Church in the direction of the true Catholic doctrine of union and association between Church and State. The Pope has found it difficult to enlighten the ignorance of the American Catholic mind on this fundamental point. There are those among the highest leaders of the Church here who still fail to see the significance of the Pope's teaching, and who fail to see that the Smith heresy tends to confine the destiny of the Church.

Only last November (1934) on the occasion of his jubilee celebration in the Catholic University, Washington, D. C., Cardinal O'Connell gave expression to the same stupid blunder, when he stated that American bishops and priests *"desire no privilege for their Church but the freedom which the Fathers and Founders of this nation guaranteed to them from the beginning."* Of course, the actions of the bishops and priests belie these words of the Cardinal, but the effect of their pronouncement was to confuse and mislead the American Catholic mind.

His Holiness witnesses with distress many other evidences of blundering and ignorance of strategy on the part of his officers here. How stupid and crude in his eyes must have been the spectacle of Archbishop Curley's insulting attack on the President? What does he think of those "traitors," as the Jesuit president of Fordham calls them,[1] some of them priests and religious, who run counter to his dearest theories of education and recommend Catholic youths to enter Godless Universities? Do not American Catholics realize that the ultimate success of Catholicism in America hinges on an exclusively sectarian education?

Pius is disgusted when he contemplates the opportunity that the Church lost through neglecting the Negro! Had American bishops had any vision, they would long since have captured the Negro's soul and his vote. No wonder Father LaFarge S. J.[2] warns American Catholics "of the deep anxiety over our neglect of the Negro felt by the Supreme Pontiff himself *who has never missed an opportunity to remind us of our duties.*"

Tactless blundering again in regard to apologetics and controversy! The Pope sees nothing but vulgarity and senseless loss of prestige in the abusive methods of American Catholic controversialists of the type of Father Gillis, the Paulist; Father Cox, the Jesuit; Father Curran, of the Catholic Truth Society; and Michael Williams, of the *Commonweal*; Patrick Scanlan, of the *Brooklyn Tablet*; and a hundred others too numerous to mention. What is his idea of controversy? "When it is necessary for them to enter into controversy," he writes, "they should combat error and resist adversaries *in such manner that the latter will know that they are prompted by rectitude and above all inspired by charity.*"

Pius XI knows only too well that the general effect of the pugnacious bitter spirit of Catholic controversialists has been to alienate public sympathy from the Church. Lack of

[1] *New York Times*, June 9, 1935.
[2] *America*, June 8, 1935.

confidence in the leadership of American bishops and priests inspired His Holiness to take personal charge of the Catholic campaign in this country. For the past few years he is "present" in this country, directing and leading the faithful. His encyclical "Quadragesimo Anno," to which I have so often referred, embodies important principles of his program and marks his entry into the American arena. It has been the source of his high repute amongst us. It prompted the non-Catholic Senator Nye to state: "I would almost be inclined to say that His Holiness furnishes the only leadership of unquestionable, world-wide authority in our critical struggle to emerge from the problems created by war and avarice." [1]

The installation of a radio broadcasting set-up in the Vatican City was a significant act of the Pope. He resolved to speak directly to Americans. He has done so frequently. When, last Easter (1935), he sang the solemn High Mass in St. Peter's he was heard clearly over the networks of the Columbia System and the National Broadcasting Company. To quote the *New York Times:* "The clear voice of the Pope was distinctly heard. . . . The chanting of the famous Sistine Choir, the tolling of the bells of St. Peter's, the silver trumpets and *the repetition of shouts from the great multitude acclaiming the Pope with the familiar 'Viva il Papa Re' conveyed the pageantry and color of the service to* listeners. . . . The broadcast closed with the Pope delivering the Papal benediction to the world at large."

His Holiness, as we have said above, knows the value of the publicity he enjoys in this country. He knows the nostalgia that the cry "Viva il Papa Re" causes in the hearts of many Catholics. He knows that the eulogies showered upon him prepare the public mind for his leadership. It was he

[1] *America,* April 20, 1935.

who inspired the launching of the Legion of Decency drive. He called it "a glorious campaign" and lent it his name. At his behest the bishops began their assault on the Calles-Cardenas regime in Mexico. The mobilization of the Knights of Columbus, which aimed at arousing enthusiasm for Catholic Action among laymen, was blessed and encouraged by Pius. The various instruments for educating Catholics in Catholic Action derive from the Pope's inspiration. As we have seen, he is working with and through Father Coughlin, although it is impossible to tell how long he will continue to do so. He may be inclined, at any time, to exchange Father Coughlin for some tactical advantage—let us not forget that he is always ready to bargain. Against Neo-Paganism and Communism he keeps up an incessant fight through Catholic organizations. Meanwhile through his Press he reminds Americans that to the Church alone belongs the right of reforming the social and moral order.[1]

The factor that told in Europe for the success of his diplomacy is telling here also, namely, the spreading fear of Communism. Rightly the public senses that the one dependable, powerful, fighting foe of the Red Peril is the white-garbed monarch of the Vatican City—the world's king of kings.

The capitalists of America welcome the "presence" in our midst of the Catholic Generalissimo. They realize that his superlative leadership of the Catholic forces is their safest bulwark. Gladly would they exchange a few amendments to the Constitution for a guarantee from Pius XI that the Communists would be suppressed. Wholeheartedly they echo his words: "We cannot contemplate without sorrow the heed-

[1] "To the Church and to the Church alone belongs the leadership of social forces for reform and human improvement," said Pius X.

lessness of those who seem to make light of these immediate dangers [of Communism] and with stolid indifference allow the propagation far and wide of those doctrines which seek by violence and bloodshed the destruction of all society." With equanimity also, the capitalists regard the Catholic effort to salvage the Negro race. So long as the Negro remains a drifting hulk in our national life our economic stability is menaced.

Pius XI is not afraid of Protestant opposition to his plans. As he declared recently when canonizing two Englishmen and inviting England to return to the "one true fold": *"Non-Catholic sects are divided more than ever. The Apostolic See remains as the only foundation and pillar of truth."* He counts, not without reason, on multitudes of politically-minded Protestants jumping on his band-wagon when his victory is assured. He is aware that the slogan "One religion is as good as another" closely expresses the American idea, and that as soon as he can justify Catholicism in the eyes of Americans he can have as many of them as he wants in his fold. In the enthusiasm of Father Coughlin's non-Catholic following for his doctrines, he has ample proof before his eyes that many Americans will accept him as their Papa Re so soon as he "explains himself" to them.

Meanwhile through Catholic Action the papal influence and papal ideas are irradiating every sphere of life. The subtle aroma of Catholicism is permeating the national thought. Here, there and everywhere propaganda is busy "making America Catholic." Every sixth man is already a Catholic and every sixth woman and every sixth child. From obscure and lowly beginnings Catholicism has grown into a vast and powerful order. Now at its zenith of energy, led by the masterful and astute Roman pontiff, it throbs with life and pride.

Day by day the rank and file of the Church are mentally inflamed as they hear or read of the mystical doctrine of the Church's miraculous existence and as they are reminded of the justice and necessity of the Church's claim to dominance. "Men have tried," said a recent preacher in St. Patrick's, "to bury the Church, to explain away its miracles. Students of government have pointed to supposed flaws in its policies. . . . Yet is there one of them that can explain why she has not passed away with the empires that died during her first nineteen hundred years? Her resurrection century after century cannot be explained unless one recognizes the power of God in her."

Here in America we are witnessing another of those "resurrections" which may mean for us sooner or later submission to the spiritual overlordship of the Holy See.

Who can place a limit to the Catholic objective in this country? Re-open diplomatic relations with Rome? Though gratified by such a concession, why should Catholics be content with that? Accord to them the right of exclusive censorship over books, plays, amusements and the Press. The Church would accept such office without giving thanks for it, for she would regard it as her exclusive right to enjoy it. Amend the Constitution so as to allow State Legislatures to apportion public moneys to the support of Catholic schools and institutions. The Church would grudgingly admit that a long-delayed obligation was being met by the country. Go further, and amend the Constitution so as to recognize the jurisdiction of her Ecclesiastical Courts and *establish* the Catholic Church as the official Church of America. At this point the Church would begin to relax and smile with content. But still she would demand more and more of us. She would have charge of the departments of philosophy and history in all our universities; she would have large sections of her Canon Law incorporated into the State Laws; she would insist on being empowered to exercise certain essential inquisitorial rights—not, of course, Torquemada stuff—but a modernized and civilized Holy O.G.P.U. She would not ask for any measures to be taken against Protestant denominations so long as they did not criticize her or cross her path or encourage Freemasonry or officially endorse eugenics and birth control. Protestant sects would be tolerated and treated in a kindly way *subject to what she would consider necessary and reasonable restrictions.*

Never was the Catholic Church in any country in the world since Christendom began so rich, so highly organized, so influential, so loyally soldiered by her subjects as she is today in the United States. Never had she a more accomplished and resolute Generalissimo than Pius XI. Never was she tempted to make a supreme effort by stakes more large and glorious than those at issue here and now.

The effort, the fight, may be drawn out. It may last for five or ten years. Even if it last for twenty—what is twenty years in the life of Rome? The fight must be fought to a finish—opposition must be worn down if it cannot be swept away. Rome's immortal destiny hangs on the outcome. That destiny overshadows the land.

Were Rome to fail to dominate American thought and American lives, her civilization, her moral code, all her glorious incredible dogmas would perish from the earth. Should Rome triumph, she will ascend to a higher state than ever she has enjoyed heretofore. Therefore she must win—if it

be given her to win what, as she claims, God has promised—
what her Prophets have foretold. Then will the vast West
be hers wherein to set up anew her earthly kingdom. And in
the fight, as she has ever fought when battles were most
desperate in the past, Rome will use steel, and gold, and
silvery lie. Rome will stoop to conquer.